Stone Men

Palestinian stonemason at work.

Stone Men

*The Palestinians
Who Built Israel*

Andrew Ross

VERSO
London • New York

First published by Verso 2019
© Andrew Ross 2019

The moral rights of the author have been asserted

1 3 5 7 9 10 8 6 4 2

Verso
UK: 6 Meard Street, London W1F 0EG
US: 20 Jay Street, Suite 1010, Brooklyn, NY 11201
versobooks.com

Verso is the imprint of New Left Books

ISBN-13: 978-1-78873-026-6
ISBN-13: 978-1-78873-028-0 (UK EBK)
ISBN-13: 978-1-78873-029-7 (US EBK)

British Library Cataloguing in Publication Data
A catalogue record for this book is available from the British Library

Library of Congress Cataloging-in-Publication Data

Names: Ross, Andrew, 1956- author.
Title: Stone men : the Palestinians who built Israel / Andrew Ross.
Description: London ; Brooklyn, NY : Verso, 2019. | Includes bibliographical
  references
Identifiers: LCCN 20180415521 ISBN 9781788730266 | ISBN 9781788730297 (US
  ebook)
Subjects: LCSH: Construction industry–Palestine. | Stonemasonry–Palestine.
  | Stonemasons–Palestine. | Palestine Arabs–Employment–Israel. |
  Arab-Israeli conflict–Economic aspects. | Labor
  supply–Palestine–History.
Classification: LCC HD9715.P2 R67 2019 | DDC 331.7/69310089/927405694–dc23
LC record available at https://lccn.loc.gov/2018041552

Typeset in Fournier by MJ & N Gavan, Truro, Cornwall
Printed and bound by CPI Group (UK) Ltd, Croydon, CR0 4YY

Contents

Acknowledgments

I n the course of researching this book, I learned quite a bit about
stone. But it was only after I started writing that I realized how
much this interest had been latent since those years I spent in high
school and college working on construction sites and in the precast
concrete company where my brother Martin was also employed as
an accountant. During that period I picked up some skills on the
job and also some valuable life advice from fellow workers. I prize
the sensuous memory of the materials that we handled: the feel of
thick concrete scooped up on a shovel, the tang of fresh mortar
and cement, and the heft of bricks balanced on a hod. Many of the
workers I interviewed in the West Bank and Israel—in the quarries,
factories, and building sites—were doing similar kinds of jobs and,
in some cases, using the same materials. However remote from their
circumstances, this personal connection to their craft and toil helped
me write the book.

I owe many debts to colleagues and friends who read the manu-
script at earlier stages: Zachary Lockman, Amin Husain, Tyler Bray,
Julie Livingston, Maggie Gray, Kareem Rabie, and Eyal Weizman.
They improved it with their suggestions, and, in some cases, scrupulous attention.

In the West Bank, I could not have done this research without the
assistance and warm company of my Bethlehem circle: Mohammed
"Habshe" Yossef, Amina Salah, Bara'h Odeh, Mohammed Abu
Srour, and the staff from Aida Camp who worked at the Al-Karmeh

restaurant. I want to acknowledge the help of Magid Shihade, Salim Abu Jamal, Nithya Nagarajan, Shatha Safi, and Fida Touma in Ramallah. In Jaffa, Sami Abu Shehadeh and Badawi Farra, and in Tel Aviv, Rachel Giora, Sharon Rotbard, and Assaf Adiv, were all generous with their time and insights.

Many thanks to my New York affinity group: Nitasha Dhillon, Amin Husain, and Yates McKee; to the extended cast of Decolonize This Place (Amy Weng, Marz Saffore, Crystal Hans, Kyle Goen, Moana Niumeitolu, and Lorena Ambrosio); and to the other intrepid members of the MTL/ Palestine film crew: Tarina Van Den Driessche, Michael Clemow, and Eric Coombs Esmail.

I would also like to mention others who helped with queries and advice: Daniel Monterescu, Mark LeVine, Suad Amiry, Alexander Petti, Maya Wind, Hadas Keda, Sunaina Maira, Rose Asad, Paula Chakravartty, Sandy Hilal, Salim Tamari, Tareq Radi and Artemis Kubala.

Last but not least, I thank my editor, Andy Hsiao, at Verso; his deep support for this book and his efforts to enliven my prose were most welcome.

Author's Note

Much of this book is based on interviews conducted over the course of three years (2015–18) in the West Bank, East Jerusalem, and Israel. I have changed the names of many persons quoted in these pages to protect their identities. Some of my interviews were conducted in English, but most were in Arabic, in the presence and with the assistance of real-time translators.

In the text, I refer to indigenous residents of Palestine before and during the British Mandate (1922–48) as Arabs. After 1948, I refer to them as Israeli Palestinians if they are Arab citizens of Israel, or simply Palestinians if they are from the West Bank and Gaza. In places, I also refer to "West Bank Palestinians" who commute to work inside Israel. "Palestine" is not an easily recognizable geographic and political body (only Area A of the Occupied Territories is nominally under the control of the Palestinian Authority or Hamas), so I have tried to avoid using the name to refer to a national or physical entity. Instead, "Occupied Territories" is more generally used in these pages, and it refers to the 22 percent of historic Palestine that Israel has occupied since 1967.

Because of the many obstacles to access, I regret I was not able to do any research for this book in Gaza.

Preface

Point of Entry

Who built the seven gates of Thebes?
The books are filled with names of kings.
Was it the kings who hauled the craggy blocks of stone?
And Babylon, so many times destroyed.
Who built the city up each time?

— Bertolt Brecht, "A Worker Reads History"

Kibbutz Ginosar, on the palm tree–lined shores of the Sea of Galilee, seemed like an agreeable place to spend the winter and spring months of 1979. The communal farming ideal of kibbutz life promised a welcome respite from the paramilitary discipline and heavy weather rigors of the North Sea oil rig where I had worked since graduating from university in Scotland. A volunteer stint on a kibbutz had become a fixture on the international circuit favored by young European travelers. The lifestyle on offer was tailor-made for late hippy souls like myself: morning labor in the fields, creative relaxation in the afternoons, and libertine revelry after sundown.

The other volunteers, European and North Americans, were a freewheeling, cosmopolitan crowd. Some of us were well aware of our value to the kibbutz as a source of free labor, though we got some payback from the after-hours routine of provoking the more austere kibbutzniks with our unruly ways. Because I had some literary skills, I was nominated to be the resident playwright, responsible for scripting skits that we staged at the back of Field 17, our "night-club." It was not difficult to find timely material nearby for these routines. Israeli forces had recently withdrawn from their first invasion of southern Lebanon (Operation Litani), but PLO fedayeen encampments were still close enough to the Israeli border to lob Katyusha rockets into the Lower Galilee. Twice during my stay in Ginosar, these rockets landed in the vicinity of the kibbutz. On each occasion, within half an hour, Israeli jets swept down over the water en route to pounding the PLO guerrilla positions thirty kilometers to the north. The asymmetry in the sky was plain to see, and, from what I could tell, it infuriated most of the volunteers, eclipsing any fears we might have had about our own safety. Among this peace and love crowd, sentiment clearly ran against the overmilitarized Israeli forces, and it was easy to stir up the nightclub audience by injecting dark comedy into our on-stage satires.

While the kibbutz carefully cultivated its image as a protected haven, insulating residents from external events, it was obvious to many of us that the region was in turmoil. The primary cause was conflict over the stepped-up expropriation of Palestinian land, as part of the latest Israeli effort to "Judaize the Galilee." This campaign had been ongoing since 1949 when Israeli authorities extended Plan Dalet (the blueprint for cleansing villages and increasing Jewish presence in the predominantly Arab region) to prevent Palestinians evicted during the *Nakba* ("catastrophe" in Arabic) from returning to their homes. The government renewed the campaign in the 1970s, resulting in a series of land confiscations and new settlement building. In response, Israeli Palestinians declared a national strike in March 1976, and demonstrations were staged in every community, with solidarity actions occurring in the West Bank and Gaza and in Lebanese refugee camps. This insurgency, subsequently known and commemorated each year as Land Day, marked the onset of a new wave of indigenous nationalism, with Palestinian citizens of Israel participating in large numbers for the first time since 1948.

Since Ginosar was a liberal, if no longer an aspirational socialist, community, volunteers like myself tended to assume the kibbutz was not complicit in this lawless land-grabbing. Its past record was more questionable, however, as we would have learned had we looked more closely, especially to the career of Yigal Allon, one of Ginosar's founders, and lauded to this day as its most notable member. An exemplary sabra (native-born) pioneer, Allon was a national hero by the time of Israel's independence, personifying the soldier–politician generation of Ashkenazi Jewish elites weaned on kibbutznik and labor movement values. In his early career as a Haganah commander, he assisted the ruthless British suppression of the Arab Revolt (*al-nahda al-kubra*) of 1936–39, the nationalist uprising against the Mandate administration's policy of allowing open-ended Jewish immigration. It was during this campaign that he learned the brutal counterinsurgency tactics of collective punishment from Orde Wingate, the ardent Zionist who created the joint British–Jewish commando units known and feared as the Special Night Squads.

In 1941, with encouragement from the British Command, Allon helped found the Haganah's crack Palmach commando force at Ginosar and served as one of its first company commanders. In that capacity, he coordinated Operation Yiftach, the ethnic cleansing of the Eastern Galilee that occurred in advance of the British withdrawal from historic Palestine in May 1948. His troops invaded and evacuated the regional center of Safad along with dozens of villages and towns. Subsequently, Allon directed the smaller Operation Broom (Operation Matate), which "swept away" Arab villages and Bedouin encampments on the Tiberias–Rosh Pina road, a strategic throughway that passed by Ginosar.[1] After the houses were blown up and the tents burned, the residents were chased off across the lake toward the Syrian border.

In an interview with filmmaker Eyal Sivan, Palmach machine-gunner Yerachmiel Kahanovich elaborated on Operation Broom:

ES: Operation Broom, what is it? You simply stood in line and just ...

YK: Yes, you march up to a village, you expel it, you gather round and have a bite to eat, and go on to the next village ...

ES: But how?

YK: You mean by shooting?

ES: How do you mean?

YK: We shot, we threw a grenade here and there. Just listen—there's one thing you have to understand: at first, once they heard shots they took off with the intention of returning later.

ES: But, wait a sec, that was before May 15, that was before the Arab armies came ... Operation Broom then. How does it happen? Do you receive any information? Is it an organized campaign? ...

YK: Yigal Allon himself planned it. We moved from one place to the next.

ES: What places? Can you tell me?

YK: We passed by Tiberias and moved from one village to the other, from one to the next.

ES: So you had orders to expel and clean up the villages?

YK: And then go home.[2]

Both of these military operations were part of the well-coordinated Plan Dalet strategy, overseen by David Ben-Gurion and an inner circle of military chieftains, to terrorize and expel as many Palestinians as possible. After Allon's death in 1980, Kibbutz Ginosar built a museum to memorialize him. One of its galleries presents a stirring account, in images and martial odes, of the Palmach and its exploits during the *Nakba*. The walls feature some of Allon's words, showcasing the doctrine of "purity of arms" that is supposed to govern the conduct of Israel's military—"Whoever replaces the tragic necessity of defense with the joy of fighting overturns the entire purpose of our campaign"—and his personal egalitarianism—"I can promote you to the rank of sergeant but you will need to receive your authority from your privates." On other floors of the museum, the curators depict Allon as a promoter of amity between Arabs and Jews, especially through the annual Spring Gatherings that he convened in Ginosar to welcome Palestinian notables from all over the Galilee.

But his military deeds, as Israeli revisionist historians have shown, confirm that he was one of the most reliable executors of Plan Dalet, interpreting Ben-Gurion's will in the most aggressive fashion. It was Allon who used scaremongering in a "whisper campaign," as he phrased it, to "force the tens of thousands of sulky Arabs who remained in Galilee to flee."[3] In his own Palmach memoirs, he openly espoused the language of ethnic cleansing to describe the campaign's military goal: "We regarded it as imperative to cleanse the interior of the Galilee and to create Jewish territorial continuity in the whole of Upper Galilee."[4] Immediately after the June War (or *Naksa*—"relapse" or "setback" in Arabic) in 1967, Allon presented a detailed plan for taking over and dividing up the Occupied Territories. Although it was never officially implemented, policymakers have adopted, and are still abiding by, its core principle—to settle, with a view to annexing, the most thinly populated Palestinian lands of the West Bank while preserving the demographic balance of a Jewish majority. This alternative formula for ethnic cleansing has been used as a rule of thumb to authorize land grabs, even by settler zealots who use biblical scripture, not the Allon Plan blueprint, as their aspirational guide.[5]

Needless to say, the fond memories of Allon that I heard kibbutzniks recount (he died not long after my Ginosar stay, while campaigning for leadership of the liberal Alignment Party) would not have been shared by the Arab villagers who were chased out of the region by his Palmach forces, nor by their relatives who managed to stay on, struggling to earn a livelihood as hired hands in area kibbutzim and other Jewish enterprises. Neither did it occur to me when I started at Ginosar that I was doing work that might otherwise have been contracted out to one of them. I was far too caught up in the agrarian romance of working with the soil as part of a commune. For my daytime labor, I was allocated to the grapefruit orchards, where I snagged the job of treating trees afflicted with gummosis, an infectious rot manifested by gum bleeding from lesions on the trunk and branches. To doctor the diseased trees I had to carve out the weeping sores and apply a chemical remedy. But it was not a full-time task, so I was commandeered, on occasion, to join the small fishing fleet on the lake or, whenever extra hands were needed, for banana harvesting.

At the end of one of my shifts in the banana fields, as the crew lingered before dispersing, two members of the work team peeled off and walked out toward the road that bordered the kibbutz. They did not have the loose-limbed swagger of the typical kibbutznik male and were clearly outsiders, heading home. Quizzing my work mates, I learned that they were Palestinian day laborers, and that others,

The author in Ginosar orchards, 1979.

like them, were employed in other parts of the kibbutz economy, including the lucrative hotel facility, Nof Ginosar. Who were they? Where did they live? How well were they paid? And how did they feel about working for kibbutzniks who had possibly taken over some of their ancestral lands?

These questions I might have followed up on, but I was not called back to the banana groves, and I left shortly afterward to travel in Egypt. Yet my brief encounter with the Palestinian field hands turned out to be the seedling for this book, though it germinated very slowly, since a full thirty-six years would pass before my return to the region. In 2015, some friends were making a documentary film in the West Bank and asked me to join the crew. They were in need of an analyst to look at the employment options available to Palestinians who had lived under military occupation and enforced poverty for the past fifty years. We began by interviewing men and women crossing West Bank border checkpoints to work inside Israel. In the course of the filming, I realized that I was finally asking the questions I had lightly formulated for myself decades before, and the responses of the workers standing in line for hours on end inspired me to ask many more as this book developed and spun away from the film.

On that first return visit, the film crew decided to make a quick trip to Ginosar to see what remained of the socialist idealism that had come under direct threat, at the time of my original stay, from the watershed election of Menachem Begin's Likud Party in 1977. Generous state subsidies to kibbutzim fell off during Begin's term, and a steady march toward the privatization of every facet of community life set in. For the younger Ginosar members whom I interviewed in 2015, the collectivism I had witnessed in 1979, which included shared clothing and work tasks, communal kitchens, centralized child-rearing, and participatory budgeting, all lay in the remote past. The everyday norms of these current residents were quite the opposite: private home ownership, household dining and parenting, differential pay grading, and a cash economy for almost all goods and services. On a later visit of my own, I listened to sweetened reminiscing about the old days from several elderly members, though none of them complained about their improved standard of living in recent decades. Over time, Ginosar has become Israel's biggest banana producer through the global operations of its agricultural company, with holdings distant from its Galilee base, and some fields even close to Gaza.

What became of the volunteers? A wood sculptor, whose studio was housed in the only remaining cabin from the old "volunteers' ghetto," gave me a blunt assessment: "People like you were no longer needed in the fields after the Thai workers came." (Migrants from Thailand have formed a large part of Israel's agricultural workforce since the mid-1990s.) Another veteran member reported that African students also tended Ginosar's crops, as part of an educational program. "The Arabs," he added, "are only employed in the kibbutz's hotel." This man had fought in several wars, including the Lebanese invasions, and mused that much strife "would have been avoided if my friend Yigal Allon had become prime minister in the early 1980s—he really understood how the Arabs think." On American policies, he drew a hard line, opining that "Trump is good for Israel, though maybe not so good for the US, while Obama, I think, was really an Arab all along."

Could Israeli Palestinians live in Ginosar? I asked a more recently established resident, watering the vegetables in the yard of his cottage.[6] He smiled knowingly, and ventured, "Well, you know that Arabs are quite different from us, so they would not fit in. They would not want to come and live here anyway." Shortly afterward, I ran into two female Arab employees about to enter the Nof Ginosar hotel. "No, we could not live here," one of them confirmed, "but the job and the pay are OK." She worked in housekeeping, and her colleague was in the kitchens. "We are supposed to be out of sight," she added. In that respect, their job descriptions were little different from those of ethnic minorities who clean hotel rooms or assist with food preparation in many of the rich countries of the world. But the Jewish employment of Arabs has never been a straightforward contractual arrangement, and least of all on a kibbutz, whose origins lay in the bitter struggle to "conquer" Arab competition in the early twentieth-century labor market.

Haaretz, Israel's leading liberal newspaper, had recently carried a story about Ginosar's joint ventures with illegal settlements across the Green Line (the 1949 Armistice, or pre-1967, border) in the northern Jordan Valley. For several years, the kibbutz had been cultivating banana groves in the West Bank on Palestinian land seized by the religious moshav settlement of Shadmot Mehola. The higher temperatures and accessible water resources of the Jordan Valley allowed growers to go to market early in the season when prices were high. But these profits came at an even higher price for the region's Palestinians, who had seen their lands confiscated over the years or closed off by the military (87 percent of the Jordan Valley land in the West Bank is now off-limits to Palestinians, in tune with the original Allon Plan to take over the entire region), and whose wells had run dry as more and more water was diverted to service Jewish settlements.[7] The Ginosar/Mehola banana groves were now receiving up to 40 percent of the amount of water that was allocated by Israeli authorities to the entire village of Ein al-Beida, with almost 2,000 residents. The barely disguised goal of this form of "water apartheid" was to reduce supplies until the villagers were forced to move out.[8]

Another recent *Haaretz* article documented how Jamal Fukhah, a fifty-six-year-old Ein al-Beida villager, was employed by Ginosar in these groves (on a sixteen-hour overnight shift, seven days a week) at substandard wages, and had been abruptly fired without any severance pay. He was paid 6.50 shekels an hour (less than $2) in cash, an apparent violation of the landmark 2007 Israeli High Court of Justice ruling that Palestinian workers on West Bank settlements had to be paid the same minimum wage—23 shekels an hour, at that time—and offered the same social welfare benefits as workers in Israel.[9] Fukhah shared the predicament of many West Bank villagers. Starved of any other employment, including across the Green Line itself, they had little choice but to take the settlement wages, even if they were lower than those offered to imported Thai laborers.

That 2007 ruling is routinely flouted by settlement employers, who regard the military overseers of Area C (60 percent of West Bank territory that is under Israeli civilian and security authority) as the real source of authority. This noncompliant stance results in severe human rights violations. In 2015, just before our film crew visited Ginosar, Human Rights Watch issued a devastating report on the extensive use of Palestinian child labor on the Jordan Valley's Jewish settlement farms. Children as young as eleven were being forced to drop out of school to work in the fields to help their families overcome one of the world's highest poverty rates. The children's heavy manual work was chronically underpaid and often involved contact with hazardous pesticides.[10]

Outsourcing from rich to poor countries is routinely driven by the attraction of cheap labor and weakened environmental regulation. Israeli employers are able to enjoy such advantages simply by moving their business a few miles across the Green Line to the agricultural and industrial zones of settlements, where the gray zone of exception permitted by the Occupation allows them to circumvent Israeli laws and international human rights conventions. Palestinian laborers crossing the Green Line in the other direction are better paid, and, in principle, are entitled to social insurance benefits, but they make the journey under duress, and they are herded and humiliated en route through checkpoints. Yet without their steady toil, dependability, and applied skills, neither Israel nor the settlements that are gobbling up the West Bank would exist in anything like their current form. As I recount in the pages that follow, nowhere is this more evident than in the construction sector. Year in and year out, the hands that built Israel's houses, schools, factories, offices, roads, bridges, and even its separation barriers, have been Palestinian. How should those decades of effort be recognized, tallied, and rewarded?

Introduction

Your insistent need to demonstrate the history of stones and your ability to invent proofs does not give you prior membership over him who knows the time of the rain from the smell of the stone. That stone for you is an intellectual effort. For the owner it is a roof and walls.

—Mahmoud Darwish[1]

Palestinians honor the olive tree as an abiding symbol of their ethnic heritage. By some estimates, more than a million trees have been felled by Israeli bulldozers, uprooted by soldiers, or burned by West Bank settlers since 1967.[2] The groves that remain have acquired a more exalted status. While their role as a primary source of income has diminished, they are more and more identified with the Palestinian people's steadfast attachment to land that is constantly at risk of seizure or theft. All across the world, people now recognize the olive tree as an icon of Palestinian survival, but much less is known about the significance of the limestone outcroppings that poke through the surface of the orchard soil. Though they are often an affliction to olive growers, these stone deposits are now Palestinians' most valuable natural resource. As this book documents, they have long played a key role in the ongoing drama that pits the Palestinian people against their colonizers.

The central highlands of the West Bank harbor some of the best quality dolomitic limestone in the world, and the business of stone quarrying, cutting, fabrication, and dressing is the Occupied

Territories' largest private employer and generator of revenue, supplying the construction industry in Israel, along with several Middle
Eastern countries and even more overseas. According to the Union
of Stone and Marble, its sector earns $450 million in sales and boasts
more than 1,200 firms and between 25,000 and 30,000 jobs, and it
accounts for almost 25 percent of national industrial production.
Its output is the single biggest industrial share (5–7 percent) of the
Occupied Territories' GDP, and overall reserves of stone are valued
at $30 billion. Remarkably, for such a small population, by 2014,
Palestinians were the twelfth largest stone producers in the world
(producing 22 million square meters of goods annually), ranking
just behind the United States and ahead of Russia.[3]

The West Bank has two abundant natural resources—stone
and water—that are notably scarce in Israel and therefore in great
demand. Under the Oslo Accords, Israel can siphon off up to 80
percent of West Bank water reserves from the Sea of Galilee and
the rain-fed mountain aquifer by deploying advanced technology to
pump from the lowest levels. By contrast, Palestinians quarry most
of the subsurface stone, and they own all of the factories and workshops where the cutting, fabrication, and finishing is done. While
the Occupied Territories are rarely compared to countries that are
economically reliant on the extraction of a single resource, they
do have something in common with oil producers like Angola or
Nigeria, where activists struggle to protect their fellow citizens from
environmental harm on the one hand and from predatory profiteers
and kleptocratic officials on the other. In fact, West Bank stone is
sometimes referred to as "white oil," and its people suffer, in their
own way, from the "resource curse" that delivers a range of problems, along with some prosperity, to countries with such a precious
natural asset.

In the case of Palestinians, the Israeli demand for their stone
presents a paradox. Aside from the cheap, skilled labor of construction workers, stone is the primary Palestinian commodity that
Israelis need to physically build out their state, along with their
ever-expanding West Bank colonies. Palestinian quarries have long
supplied the raw material for building the houses of Zion, while

Palestinian towns and villages supplied the builders. By far the majority of Palestinian stone (more than 70 percent) finds its way into the Israeli market, underpinning the dependency on the occupying power. In fact, stone makes up half of the country's exports across the Green Line, though much of it is also used in the West Bank to construct "facts on the ground" (Jewish settlements and security infrastructure established prior to any legal recognition).

But the industry is no less central to Palestinians' efforts to erect their own physical bulwarks against the Occupation and settler expansion. Everyone, on both sides, wants to reinforce their presence and claims on territory, and so the use of local stone—weathered, in some cases, to give a vintage appearance—suggests an authentic, long-standing connection to the land. Far from inert, then, the stones of the West Bank—and not just the smaller ones that the much-lionized "children of the stones" throw at soldiers—are an expressive frontline ingredient of the landscapes where the national conflict is played out.

With these ample deposits under their feet, it is no surprise that the region's stonemasons developed top-notch artisanal skills and have long been venerated and sought after for their services. During the Ottoman and British Mandate eras, every large village in historic Palestine hosted a master mason who designed and constructed homesteads and common-use buildings. These craftsmen and their crews inherited and passed on tools, techniques, and know-how, serving as stewards and modernizers of the regional Arab vernacular styles.[4] Without any professional training in design or planning, they built palaces, hilltop villages, and township cores that are much admired today as examples of "architecture without architects." From the mid-nineteenth century, the masons were regionally employed in city building—in Jaffa, Haifa, Acre, Hebron, Jerusalem, and Bethlehem—and later, when other Arab countries in the region needed their expertise, in nation-building. Indeed, it would be no exaggeration to say that the "stone men" of Palestine have built almost every state in the Middle East except their own.

Of all these countries, Israel has been the biggest beneficiary of Palestinian manpower and raw materials. Despite efforts, early and late, to exclude them from the building trades, Palestinians have played an essential role in the physical and economic construction of the Zionist "national home." This has been the case from the turn of the twentieth century when the Jews of Ottoman Palestine, whether Sephardic and partly assimilated, or Ashkenazi Zionists and largely separatist, depended on their building skills. Palestinians' contribution to construction was stepped up during the modernizing wave of economic expansion under the British Mandate, and it continued after 1948, when the newly established state of Israel used their labor to help house the influx of Jewish immigrants. Since 1967, when the West Bank was secured as a reservoir of cheap labor, Israel's dependency on Palestinian workers has proved difficult to shake off.

During the Mandate era, Zionist leaders aimed their policy of Hebrew Labor (*avoda ivrit*) at the exclusive use of Jewish workers in Jewish-owned businesses. But since many employers, especially in construction, continued to prefer the cheaper and more proficient Arab workers, the efforts to enforce this embargo, even when it was backed by force, were only partly successful. Sectors of the construction workforce were Arab-free only in the years immediately after 1948, when the Palestinians who remained in the new Israeli state were under military lockdown. Within a few years, however, they could once again be found everywhere on building sites, and, after 1967, they were joined en masse by their West Bank brethren. At the peak of the open borders era (which ended in the early 1990s), up to 40 percent of the West Bank and Gaza workforce was employed inside the Green Line, primarily engaged in construction, and generating a significant share of Israeli GDP. Even after the Israeli authorities imposed a collective punishment for the first intifada (1987–91) by canceling work permits and importing overseas migrants (from Romania, Bulgaria, Turkey, Poland, Nigeria, and China) as a replacement workforce, they were unable to stamp out employers' abiding preference for Palestinian labor.

In the first quarter of 2017, the number of West Bank Palestinians employed to meet Israel's housing shortage surpassed the pre-intifada levels, with almost 140,000 inside the Green Line and 24,000 in the settlement colonies, and many more working there without permits.[5] In 2016, Israel's National Economic Council projected a need to build an additional 1.5 million homes before 2040.[6] Since the gross monthly cost of employing Palestinians is less than half that of Israeli or foreign workers (whose housing and welfare needs are a social cost), this long-term need virtually guarantees a protracted demand for Palestinian builders.[7]

What have Palestinians earned collectively from all of these indispensable contributions, and how should these efforts be recognized in the political debate about the future of the lands of historic Palestine? What kinds of rights accrue from the century or more of toil they have devoted to the construction of the Zionist project prior to 1948, the Israeli state, the West Bank settlements, and the Occupied Territories themselves? After all, the long inventory of Palestinian labor includes a principal share in building the infrastructure of modernity under the British Mandate (roads, railways, ports, telecom lines, an airport, and other public works); the "first Hebrew city" of Tel Aviv; all the Arab towns and cities that were taken under Jewish control after the *Nakba*; the ever-expanding metropolis of "unified" and Greater Jerusalem; and the red-tiled hilltop settlements on the West Bank along with their grid of bypass roads, barrier walls, super-highways, and other security structures. All told, Palestinian workers have had a decisive hand in most of the fixed assets on the land between the River Jordan and the Mediterranean coast.

Should claims arising from this long record of labor participation be part of the "final status" settlement between Israelis and Palestinians? Talks about a permanent settlement have been on hiatus for more than a decade, but if and when they resume, the thorny matters of restitution of property, compensation for losses and moral suffering, and the right to return for refugees will still be on the table. In recent decades, and following the example of German reparations for wartime Jewish harms and losses, every international instance of conflict resolution has addressed the claims of displaced populations. The UN Basic Principles and Guidelines on the Right to a Remedy and Reparation for Victims of Gross Violations of

International Human Rights Law outlines five forms of reparations: restitution, compensation, rehabilitation (including psychological care and legal/medical services), moral satisfaction (apologies and commemoration), and guarantees of nonrepetition. To date, Israeli negotiators have only been prepared to talk about very limited amounts of monetary compensation. The international consensus favors a comprehensive settlement that includes all of them.

Several estimates, drawing on a variety of archives, have been published of the sums and the financial remedies involved, and so there is no shortage of documented evidence to support the claims. To cite one example, Thierry Senechal and Leila Hilal suggest a total of $3.4 billion in refugee losses incurred during the *Nakba* ($297 billion in 2009 dollars), based on their survey of the following damages: loss of rural and urban property, movable assets, bank accounts, businesses, communal property, religious endowments, Arab share of state property and infrastructure— roads, hospitals, railways, seaports, airports, schools, irrigation networks, public buildings—along with loss of livelihoods and employment.[8]

This kind of reparative justice is primarily about repaying debts from the past, but how can the remedies assist more directly in securing a different kind of future? The premise, suggested in this book, that Palestinians have earned civil and political rights through their cumulative labor, presents one of many pathways beyond the apartheid-style status quo. As the policies of the Trump and Netanyahu administrations (including, but not limited to, the 2018 relocation of the US embassy to Jerusalem) further foreclose any prospect of a practical partition (the "two state solution"), and as momentum steadily builds behind some vision of a single democratic state within the same boundaries as historic Palestine, it ought to become more admissible that equity earned from building the state translates into political rights within it.

Generations in the Trade

Amir Younis had not plied his trade for a decade or more, but he kept himself busy by selling sundry items out of a hole-in-the-wall grocery store: candy, detergent, rice, cigarettes. Eager to reminisce about his working life as a stonemason, he needed no coaxing to retrieve a set of tools he kept in a drawer of the shop desk. There were chisels and hammers of varying sizes, their shape and function unaltered from generation to generation of use. "This one is for doing *taltis,* that one for *tubzeh,* and those for *mattabeh* and *msamsam,*" he explained, referring to common styles of stone dressing. "These are all popular in Israel, Jordan, and Lebanon." He picked up a stone block outside the store and showed me how to chisel the most roughly hewed, in the *tubzeh* style, chopping at the surface with a series of angled hammer blows.

We were in Beit Fajjar, a village eight kilometers south of Bethlehem and a renowned center of the stone industry, where the story Amir told me about the men in his family history was fairly commonplace. "My father taught me and my brothers how to cut and finish stone, because that's what everyone here does, and I followed my older brother to Jordan in the 1970s. There was lots of work there and it paid a lot better than you could get here in Palestine." What did you do there? "We built Amman," he replied, matter of factly, "and they even gave me a Jordanian nationality card." He explained that "when I was stopped at the border, I told them I had a Palestinian wife and a Jordanian one, and the guard said, 'You look like you belong to the Jordanian wife,' so he

Photo by author

Amir Younis, chiseling in the tubzeh *style.*

gave me the card, and I worked there until 1989." It was a joke knowingly told in male company, but the telling of it disclosed a migrant worker's intimacy with unpredictable encounters at border crossings, and, in this case at least, with the flexible mobility enjoyed by West Bank Palestinians as they entered and left the East Bank during this period.

At this point in the conversation, his brother, Mohammed, entered the store, and took over the story, recounting how he took crews of ten men and more to Jordan from Beit Fajjar, along with truckloads of stone blocks. "The Jordanians needed us," he explained, "they were Bedouins who didn't know how to build anything." Mohammed was subsequently offered work in Riyadh for much higher pay. "My children didn't want me to be away for too long, so I said no, but lots of others went." Indeed, the 1970s and 1980s were golden years for those Palestinian workers, many of them highly skilled and educated, who migrated to the Gulf states on the back of the oil boom to build out and service the national infrastructures of these fledgling states. Some of these migrants became large manpower contractors in their own right, while others founded construction empires. For the less fortunate, their high-earning sojourn was terminated by the ill-fated decision of Yasser Arafat (an engineer who also did his share of construction contracting in Kuwait) to pledge PLO support for Saddam Hussein during the 1991 Gulf War. In retaliation, hundreds of thousands of Palestinians were forced to leave the Gulf—during and after the war, as many as 400,000 left Kuwait alone.[9] "Many people I knew had to come home," Mohammed recalled, "and there was even less work for everyone back here because the Israelis were closing the border around the same time."

In retrospect, Mohammed and Amir had been wise to return from Jordan a few years earlier to finish building houses for their children and start a stone factory in the village. Amir's son, Omar, was continuing the trade. Thanks to his father, he knew how to chisel, but he told me that he preferred to work in a factory, operating a machine that did the cutting and polishing. "Exports are more profitable," he explained, "and many of the buyers are from countries where they want polished or brushed stone, not the chiseled kind." The *tubzeh* hand-crafted work could not be automated, he reported, and "although you get paid a little more for doing it, the demand for that kind of stone finish is all local, only from Palestinians and Israelis." "Besides," he smiled, "the machine is much easier on my back, I don't have my father's strong spine."

Omar was also a steward in the workers union, formed in Beit Fajjar in the 1990s as a counterweight to the powerful Union of Stone and Marble, which served the interests of factory owners. Like everyone I interviewed, whether they were workers or owners, Omar railed against the restrictions placed on the industry by Israeli officials and soldiers. Though they bought 75 percent of the Palestinian product, the Israelis did all they could to obstruct the business of extraction and fabrication. "They take away our tools, the machines in the quarries, the roads we need to use," he declared angrily, "and in the end, they will take everything away from us."

Omar's own son, Marwan, worked in the same factory but, unlike his elders, he seemed to have no passion for stone. It looked as if the craft of masonry was going to skip his generation, though it was by no means a dying trade. A reticent nineteen-year-old, he was searching for an escape. "This work is too hard for me," he confessed, "I'd rather be a mechanic, though I will probably go to work in Israel soon, like my friends. None of them are in the factories or quarries, and they earn much more than me." He was too young to qualify for an Israeli work permit (only available to married males, aged twenty-two or older), so he would likely be joining the army of unregistered workers who crossed the Green Line illegally.[10] Most of them would be building houses and infrastructure with stone products—slabs, tiles, and aggregate—that originated in places like Beit Fajjar. A supply line of labor and materials ran between these locations, but it was especially fraught with danger for the undocumented. Even for workers with permits who faced the ordeal of the border checkpoints, there was no end of hardship and harassment. "I am not scared," Marwan retorted. "Palestinian men who are my age are fearless."

Stone Men draws on hundreds of interviews, over the course of three years, with male factory employees, like Amir, Mohammed,

Omar, and Marwan, and construction workers who either toiled in
West Bank settlements or crossed the Green Line to work in Israel.
Like many workers in the building trades, they tended to be quite
conservative in their political views. Certainly, they had opinions
about the national issues that consume Israeli–Palestinian relations,
but their daily struggle for survival was a much higher priority
than worrying over the seemingly intractable state-level conflict.
Their resilience as breadwinners in a male trade, their sense of
dignity as workers, and their aspirations as Palestinians weighed in
the balance against their typically harsh treatment by employers,
contractors, soldiers, and officials on both sides of the Green Line.
In Zionist histories, their forefathers appear only as a "foreign"
threat to the would-be rugged Jewish pioneers who carved out their
embryo state.

For the last fifty years, their livelihoods have been tossed around
as colonial bargaining chips, "permitted" to work for the occupier in return for keeping the peace. Regardless of their typically
thankless reception or maltreatment, they have almost always been
there, resolutely filling the slots in the production line that connects
the quarries to the construction sites. Unaccustomed to having
an audible voice, let alone a public profile, the other side of their
dependency was their resolute will to show up for work. Despite all
the obstacles and humiliation thrown in their paths, their tenacity
on the job has even been hailed as the way of the *samedin* practicing
the resistance philosophy of *sumud*, or steadfastness, developed by
Palestinians after the 1967 war.[11]

This historic contribution has not garnered a lot of attention
outside of the Occupied Territories. International watchers of
regional affairs and solidarity advocates have primarily focused,
and with good reason, on the ongoing calamity of Zionist land colonization. The tragic story about the steady loss of their land has
overshadowed how Palestinians earn their livelihoods and under
what browbeaten circumstances. Yet before the large-scale military
conquests of land occurred, in 1948 and 1967, the long-running
Zionist campaign to dominate the regional employment market,
known as the Conquest of Labor (*kibbush ha'avoda*), was by far

the most consequential conflict during the British Mandate. Its origins lay in the Labor Zionist doctrine of Jewish self-reinvention, whereby settlers were urged to vanquish the legacy of traditional Jewish middleman occupations by throwing themselves into manual labor. But leaders of the new Yishuv (the Zionist immigrant community in Palestine) rapidly transformed this concept into a militant strategy to win and then consolidate an exclusively Jewish share of the labor market. When Hebrew Labor became a keystone separatist policy within the new Yishuv, the more radical settler groups, including the anti-Zionist Palestine Communist Party, who pushed hard for co-existence and joint organizing among Arab and Jewish workers, found themselves on the sidelines.

Notably, the enduring conflict between the Jewish and Arab populations of Palestine began in workplaces long before Jewish control arose from conquest on the battlefield. After the *Nakba*, Palestinian workers no longer posed an immediate threat to Jewish jobs, though their labor was still considered indispensable. After 1967, Palestinians in the Occupied Territories would become a cheap, and almost wholly dependent, resource to be utilized at will for Israeli needs, as well as a negotiating asset in the game of "jobs for peace." In the course of these decades, the Zionist sense of purpose shifted decisively away from labor war toward land acquisition. Even with this more single-minded goal, the circumstances of Palestinian employment still had a strategic role to play beyond Israel's labor needs. As rural Palestinians on the West Bank increasingly became wage laborers on Israeli construction sites, their attachment to the land weakened, and this has made it easier for the authorities, and settlers, to confiscate or steal.

Separation and Mimicry

One of my interviewees, waiting patiently in a checkpoint line to cross over for his shift in a Jerusalem suburb, had this to say about his line of work: "They demolish our houses while we build theirs." It was not an uncommon observation, but his blunt formulation was especially compelling to me. The asymmetry was plain enough, and since, for many Palestinians, the family home is almost as revered as an olive grove, its destruction is seen as an especially malicious act. But I was also struck by what his comment suggests about the interdependence, however lopsided, between the two parties. For all the hostility whipped up by colonial policies, Arab–Jewish relationships have always been intertangled (and prone to outbreaks of mimicry), whether under circumstances of uncertain co-existence or forced separation.

In the early years of Zionist settlement, Jews had no alternative but to learn skills and techniques from Arab masons and builders who were accustomed to working with local stone. But in the course of constructing Tel Aviv—to be built, ideally, by Jewish hands—municipal leaders tried to substitute cement and concrete for the *kurkar* sandstone readily available on the Mediterranean coastland. In time, they would come to lionize concrete as the signature mark of Israeli modernity, but the original choice was made in order to cut out the Arab stonemasons of Jaffa. Subsequently, Jewish decision-makers selected building materials and styles to ensure that the face of the new Jewish settlement looked nothing like its predominantly "Levantine" surroundings. After the *Nakba*, the wholesale demolition of Arab villages and the makeover of urban quarters further reinforced this drive to eradicate the legacy of Ottoman Palestine, while the rule of concrete held sway over the build-out of the new state. When officers of the Jewish National Fund launched their drive to plant forests (and recreational parks and nature reserves) over the ruins of Ottoman-era villages in order to conceal the evidence, they purposely favored the European look, and fast growth, of Alpine conifer species over indigenous fauna.[12]

After 1967 and the annexation of the Old City in East Jerusalem, the direction of Zionist flight away from the heritage of the region went into reverse. The excavations of "biblical archaeologists" sparked religious-mythical interest in the landscape of Jewish antiquity. Israelis began to see the stones of Palestine through new eyes. They would no longer be spurned as the crumbling legacy of a backward civilization; now they arose from holy ground and were reminders of an ancient Jewish birthright to be reclaimed as part of what Shlomo Sand called the "nationalization of God."[13] A more secular appetite for the real estate value of antique stone buildings ran parallel with this religiously driven turn to heritage. Gentrifiers, with their neotraditional appreciation for vintage walls and decorative features, brought about a transformation in Israeli taste. Their market preferences swept through the remnants of old Arab districts in Jaffa, Acre, and Haifa, saved in the nick of time from the Hebrew bulldozer. By 2015, when I began my reporting in Jaffa, Ottomania had reached fever pitch. Some restored buildings bordering the old city were fetching the highest real estate prices in Israel, and *kurkar*, the local sandstone that had been shunned a century before by Tel Avivians, was a sought-after item.

Nor has Jerusalem, ground zero of antiquity, escaped the neotraditionalist turn. Realtors and their clients increasingly covet "Arab houses" and old tile stones or interior decor. Yet that city was spared from the mid-century cult of concrete by a 1918 British municipal ordinance mandating that all buildings use local limestone, and so there is more of an aesthetic continuum between the Ottoman past and the Zionist present. After the occupation of East Jerusalem began in 1967, Israeli planners established suburban satellites on the perimeter of the vastly expanded municipal boundaries. In accord with the ordinance, all of the new building on this spreading periphery was dutifully clad in "Jerusalem Stone," quarried from the West Bank highlands. As more and more commuter colonies sprouted well beyond the Green Line on Palestinian hilltops, the authorities drew on the same limestone supply to signify to the world that these settlements would one day be seen as a natural part of Greater Jerusalem.

The newfound Israeli craving for local stone is echoed in West Bank towns and villages, but there the push for conservation is not driven by market fever or religious zeal. Preserving and restoring vintage buildings is a way for Palestinians to protect them from seizure and demolition by settlers, while the architects, engineers, and workers who are breathing new life into the old houses also see themselves as fostering national pride. A different kind of mimicry has sprung up on West Bank hilltops in the form of master-planned residential developments (like the controversial

"Palestinian settlement" of Rawabi) that owe more than a little to the red-tiled Jewish colonies on the other side of the valleys. Intended for the West Bank's new creditworthy middle class, these planned communities draw on the same Palestinian construction workforce as the Jewish settlements, and their investors belong to a domestic capitalist class waist-deep in joint ventures with their Israeli counterparts.

The long history of Jewish dependency on Palestinian labor and resources has not necessarily led to any positive recognition for Palestinians; it has been accompanied at almost every step of the way by discrimination, degradation, and exploitation. Nor are there any practical prospects today for a more equitable post-Occupation arrangement. Foreign and regional powers are more interested in sowing conflict and division than in brokering just solutions. But for working people at least, squeezed on both sides of the Green Line by the economic scourge of neoliberalism, the case for common cause and innovative labor organizing is steadily growing. In the last several years, in the Occupied Territories and Israel, new trade unions have emerged, independent of the circles of government power in Ramallah and Jerusalem. These organizations now have strong cooperative ties with NGOs that advocate for the labor and human rights of foreign migrants and West Bank Palestinians employed in Israel or the settlements and often under the same umbrella as exploited Israeli Jews and Palestinians.

Efforts at joint organizing among Palestinians and Jews are still in a fledgling stage, and although they recall the early twentieth century socialist dreams of co-existence at the core of a workers commonwealth, they arise out of quite different conditions and in response to a different stage of capitalist development. For one thing, global investors are attracted, as elsewhere in the world, to the region's precarious labor pools, freed up by decades of deregulation and casualization. In addition, the Occupation has helped to concentrate a vast degree of economic power within a handful of oligarchic family empires, in both Israel and the Occupied Territories (while delivering more and more political power into the hands of settler elites who have infiltrated the top echelons of the Israeli government and military). As a result, Israel boasts one of the highest wealth gaps among members of the Organisation for Economic Co-operation and Development, while in the West Bank, there is a vast income gulf between working-class households and the Palestinian Authority's upper management and its associated capitalist circle.[14] These disparities are dwarfed by the economic impact of Occupation; Israel's 2016 GDP per capita was almost $34,000 while the Palestinian GDP per capita that year was less than $2,000.[15]

The Ongoing *Nakba*

Readers familiar with the annals of settler colonialism know how the labor of indigenous populations was typically exploited at the same time as land was seized from them and how the one form of injustice facilitated the other. Israel/Palestine offers a stark example of this dual extortion and is most often compared to apartheid-era South Africa, whose Bantustan labor reservoirs and pass law system have much in common with the increasingly fragmented cantons and permit regime of the Occupied Territories.

There is no uniform blueprint for settler colonialism, and there are many factors that make Israel a singular case. Among these are the Zionist appeal to deep antiquity and biblical scripture to justify the imposition of a Jewish homeland on Palestinian soil; the eccentric definition of "Jewish nationality" (not recognized in international law), which offers Israeli citizenship to Jews worldwide—and the corresponding legal nonexistence of Israeli national identity[16]; the long-established UN recognition of inalienable Palestinian rights, including the right to return, and the even stronger record of indictments against Israel's conduct as an occupying force; and the unique legal status, under UNRWA jurisdiction, of more than five and a half million registered refugees worldwide (only slightly less than the total population of Palestinians resident in the lands of historic Palestine).

This book does not take up any lines of comparison with other settler colonial examples. Nor is my goal to add to the bulging stockpile of "solutions" for ending the Occupation.[17] *Stone Men*

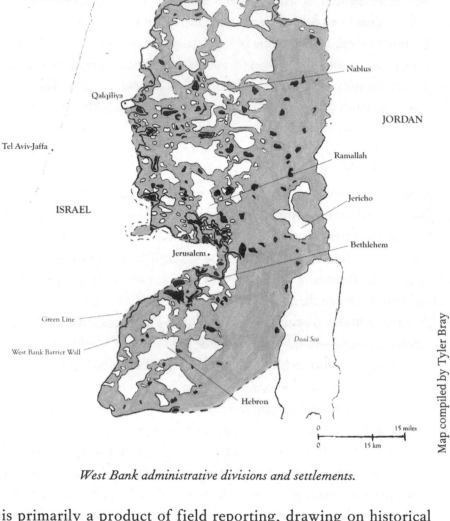

Areas A & B
Israeli Municipality
Israeli Settlements

Jenin

Mediterranean Sea

Nablus

Qalqiliya

JORDAN

Tel Aviv-Jaffa

Ramallah

Jericho

ISRAEL

Bethlehem

Jerusalem

Green Line

Dead Sea

West Bank Barrier Wall

Hebron

0   15 miles
0   15 km

Map compiled by Tyler Bray

West Bank administrative divisions and settlements.

is primarily a product of field reporting, drawing on historical scholarship as and when required. Nonetheless it can be read as a contribution, in its own way, to the debate about a decolonized, successor state. With no end in sight to the ongoing land grab— as early as 2010, according to Israeli NGO B'Tselem, as much as 42 percent of the West Bank was under the jurisdiction of local and regional Jewish settlement councils[18]—the talking points of that debate are pivoting rapidly away from the viability of a partition between separate states. Tectonic shifts in regional politics among the powerful Arab states are hastening on this transition. Advocates of a just settlement focus more and more on ways of equalizing the civil and political rights of all who currently reside in (and who would be entitled to return to) Israel and the Occupied Territories.[19] There already exists a de facto single state on these lands, roughly corresponding to the pre-1948 geographical shape of Mandatory Palestine. What kinds of evidence and testimony would help to secure equality of citizenship and basic democratic rights for all of its current and future populations? Should it include the long record of labor contributions outlined in this book?

Bonded, indentured, enslaved, or ethnically persecuted workers who built other nations have struggled, on a related basis, for some kind of state-level recognition. In the United States, the hard labor of African, Irish, Chinese, and Mexican Americans has often been held up as a justification for earning full inclusion and civil rights, and, in the case of the descendants of slaves, as grounds for economic reparations. Undocumented immigrants facing deportation today often stake their claim to residence on the basis of their labor. As far as I know, no formal suit of this kind has been filed, and some related pledges—like General Sherman's promise of forty acres and a mule as recognition of African American freedmen's right to own land they had worked as slaves—notoriously went unfulfilled. But, over time, the moral force of the argument has played into the civic and legal acceptance of the rights of these "laboring" populations.

Despite its many inequities, including the perpetuation of white supremacy, the United States has become a multiethnic society, capable of absorbing a range of immigrant identities. Israel is no such thing (least of all a "nation of immigrants"): its lawmakers vigorously oppose the granting of any rights to foreign workers or to their Israeli-born children, let alone to refugees entitled to protection under international conventions. A Jew who sets foot in Israel for the first time enjoys national rights that cannot be accorded to its own Palestinian citizens, let alone those from the Occupied Territories, or migrants who have spent much of their lives working in Israel, building homes, hotels, museums, and shopping malls in cities and suburban subdivisions, not to mention the segregating landscape of bypass roads, separation walls, and prisons.

Settler colonialists, especially in North America, often appealed to John Locke's labor theory of property to justify their expropriation of land from indigenous peoples. According to their version of Locke, if the colonists "improved" land by mixing their labor with the soil, they were entitled to own it. Clearly it helped to be able to argue that the land had been neglected or underused by the indigenous population (considered to be a waste of God's bounty to humankind), and even better if it were designated as "vacant" wilderness. Zionist settlers made good use of this formula in their approach to redeeming what they called the Land of Israel; for many decades, "making the desert bloom" was a serviceable mythology, and it still passes muster in some quarters.[20]

In Locke's theory of property, as Marx pointed out, it makes little difference if would-be owners base their claim on their own toil or on their use of hired labor; in either case, the property belongs to them. The later industrialization of wage labor only magnified this patently unfair outcome. Under the factory system, Locke's ideal of property earned through an individual's effort fell apart (though it lives on today in the case of creative or intellectual property, where authors, broadly defined, have limited rights). Workers employed in waged labor are generally excluded from any equity rights to the fruit of their labor. This rule also applies to the labor of construction, even though a built asset can greatly increase the value of the land on which it sits. Typically, the principle of sweat equity applies only to the value earned from an owner's personal investment of effort. The toil of a waged laborer on the same building or enterprise is regarded as a more limited contractual matter, altogether separate from property and use rights.

But what if the workers in question are not freely contracted and instead are bound by tight, even coercive, constraints placed upon them by the employer group? And what if the land on which they are instructed to work has been illegally taken from their own people? On an individual basis, evidence of these inequities might support a compensation claim, but the collective plight of the post-1948 Palestinian worker merits a longer view and a different kind of approach. Surely, in the case of state-level justice regarding territorial sovereignty, full political rights, and citizenship, the overall worth of Palestinians' aggregate labor contribution to the assets encompassed by the state ought to be considered as an equity component. Israeli policies, at least since 1948, were designed to make those contributions all but compulsory. That so many Palestinians had no alternative but to work for their occupiers—and were all but forced to do so—further strengthens the case for a remedy that includes political recognition as full citizens in a unitary state.

Under UN Resolutions 194 (1948) and 3236 (1974), the forced transfer of Palestinians from their land and homes in 1948 and 1967 established Israel's responsibility to acknowledge the former owners' right to return to their property. Far from a single historical event—since it continues to this day in each act of confiscation, demolition, and eviction—the ongoing *Nakba* (*al-Nakba al-mustamera*) has extended these liabilities, adding new entries to the list of wrongs that might present grounds for restitution and reparations in any final settlement. One of the longest running injustices, and intimately connected to this long *Nakba*, was the making of a tractable and dependent workforce—a reservoir of unfree, and all but compulsory, labor.[21]

The sharp constraints placed on Palestinian livelihoods today may appear remote in time from 1948, but they are integral to, and inseparable from, the *Nakba*'s unfinished program of dispossession, expulsion, and asset transfer. Indeed, the prototype for these labor controls was the immediate post-1948 treatment of Israeli Palestinians, whose limited movement was subject to military say-so. It was through the filter of these tight travel constraints that their cut-price labor was first made available to Jewish employers from the early 1950s. Later, in the course of the Occupation of the West Bank and Gaza, the administration of those constraints was finessed through the growth of a convoluted permit system, ubiquitous restrictions on movement, mass incarceration, torture, wage theft, advanced surveillance, and the intensive discipline and humiliation served on workers at checkpoints. Using the strategy of economic pacification (jobs in return for acquiescence, and in some cases, collaboration with Shin Bet, the Israeli security agency), alongside the tactic of collective punishment (border closures and permit cancellations as retribution for the intifadas or autonomous acts of resistance), the authorities have been able to fine-tune their management of Palestinians' existential need to access the Israeli labor market.

At no point was this "need" ever produced by a competitive labor market. It was devised, shaped, and perpetuated, under threat of penalty, by the occupying force. Israeli policymakers sought to block economic development in the West Bank and Gaza by depressing wages, reinforcing dependency, and shoring up poverty. The intended outcome was that, for most households, the alternative to working for the occupier would be a starvation wage. As one of my interviewees put it, "if we didn't have work inside Israel, we would have to eat each other." Given the high levels of food insecurity and chronic malnutrition among the Palestinian population, and especially in Gaza and parts of Area C, his comment was a particularly dark joke.

1

Conquest and Manpower

In Palestine we do not propose even to go through the form of consulting the wishes of the present inhabitants of the country ... The Four Great Powers are committed to Zionism. And Zionism, be it right or wrong, good or bad, is rooted in age-long traditions, in present needs, in future hopes, of far profounder import than the desires and prejudices of the 700,000 Arabs who now inhabit that ancient land.

  —Lord Arthur Balfour, Memorandum to Lord Curzon, August 11, 1919

Mapai [the Israeli Labor Party] holds the orthodox Socialist view concerning "imperialism," which it regards as something inherently evil. It might therefore have been expected to be an ally of the Arab workers in their struggle against British "imperialism." This is however not so, because its Zionism, on all occasions, takes precedence over its socialism.

  —George Mansour, "The Arab Worker under the Palestine Mandate," 1937

In many parts of the world, the grisly upshot of settler colonialism was the (near) eradication of indigenous populations.[1] Zionist settlement of Palestinian lands might have been little different had it not proceeded at a time when the great empires of the modern era were winding down and cracking apart. The Israeli land grabs of 1948 and 1967 ran directly against the headwinds of decolonization elsewhere in the region and the world. Subsequent Israeli treatment of Palestinian refugees and occupied peoples fell afoul of canons of international law that had pivoted away from supporting the European doctrines of conquest. For those and other reasons, Zionist colonists were unable to forcibly transfer all of the inhabitants of Palestine in line with what Zionist founder Theodor Herzl described as the need "to spirit the penniless population across the border ... whilst denying it any employment in our own country."[2] In 1937, David Ben-Gurion wrote that "I support compulsory transfer. I don't see anything immoral in it,"[3] and Joseph Weitz, the director of the Jewish Agency's Land Department, spelled it out:

> The only way is to transfer the Arabs from here to neighboring countries, all of them except perhaps Bethlehem, Nazareth and Old Jerusalem. Not a single village or a single tribe must be left.[4]

After 1948, when they attained an unassailable demographic advantage (Ben-Gurion aimed for an 80 percent Jewish majority), Israeli leaders opted for hardship policies often referred to as "soft transfer" or "silent expulsions" (in which Palestinians would self-deport) or more varied forms of ethnic cleansing such as settlement expansion on confiscated land. At the same time as the settlers took over lands, they commandeered the labor of indigenous Arabs to build the settler state. These two developments were not unconnected. Turning rural male Palestinians into wage workers—as kibbutz field hands, tilers and plasterers on Israeli construction sites, or all-purpose laborers on West Bank settlements—meant that their hold on the land was weakened, making it easier to seize.[5] But long before settlers gained the upper hand as employers and occupiers, they had to compete for, and win, a decisive share of the labor market—a story that began in scrappy fashion in Ottoman Palestine, generated no end of friction during the British Mandate, and reached its bloody climax in 1948.

Those early labor market conflicts cast the die that would shape the future career of apartheid-style segregation in Israel/Palestine.[6] They also determined how control of the Palestinian workforce, after 1948 and 1967 and to this day, became the key to the building out of the Israeli state and its expansion into the West Bank. That is why, in planning how to write this book, I realized I would need to review the history of employment in early twentieth century Palestine and to do so through the lens of the construction jobs that are my primary interest in these pages. In the first three formative decades of the century, the often bitter contention over jobs and livelihoods fueled the steady growth of both Zionist and Palestinian nationalism. The outcome was violent and unequal; after the *Nakba*, it bred a cruel dominion, and later an occupation, that continues to violate international norms and laws. But the version of that history which I will present in this chapter shows that in spite of the early settler resolve to "purify" workplaces as exclusively Jewish, or the later government efforts to replace Palestinians with migrant workers, the physical unfolding of Zionism on the land has always been a project that both relied on Arab workers and was indebted to them in ways that have yet to be fully reckoned with.

A European Wage in the Middle East

Because of my own point of entry sketched earlier (see the Preface), I chose to begin with the founding of Kibbutz Ginosar itself, as a tactical Zionist outpost, in the heat of the anti-colonial Arab Revolt (1936–39). In common with other rudimentary settlements established in the Eastern Galilee during this period, the founders of Ginosar intended to secure a Jewish presence on militarily strategic portions of Arab territory. But the other goal behind their formation was to carve out a sustainable Jewish niche in the labor market, where previous efforts at agricultural settlement had failed.

In 1934, Ginosar's young founders struck camp in the Jewish settlement at Migdal (just outside the village of Majdal, allegedly the birthplace of Mary Magdalene), on a ridge overlooking the western shore of the Sea of Galilee. There they awaited allocation from the Jewish Agency, the leading Zionist organization, which had teamed up with the Jewish National Fund (JNF) to buy Arab land from absentee landlords. In March 1937, when the paramilitary Haganah command encouraged them to secure the strategic road between

Tiberias and Rosh Pina, the group moved down on to the traditional lands of Ghuwayr Abu Shusha (the Arabic name for Ginosar's location) to occupy a portion of the 5,000 dunums (a dunum is a quarter acre) that had been purchased by JNF rival, Baron Edmond de Rothschild's Palestine Jewish Colonization Association.[7] Once in place, they hastily erected a "tower and stockade" (*homa umigdal*). Thrown up overnight to outfox the British authorities, this kind of fortification—a watchtower and four shacks, surrounded by a gravel-filled wall and a barbed-wire perimeter fence—was utilized by dozens of start-up kibbutzim during this period.[8] Under Ottoman law (adopted by the British), an illegal building could not be demolished once a roof was added; hence the hurried nocturnal effort to raise up a structure, no matter how rickety.[9]

Once the stockade was in place, and after the Arab Revolt was brutally suppressed by the British (with Zionist paramilitary assistance), the Ginosar group dug in and expanded its holdings, though only after a violent conflict over water rights with the neighboring Ghuwayr Abu Shusha villagers (which resulted in two Arab fatalities and the subsequent imprisonment of ten kibbutz members).[10]

Many of these founder members, who included Yigal Allon, freshly graduated from Kadoorie Agricultural High School,

Ginosar pioneers in settler guard uniforms, with watchtower, 1937.

Courtesy of Kibbutz Ginosar

were ardent disciples of A. D. Gordon, a prominent advocate of the Labor Zionist doctrine that would become a dominant strain among other Yishuv leaders like Ben-Gurion, Yosef Brenner, Golda Meir,

Aerial view of Ginosar stockade, 1937.

Courtesy of Kibbutz Ginosar

and Berl Katznelson. In accord with Gordon's teachings, these pioneers believed that true possession of land was something that had to be earned, not through forcible acquisition, but through their labor with the soil. For this kind of Zionist, manual work was hallowed as an act of individual redemption, and this labor was an anvil on which to forge the self-reliant mentality of Jewish nationalism. Yet Ginosar, like other kibbutzim, would get an economic boost from the annexation of stolen land. During the *Nakba*, the kibbutzniks took over neighboring Arab lands in Ghuwayr Abu Shusha, whose residents were expelled as part of Yigal Allon's Operation Broom.[11]

A charismatic zealot, Gordon had settled in Degania (the first *kvutza*, a kibbutz prototype), ten miles to the south of Ginosar, in 1919, and his influence grew considerably through the Gordonia and *Hapoel Hatzair* (Young Worker) movements in the decade following his death three years later. His teachings were a cocktail of Tolstoyan communalism, Jewish mysticism, and neo-Marxist productivism, but his assertions about Zionism were often disarmingly candid:

> we come to our Homeland in order to be planted in our natural soil from
> which we have been uprooted, to strike our roots deep into its life-giving

substances, and to stretch out our branches in the sustaining and creating air and sunlight of the Homeland.[12]

Gordon's views were aligned with formative Labor Zionists like Ber Borochov (buried in the Kinneret cemetery, also just to the south of Ginosar), who argued that, historically, Jews had seldom been allowed to occupy productive positions in society, either as artisans or farmers, but had been relegated to middlemen occupations in trade, finance, and services. Settlement in Palestine held out the promise of a Jewish peasant-proletarian nation, with agrarian roots, and a producer base in control of its economic and spiritual destiny. To fulfil this aspiration, Gordon and other Labor Zionists tried (with only partial success) to steer their acolytes away from the kind of *urban* proletarian identity advocated by other European socialists and onto the redeeming land itself.

Gordon allegedly coined the slogan of "Conquest of Labor" to evoke the personal struggle of Zionist settlers, through manual toil on the land, to bring forth the muscular personality of the New Jew.[13] In practice, the term became inseparable from the concept of "Hebrew Labor," which he and others took up as the rallying cry for barring Arabs from employment in Jewish enterprises. Nor can the darker meaning of Gordon's "conquest" be ignored when put in the context of colonial settlement. Who was being conquered? Gordon's deferential "inner Jew," deprived, by generations of Gentiles, of the right to serve as the natural backbone of the economy? Or the Arab fellahin peasantry, many of them already struggling as indebted tenant-farmers, who would be chased off these lands and their own ancestral small holdings in the years to come? Gordon's "religion of labor" was a powerful motivator for the partisan mentality of kibbutzniks who imagined they were building an agrarian socialist paradise. But it was also a convenient, and increasingly unsubtle, fig leaf for the land colonization project of Zionism.

In some respects, Gordon's creed had a clear affinity with Locke's labor theory of property, and, although they acquired their early colonies through market land purchases, Zionist settlers increasingly promoted their cause through the widely circulated mythology about the "barren wasteland" of Ottoman Palestine and the settlers' vaunted success in "making the desert bloom." Just as in North America, the settlers often intruded on precapitalist systems of land commons. In Palestine, these were either *miri,* or state-owned, land where grazing and growing rights were granted by usufruct to peasants, or the more egalitarian *musha* (accounting for 50 percent of land ownership in Palestine), a communal form of production that evenly shared out the fertile and poor lands through periodic redivision among village clans.[14]

Socialist settlers with modest, assimilationist goals might have adapted to, and flourished within, these systems, but Jewish agricultural settlement was increasingly driven along a narrower, nationalist track and would be steered ultimately toward maximal control of territory, interpreted as a claim of ancient right on the Land of Israel (Eretz Israel). Initially, however, the collective enterprise of the kibbutz presented a technical solution to the economic challenge faced by Jewish settlers in Palestine since the 1880s—how to generate a "European standard of living" from a Middle Eastern agricultural livelihood.

In the late nineteenth century, early Jewish colonists (the "Lovers of Zion" from Eastern Europe) tried, and failed, to subsist on lands near the coast and in Eastern Galilee that had been purchased from absentee owners residing in Damascus, Aleppo, and Beirut. Baron Edmond de Rothschild converted these colonies into cash-cropping plantations, drawing on the colonial Algerian model and aimed at the international export market. This was a labor-intensive system, and Rothschild found the cost of employing Jewish settlers with little agrarian experience to be prohibitive, given the abundant availability of Arabs with unmatchable skills in regional agriculture and with low-cost household economies of their own.

After Rothschild turned over the titles of these colonies to the Palestine Jewish Colonization Association in 1898, a new wave of planters were allowed to establish privately owned *moshava* farms, but they too favored the cheaper and more capable Arab hands. Jewish workers appealed to these new owners to employ them on the basis of shared ethnicity and at higher pay, arguing that it was unjust to reduce Jews to Arab standards of living, but the planters would not do so unless they worked for an "Arab wage," to be topped up from international Zionist funds. None of these agricultural efforts to employ the Jewish settlers succeeded in providing year-round livelihoods, and so large numbers of them left the region.[15]

Another doomed effort to create a sustainable Jewish workforce involved the importation of Yemenite Jews from 1909 to 1914 to take the low-skill agricultural jobs, again at "Arab pay." Affronted by being physically segregated and consigned, like a lower caste, to the more routine tasks, the Yemenites resisted and ended up competing for the better, higher paid jobs that were reserved for Ashkenazis.[16] In some respects, the unequal economic status of Israel's Mizrahi Jews (Arabic-speaking and from Arab cultural backgrounds) originated in this early conflict and has endured to the present in the form of a gap in income and status between Mizrahi and Ashkenazi populations. The long-standing social and cultural denigration of these "Oriental Jews" in Israeli society can also be traced to the racist assumptions of early Zionist settlers that Yemenite Jews and their Sephardic brethren were only fit to be "hewers of wood and drawers of water."[17] To this day, the lower economic and social standing of the Mizrahi is bolstered by the Israeli equivalent of what W. E. B. Du Bois called a "psychological wage" offered to impoverished European Americans on account of their whiteness: you may be poor, but at least you are not Palestinians.

Ultimately, it was the solution of producer collectives, operating on the principles of self-labor and mutual aid, that proved to be the only sustainable economic arrangements for exclusively Jewish agricultural employment. These took a variety of forms: the *moshav ovdim*, or small-holders cooperative; the fully collectivized settlements of the kibbutzim; and the "middle-class" *moshavim*, which did not prohibit the hiring of Arab day labor. Pooled resources, group purchasing and contracting, and communal cooking and living proved to be more cost-efficient than a household system based on individual wages. The savings were supposed to cover the additional expense of "culture," considered indispensable for the literate Ashkenazi but not for the less bookish Yemenite Jews or Arabs.[18] Labor

Zionists, after all, set out to create an *advanced peasantry*, educated and ideologically committed to their new class identity, as distinct from the more organic Arab peasantry. But these kinds of communal enterprise were also heavily subsidized and could not be sustained without funding from overseas Zionists. The JNF, for example, provided forgivable loans as seed capital and handed over land that it considered "national" property, never to be sold to, or worked on by, non-Jews. These donations helped to inoculate the kibbutzniks against the contagious taint of colonialism and the presumed evil of capitalist labor exploitation.

Even with the JNF subsidies and the advantage of efficiencies from pooled resources, the settlers could not compete in the open market with Palestinian agricultural products. They could only sustain sales because of the preferential consumption of the swelling population of urban Jews. Like the Hebrew Labor policy, aimed at excluding Arabs from urban, coastal workplaces, the campaign to buy solely Jewish produce was more technically a boycott of Arab goods, and it was upheld with force. With full encouragement and financial backing from Histadrut trade union officials, enforcers issued death threats to, and physically assaulted, Jewish business owners who employed Arab workers; they organized often violent pickets of these workplaces that resulted in property destruction and serious injuries, and they destroyed produce from Jewish agricultural colonies that hired Arabs, along with Arab products popular with Jewish consumers.[19] Inevitably, these boycotts generated reciprocal action on the other side; during the general strike called for in mid-April 1936 that launched the Arab Revolt, Arab participants withdrew patronage of Jewish goods and Jewish-owned businesses.

A Great Colonizing Agency

No entity was more central to the Conquest of Labor than the Histadrut, founded in 1920 as the General Union for Hebrew Workers in the Land of Israel. Far from being the product of a mass workers movement, the Histadrut was the command center of the new Yishuv, driving every aspect of Zionist settlement, from the incubation of the Haganah paramilitary defense force to the hard-nosed enforcement of Arab exclusion from workplaces.[20] Golda Meir described it as "a great colonizing agency," and it functioned like a provisional Jewish state in Mandatory Palestine. In the years after 1948, it would grow into a behemoth, distributing welfare services and public goods; steering social, economic, and foreign policy; and, in its capacity as a corporate enterprise (Israel's largest non-state employer), controlling wages, pensions, and medical benefits for the vast majority of the national workforce. At the peak of its power in the 1980s, 85 percent of Israeli workers were members, of which more than 280,000 were employed by Histadrut subsidiaries.[21]

From the outset, the federation's leadership, anchored by Ben-Gurion, its first general secretary, strongly resisted any effort to integrate Arabs and Jews into the same organized trade union unit. This meant pushing back against the socialist beliefs of many Jewish immigrants. How could a workers' society be created without full equality and class unity for all? In Europe, anti-Zionists hoped that "the Jewish Question" would be resolved through the triumph of socialism. Many Ashkenazi settlers saw their efforts to become pro-letarianized as part of that same struggle for socialism in Palestine. They clung to the belief that their zeal and fraternity would help the Arab peasantry shake off its bonds to effendi landowner exploiters and that urbanization would bring forth a new and modern working class, composed equally of Arabs and Jews.

Yet the Histadrut did all it could to ensure that the primary result of Jewish proletarianization would be a new Jewish nation, rather than a new multiethnic working class.[22] Conflict between worker and employer could not be avoided. It was, after all, the reason a trade union was necessary. But wherever these differences arose, the Histadrut leadership lobbied Jewish owners to put the nationalist interest before profit and exhorted workers to tamp down their wage demands in the interests of Zionist unity. The key to labor peace, the federation's leaders insisted, was a Jewish-only workforce, and they seldom failed to remind recalcitrant Jewish employers that the grisly alternative would be "Arab violence."[23] In a 1930 address to the His-tadrut Executive, Ben-Gurion thundered that "there must be a war, a war of life and death" for Hebrew Labor, and again, a year later, warned that "Hebrew Labor will be solved by two paths: peacefully, by the purchase of land and farms and, if not peacefully, then behold by the path of war."[24]

Arab militancy did exist—it was not solely a bogeyman—but it arose primarily as resistance to the Hebrew Labor policy and to Zionist expansion. Nonetheless, alarmist talk about the Arab threat, combined with appeals to Jewish security and victimhood, would become a dominant strain of Zionist rhetoric right down to the present day. From the mid-1920s through the late 1930s, the Histadrut leadership and the Zionist Executive used holy war sloganeering: officials hyperbolically depicted "invasive breaches" in the "wall of Hebrew labor" as frontline battle losses, and they vilified Jewish bosses who employed Arabs as "national traitors," committing the grave sin of hiring "foreign" labor.[25] When the fearmongering failed, the Histadrut called Jewish strikes to pressure employers to lay off Arabs. The federation bused in middle-class Tel Avivians—teachers, doctors, writers, actors, and librarians—to picket orange growers defamed as "displacers" and "alienators."[26] Strikes were a persistent feature of workplaces in Mandate Palestine for almost three decades, but the Histadrut's "Zionization" of strike actions ruthlessly singled out employers who tried to save on labor costs by hiring Arab workers or who preferred them because they were less likely to protest their working conditions.[27]

Commenting, in 1937, on the yawning gulf between the Histadrut's tactics and its self-presentation as a force for the good of all working people, George Mansour, general secretary of the Arab Workers Society, observed:

> If the Histadrut had been sincere in its protestations of good will, if it had been willing to do something to improve the lot of the Arab worker in return for "penetrating into all spheres of labour" and turning the country into a Jewish fatherland, it might have done something as follows. It might have employed one quarter Arab labour with its own labour and have taught the Arabs its own skilled processes and have paid the Arab the same wage for the same work. In that case, the Arab would not have felt quite the same

bitterness that he feels now. The Histadrut never did anything of the sort. It
never employed a single Arab if it could help it; when it was forced to do so,
it paid them half the wages that it paid to its own men; and whenever it could
oust Arab from any sphere of work, it did so.[28]

In its capacity as a union, the Histadrut was obliged to represent and
protect workers. But it was also an employer, through its various
industrial arms, in construction, manufacturing, transport, health,
and (through its own Bank Hapoalim) financing. Not long after its
founding, the Histadrut had become the largest source of Jewish
jobs in Palestine, and so it exercised highly centralized control over
every aspect of workers' lives while trying to furnish them with a
"European wage." By 1933, as much as 75 percent of the Jewish
workforce were Histadrut members, and the federation's power as
a mass employer allowed it to suppress wage inflation at the same
time it was executing the Hebrew Labor policy. Balancing its many
roles came at a steep cost, but the federation's tight relationship
with world Zionist organizations meant that bankruptcy was never
a serious risk since its industrial operations would always be bailed
out with overseas funds.

The Hebrew Labor policy, which entailed higher payroll costs,
was never an easy sell among Jewish private sector employers, some
of whom worked around compliance by employing Jewish women
at lower wages than the men.[29] While foreign owners of enterprises
clearly preferred Arab employees, Zionist pressure on the Mandate
authorities harvested a sizable (and unfair, according to Arab critics)
share of government jobs for Jews.[30] In the public sector, Jews and
Arabs worked together in railways, government enterprises and
agencies like the telephone and telegraph systems, and the ports, as
well as municipal government in cities with mixed populations or an
Arab majority. Wages were still very lopsided in these workplaces
(with Arabs earning 30 percent to 50 percent less), but cooperation, even organizing, among Arab and Jewish workers was not
uncommon. In its approach to these "mixed" workplaces, which
Ben-Gurion bluntly described as an "evil," the Histadrut endorsed
the principle of joint organization under the rubric of two separate

(but decidedly unequal) unions, though its ultimate preference was for the Arab one to be a subordinate department under the wing of the Jewish mother federation.

In Zachary Lockman's scrupulous account, the railway sector in particular saw prolonged efforts at joint organizing. At one point, in 1924, members of the radical Po'alei Tziyon Smol Party of Labor Zionists took control of the railwaymen union and called for a fully integrated, "international" bargaining unit, open to all. This development (bakery workers in Jaffa and Tel Aviv made a similar declaration in 1922) posed a threat to Histadrut leaders, who pushed hard for Ben-Gurion's alternative vision of an All-Palestine alliance with two national sections. In any event, the initiative fell apart a year later when the Arab members, suspicious of Histadrut intentions and appalled by the federation's effort to "purify" workplaces elsewhere, broke away to form the independent Palestinian Arab Workers' Society (PAWS).[31]

It would be the first of several Arab labor organizations, formed by increasingly urbanized and industrialized workers, including the Arab Workers Society (1934), Federation of Arab Trade Unions and Labor Societies (1942), and Arab Workers' Congress (1945); by the end of World War II, PAWS alone boasted a membership of more than 15,000.[32] The Histadrut decried these Arab alternatives, and, in 1932, formed the auxiliary Palestine Labor League to combat the increasingly nationalist PAWS (which was equally opposed by the elite, or *ayan*, class of notables in the Arab Higher Committee).

By the early 1930s, the federation's strenuous efforts to enforce the Hebrew Labor policy had resulted in the dismissal of many Arab workers from Jewish enterprises, but the economy and labor market were expanding, even in the midst of the worldwide depression, and so overall Arab employment in the Jewish and foreign-owned private sector continued to increase.[33] The Mandate authorities gave preference to would-be Jewish immigrants with capital (more than a thousand pounds sterling) and professional training, and so their wealth and expertise flowed into the country along with a wave of refugees from Nazi Europe (150,000 between 1933 and 1935). Despite this general economic growth, Zionists invested exclusively in Jewish enterprise, which raised Jewish wages and depressed Arab ones (to a ratio of at least 2:1), generating ever sharper conflicts that culminated in the Arab Revolt.[34]

Cementing the Future

I n light of this book's chief topic, a significant effort at joint organizing occurred in 1924–25 at the Nesher cement works near Haifa. During the construction of the Jewish firm's cement factory, the owners paid the Histadrut's Jewish workers more than twice the wage of Egyptians imported to work at a discount price. The Jews, many of them communists or socialists, sought and won the cooperation of the Arab workers to strike for higher wages for all.[35] The Histadrut opposed the joint action, and, in a bid to end the two-month strike, reached a settlement with management that cut out the Arabs. The Jewish rank and file initially refused to abandon their fellow strikers, but the federation pressured them to accept the agreement, and most of the Egyptians were deported.[36]

Nesher saw another strike action just after the plant re-opened in 1925 with an exclusively Jewish workforce. At the quarries that supplied the factory, an Arab contractor was employing Arab laborers at rock-bottom wages. The Histadrut brought its Jewish factory workers out on strike because the Nesher owners would not demand the replacement of the quarry's Arabs with Jews. Analyzing the difference between these two strikes—the first united Jews and Arabs, while the second pitted Jews against Arabs—Lockman speculates that the Histadrut may have ensured that the radical Jewish "troublemakers" employed in constructing the factory, and who initially defied the union leadership, were not subsequently hired when the factory opened.[37] While the second strike did not succeed in Judaizing the quarry, the Nesher disputes illustrate the zeal with which the Histadrut intervened against joint Jewish–Arab labor initiatives. But they also show how some left-wing Jews were willing to stand by their political principles and buck the Zionist priorities of the Histadrut leadership.

This double standard continued in the course of the next decade, which saw little improvement in conditions at the quarry. Several strikes broke out in the early 1930s, and on each occasion, the Arab strikers appealed to Histadrut, and to Nesher's Jewish workers, to mount solidarity actions. The appeals were not ignored, but the responses, and the support proffered, were half-hearted at best. When the quarry workers finally abandoned these appeals after the last strike failed in 1933, Abu Houshi, head of the Haifa Labor Council, wrote a damning summary of the Histadrut's conduct: "The failure is attributable in large measure to the stance of the Jewish workers of Nesher but even more so to the indifference of the Histadrut Executive and its lack of help."[38] The federation got its way after the Arab general strike in 1936, when the British forced the entry of Jews into the quarry's Arab workforce. But the fact that the Histadrut provided replacement Jewish workers in struck workplaces and actively engaged in strike-breaking during the uprising did not sit well with communists and other leftists of the Yishuv who still prioritized working class unity above (bourgeois) Zionist exclusion. On the Arab side, the Jewish scabbing ended any remaining illusions about joint organizing.

Cement played another, more inadvertent, role in the souring of relations between Arab workers and the Histadrut's Palestinian Labor League. In October 1935, a drum purportedly containing cement broke open while being unloaded at the Jaffa port, revealing smuggled weapons and ammunition bound for the Haganah paramilitary. A huge cache of machine guns and rifles was found in other drums. Following a passive response from the British authorities, Arab leaders called for a general strike. Public agitation over the so-called Cement Incident inspired the legendary rebel preacher Sheikh Izz al-Din al-Qassam to recruit a guerrilla force, known as the Black Hand, for insurgent actions, and his martyrdom in a subsequent skirmish helped to spark the Arab Revolt several months later.

Nesher, which quickly established a monopoly in the cement business, was not just any factory. Its need to exist was proclaimed in 1902 by none other than Theodor Herzl, the most consequential champion of the Zionist movement. To this day, Nesher's promotional material gives pride of place to Herzl's comment in *Altneuland*, his influential utopian novel about the growth of a Jewish state in

Palestine: "The plan for building a homeland for the Jewish people must take into consideration the founding of a Hebrew cement factory as well."[39] Cement would literally be the raw material for the construction of the Jewish "national home" favored by the 1917 Balfour Declaration, and so for Herzl a production plant ought to be a cornerstone of the Zionist economy. Herzl had little knowledge of the state of industry or its prospects in Palestine; for him, cement was simply a symbol of modernity and a component part of the technologically advanced society he was outlining in the novel.

But as the conflicts at Nesher forewarned, the business of supplying stone for making cement (and concrete) was destined to be a politically sensitive issue. Stone quarries were an Arab labor monopoly, and the related and long-nurtured craft of stonemasonry remained firmly in Arab hands. This meant that a Zionist nation made by Jews alone would have to be built from materials other than the locally available stone used in traditional Palestinian construction. These materials would have to be under Jewish control, especially if they were to be handled and worked by exclusively Jewish laborers.[40]

In 1922, a syndicate of British Jewish businessmen set out to realize Herzl's vision by founding the Nesher Portland Cement Company in London. They purchased land near Haifa from Lebanese owners after limestone suitable for high-quality cement was located and successfully tested in the Mount Carmel and Kishon Valley regions. The subsequent growth of Nesher as the largest private company in Palestine was also helped along by protective tariff concessions granted by Mandate authorities despite being at odds with British colonial trade policies. Companies like Nesher also benefited from the subsidizing flow of "national capital" from world Jewry.[41] These substantial subventions—often in the form of forgivable loans or investments with no return—supported all aspects of Jewish-owned enterprise and allowed the tightly organized Jewish sector to develop at a fast clip.

By comparison, Arab economic development was either sluggish or heavily dependent on contracts from the Mandate authority's public works programs.[42] The economy of urban Arab communities was organized around small workshops, along with some medium-sized manufacturing firms, in tobacco, textiles, pearl, and soap, but these enterprises were outpaced (and underdeveloped) by coastal Jewish industrial output that enjoyed the overseas donations. Outside of the urban centers, the majority of Arabs subsisted in a semi-feudal economy, many of them heavily indebted from share-cropping and rent-seeking from effendi landowners and bound to traditional clan (*hamula*) networks that were resistant to change. Village social structures remained intact even when family members traveled for waged labor on government facilities or in urban foreign-owned enterprises on the coast.

Nesher's status as the private sector's too-big-to-fail champion was shared by the Histadrut's own construction arm, Solel Boneh, which was responsible for deploying Nesher's cement to develop the kind of nation-making infrastructure and housing that purely private builders might have considered too risky or unprofitable. From the moment of its conception as a cooperative for building public works in 1923, Solel Boneh received all kinds of preferential backing. When the firm won contracts from the Mandate administration, the Histadrut channeled funds to make up the difference between the government wages, pegged at Arab rates, and the federation's aspirational "Jewish wages."[43] And when the company's debts forced it into bankruptcy in 1927, it was bailed out by the Zionist Organization. This pattern of protective subsidy continued as Solel Boneh was fully inducted into the campaign to push Arabs out of its workplaces.

In a 1969 speech before the leadership of Mapai (the governing Labor Zionist's party), David Hacohen, former managing director of Solel Boneh, described the discomfort he experienced as the enforcer of these policies:

> I had to fight my friends on the issue of Jewish socialism to defend the fact that I would not accept Arabs in my trade union, the Histadrut; to defend preaching to housewives that they should not buy at Arab stores; to defend the fact that we stood guard at orchards to prevent Arab workers from getting jobs there ... to pour kerosene on Arab tomatoes; to attack Jewish

housewives in the markets and smash Arab eggs they had bought ... to buy
dozens of *dunums* [of land] from an Arab is permitted but to sell God forbid
one Jewish *dunum* to an Arab is prohibited; to take Rothschild the incarna-
tion of capitalism as a socialist and to name him the "benefactor"—to do all
that was not easy.[44]

Not easy, and yet it was done, and with conviction, by managers
like Hacohen, who went on to pursue a left-wing political career
in the Labor establishment that oversaw the expansion of the new
Israeli state. As had been the case at Nesher, the Solel Boneh leadership found it difficult to carve out a Jewish stronghold in the stone
quarries, never mind turn them into Hebrew Labor exclusion zones.
Yet Zionist nation-building demanded a dependable Jewish supply
of limestone for its building projects. After unsuccessful efforts to
penetrate the quarries in the mountains around Jerusalem, which
harbored better quality stone, Hacohen struck a deal with Tahir
Qaraman, a prominent Haifa businessman, to open a series of
mechanized quarries and kilns near the coastal city, eventually con-
solidated, in 1929, into the Even Vesid operation. Qaraman's backing
came with the condition that Arabs would be employed, but, as was
common, they were only paid at half the rate of the Jewish workers.
When the Arabs went on strike in April 1935, the Histadrut came
out against them and supported Jewish strikebreakers, but the strikers held firm, and prevailed, resulting in a huge loss of face for the
federation.[45]

Further south, at the Majdal Yaba quarry, which supplied the Tel
Aviv building boom, repeated efforts were also made to replace
Arab workers. In 1934, a campaign was launched by the Histadrut's
Tel Aviv Labour Council:

We have decided to call on those concerned, contractors, masons, labourers
and drivers to demand from them from now on to use the Jewish product
only.... It is in their power to abstain themselves, and to prevent others, from
using stones produced by Arabs. It is their duty not to allow the unloading of
stones unless they are certain that it is Jewish. ... The refusal to unload such
stone at the place of work will not only be an important step towards making

this industry Jewish, but will also prevent cheap labour from creeping into the other Jewish industries.[46]

George Mansour, the trade unionist who testified so eloquently on behalf of the Arab working class before the Peel Commission in 1937, described the strategy devised by Jewish labor agents:

> ... to send instructions to the managers of the quarry to accumulate large heaps of stones. When this had been done, they were to dismiss the Arab workers, on the ground that there was evidently no demand for stone at present. The plan was thus to persuade the workers to return to their villages. Once they were safely out of the way, Jewish workers would be introduced and the Arabs faced with an accomplished fact. The Arab Labourers' Federation of Jaffa, however, got wind of what was happening and sent word to the workers to not leave the village. The Jews waited for days, and then sent a party of 150 Jewish workers. The Arab workers refused to allow them to start working. After repeated attempts, lasting for 17 days, the managers of the quarries consented to reengage the Arab workers.[47]

The success was short-lived, however. After the 1936 strike that launched the Arab Revolt, British troops assisted the Histadrut by blocking Arabs from returning to work. But the fight was far from over. The excluded workers reclaimed a portion of the workforce during the war, prompting another Histadrut campaign to take over the quarry in 1947, which was again beaten down by strong Arab resistance.[48]

Why were these quarries such a labor battleground? The nationalist demand for "Hebrew stone," quarried and worked by Jewish hands, was clear and persistent. But the quarries were increasingly strategic for Arab nationalists, too. The stone was the region's most valuable natural resource, and the business of quarrying was one of the few nonagricultural sectors relatively free of British interference. So, too, generations of Arab masons had honed their skills on cutting and dressing quarried stone, and the protection of their knowledge within this artisanal trade carried symbolic as well as economic weight. As a result, Arab resistance to Hebrew Labor in the quarries was probably more spirited than in other sectors. The elimination of the "threat" of Arab labor after 1948 was by no means the end of the story. As we will see later in this book, the conflict over the West Bank's all-important quarries has continued to this day.

Solel Boneh's interest in controlling the quarry supply lines was dictated by its assigned role in building out the physical infrastructure of a future Jewish state. To that end, Hacohen forged

West Bank quarry, with goats resting.

Photo by author

close ties with Mandate administrators whose pragmatic colonial policies ensured that the company became the contractor of choice for the British security and transportation networks. This favoritism was reinforced during the Arab Revolt, when the firm was selected to build police stations, Tegart forts (still used today to detain Palestinians political prisoners), and military roads as part of the effort to suppress the uprising. On some of these contracts, Solel Boneh won the authority's approval to employ only Jews, and with wages augmented through the Jewish Agency. On others, the British intervened to allow striking Arabs to be replaced with Jews. In those same years, the firm's workshops also discreetly built the prefabricated huts and fences for the "tower and stockade" settlements, to which the Mandate authorities increasingly turned a blind eye.

Hacohen, who would serve in British intelligence during the war, cultivated personal relationships at all levels of the administration, from high commissioners to policemen.[49] His efforts were no small part of the loyalty network that loosely stitched together British and Zionist colonialism, the latter evolving under the protective carapace of the occupying power. It was an ambivalent relationship, to be sure, especially since militant factions like Irgun and Lehi would engage in guerrilla warfare against the British from 1944 to 1947. But the overriding factor was the strong Orientalist perception that Palestine's Jews belonged to the West and its Arabs to the East. In accord with this prejudice, the former could be trusted, and their own colonial project was, in some measure, a kindred spirit, if not a tidy outgrowth or proxy, of British imperialism. Given the influence of the Zionist lobby on Westminster, "Britain's real role as midwife of the Zionist state," in Rosemary Sayigh's words, was never in doubt.[50]

So close was the bond that Hacohen forged with British officials that, during World War II, they chose Solel Boneh for contracts to build airports, roads, bridges, oil facilities, and army camps, not just in Palestine, but also abroad, in Egypt, Syria, Iraq, Cyprus, Lebanon, Iran, and Bahrain. They awarded the contracts even when competing Arab bids came in lower.[51] Through these points of entry, the company was able to open branches in Beirut, Damascus, and other locations around the Middle East, using its presence and personnel to disseminate Zionist propaganda, act as cover for Haganah and Mossad operatives, and smuggle Jews from cities like Baghdad.

In this regard, Solel Boneh, like the Histadrut, was much more than an economic enterprise. In the years before 1948, it functioned as a vital organ of the Zionist proto-state, helping to channel Jewish immigrants and refugees toward the Yishuv and then building homes to settle them, a mission that mushroomed after independence with the huge spike in immigration. By then, the conquest of Arab labor in Solel Boneh's sector of the building trades was effectively over. Ben-Gurion's "opportunity" to win a Jewish majority in Israel presented itself with the mass expulsions of the *Nakba*, described by Israel's first president Chaim Weizmann as a "miraculous clearing of the land."[52] Then, and only then (though not for very long) were the Histadrut and its subsidiaries able to finally guarantee Arab exclusion from workplaces.

Migrant Workers in Their Own Land

For Palestine's Arab peoples, the "catastrophe" of the *Nakba* was unimaginably devastating. Before 1948, less than 7 percent of Palestine's land was under Jewish possession. (The 1947 UN Partition proposal had allocated 57 percent for a new Jewish state.) After 1948, the Arab share was reduced to 22 percent, and, in Israeli territory, only 3 percent was left, and would henceforth be under constant threat of de-Arabization from military seizures, legal chicanery, and daylight robbery. At least 750,000 Arabs (almost two-thirds of the Arab population of Mandatory Palestine) were chased out of their domiciles and off their lands (400,000 more were expelled in the 1967 June War, referred to by Palestinians as the *Naksa*, a "setback" or "relapse"), and those who remained were now an instant minority, locked down by harsh military dictates and bereft of leadership from the class of notables who had decamped. Land, buildings, businesses, bank accounts, and other possessions left behind by the refugees were looted, expropriated, and sold off.[53] In violation of UN recommendations, the Israeli government forcibly denied their right to return to their homes (the War on Return), and (re) naturalized almost 100,000 would-be citizens as if they were immigrants to Israel.

Of the 160,000 Palestinians who remained (and whom Adel Manna has boldly called "survivors"),[54] initially as many as 50 percent were internally displaced, and, to this day, up to 25 percent of the 1.7 million Israeli Palestinians are considered in that category.[55] After 1948, many were ghettoized by military rule in their towns and regional enclaves, others were corralled inside hastily built labor camps and forced to clear rubble from demolished villages, and virtually all were denied re-employment, at least initially, in former workplaces.[56] Henceforth, their livelihoods would be dependent on policies that mutated according to the needs of the new Israeli state and its priority mission of absorbing new Jewish immigrants.

In September 2017, I visited Kafr Yasif, a village in the Western Galilee, near Acre, that was not cleansed in 1948 and subsequently took in refugees from nearby villages that were depopulated and destroyed.[57] Among those were residents whose families have a long history in the building trades. One of them was Jiryas Sakas, whose parents fled from neighboring al-Birwa, the hometown of Palestine's national poet Mahmoud Darwish. "There's a reason we were allowed to remain here in this village in '48," he remarked to me, "they needed our labor because the new Jewish immigrants were being groomed for higher office, in the military and the professions." Sakas explained that his father grasped at the opportunity when Solel Boneh made it known they needed construction workers from the villages. "This arrangement with Solel Boneh really started in 1954—before then people were still reluctant to leave their villages out of fear." He recalled that, under the Solel Boneh contract, his father's crews performed demolitions on old, damaged buildings in al-Birwa itself and built replacement structures, along with larger projects like the walls and fortifications on Mount Carmel in Haifa. "There were brokers even then, with connections to the military, who were able to secure permits for workers, and of course they took a cut for themselves." His father owned two quarries, producing the chalky "lemon stone" (*naari*) still found in the village's pre-1948 buildings, but these were shut down by Israeli authorities as the cult of building with concrete took hold in the 1950s.

By the time he took over the business from his father in the early 1990s, construction was booming on the back of the ex-Soviet immigration wave. As Solel Boneh's monopoly crumbled under a wave of deregulation and privatization, Sakas's firm adapted to the new culture of subcontracting, employing a mix of locals, West Bank Palestinians, and migrant workers. "I never saw a Jewish worker on a construction site," he claimed, "nor did my father—they only worked in management." Looking back over the history of families like his, he reckoned that "we have built close to 100 percent of Israeli homes." I asked him if he felt that this deserved some larger form of recompense or recognition. "For me, it's not a matter of compensation," he replied, "it's more about the right to return. I feel we have all earned the right for the refugees to return." How feasible would that be? I asked. "Not very difficult," he responded. "Through my business, I saw how Israel physically absorbed more than a million

Russians, we can do at least the same for a million Palestinian refugees." As for monetary returns, even for displaced Israeli Palestinians like his family, Sakas pointed out that there was a long way to go: "We live off the crumbs, workers and contractors alike. The system here in Israel is not for us, we make do with the leftovers."

Sakas's account of his family's business seemed like a condensed but reliable version of the fate of Palestinians left in Israel after 1948. Cut off from contact with other Arab countries, they remained under martial law for the next eighteen years, while the military's district governors deployed measures carried over from the Mandate's Emergency Regulations (originally drafted to contain and put down the Arab Revolt). Despite the commitment, enshrined in Israel's Declaration of Independence, to "complete equality of social and political rights for all its citizens, without distinction of creed, race or sex," there was little in the post-1948 experience of Israeli Palestinians that corresponded to this description. Given their state of privation, and with the military's boot on their neck, how would these "citizen strangers," outnumbered now by a ratio of six to one, and regarded as fifth columnists, earn a living in a state that functioned as a *Herrenvolk* democracy, with full rights reserved only for Jews?[58]

Israel's policymakers were faced with the choice of creating an entirely segregated economy for the remaining Palestinians, or re-admitting them into the new majority Jewish workforce on an equalized basis, as the pro-Soviet Mapam Party advocated.[59] The first option—of a separate Arab sector—would have involved costly state expenditures, and, in any case, proved politically unacceptable, since Israeli policymakers, then as now, were bent on blocking the growth of an independent Palestinian economy. As for the second option, the Labor establishment was unable to kick the discriminatory habits established during the previous decades, and so it carried over the split market of the Mandate period, whereby Arabs had performed low-skill labor for lower wages than any Jews employed in the same industry and were barred from higher-skill jobs.[60] The government equalized public wages in 1952, but, in the private sector, differences between Jewish and Arab pay were simply normalized as the "going rate."[61]

Households that could not survive on subsistence farming or were newly landless had no choice but to hire out their male youth for day labor in Jewish workplaces, but they were required, under military rule, to secure permits to travel outside their villages. Others who were homeless (and classified by Israel as "present absentees") lived in tin shacks on the edge of their expropriated villages and were often employed by the new occupants of their former property to tend crops and renovate housing.[62] The workers with travel permits were still barred from Histadrut membership (until 1959), and so they had no labor rights or national health benefits and only scant protection from employer abuse, and they had to return to their domiciles before curfew. Others, desperate for survival wages, risked traveling without documents to work for employers always on the lookout for cheap off-the-books labor. Many were adolescents, sleeping rough on construction sites or under trees and only returning to their villages and urban enclaves on weekends, setting a pattern that continues today for unregistered workers from the West Bank.

According to a journalist's report about conditions on Tel Aviv construction sites:

> Some 3,000 Arab workers are employed in the vicinity. They go back to their villages ... only for the weekend. These laborers, some of whom are 14 and 15 years old, are put for the night in tin huts and cowsheds. They are housed 50 to a cowshed, for which each of them pays 1£ 10 a month, or a day's wages or more. In the tin huts, which leak in the winter rain, the rent is 1£ 4 to 1£ 10. The crowding is intense, the sanitary conditions appalling. There are no toilets, and the workers prepare their meals on the spot.[63]

As in other countries, where migrant workers form a highly vulnerable caste of cheap labor, a new layer of middlemen emerged, as Sakas mentioned, to profit from the informal supply line. Village headmen (*ra'is*) took advantage of their position as brokers of permits or profited from delivering a compliant workforce to employers through the black market. As for advocates of the old Hebrew Labor doctrine, they found a new lease of life in the policy of employing only "organized labor." Until its ranks were desegregated in 1959 (the new non-Jewish members could not vote until 1966, when the federation dropped Hebrew from its official name) the Histadrut's Jewish-only membership also received direct subsidies in the provision of services and access to health benefits and housing. But even after 1959, the legacy of Hebrew Labor survived in the institutional preference for employing army veterans, who are almost all Jewish.

Nor did these jobs for Israeli Palestinians come without strings attached. In exchange for the employment opportunities, however restricted and underpaid, Israel's political elites extracted voting loyalties for the Mapai Party's ruling coalition, which included an Arab list for non-Jewish voters (barred from Mapai membership until 1973).[64] They sweetened this quid pro quo by channeling personal favors, privileges, and side payments to village mukhtars, clan headmen, Bedouin sheikhs, local informants (recruited in almost every village), and religious clerics. These patronage payoffs also came with the expectation that this class of lesser notables would keep a lid on militancy within their communities. Brokers with close ties to the Israeli military were given leeway to choose who would be awarded permits to work outside of their localities. After 1967, the government retreaded this loyalty formula in the form of jobs-for-peace as a mechanism to curb Palestinian nationalism in the West Bank and Gaza.

Despite all of the restrictions and obstacles, data from official Israeli labor force surveys (which obviously do not record the extensive contribution of casual or undocumented workers) show a steady increase in the number of "mobile" workers commuting out of Arab towns and villages from the time that Sakas's father began contracting for Solel Boneh. From 1954 to 1963, the percentage of non-Jewish men employed in construction, quarrying, mining, and manufacturing increased from 27.2 percent to 43.8 percent. In the two-year period 1961–63, the Israeli Palestinian contribution to the construction workforce grew from 13.8 percent to 18.3 percent. These increases were largely due to a tightening labor market over the course of the 1950s. Overall unemployment declined from 18 percent in 1953 to 3 percent in 1963, and, with full employment on the horizon, many of the restrictions on Arab movement were lifted, first in the northern regions in 1957 and then everywhere (except Jerusalem) in 1959.

As Arab penetration of construction grew by leaps and bounds, the sector saw a steady decline in the employment of new Mizrahi immigrants, who had been recruited initially from Arab countries as a replacement low-wage workforce after 1948 but who were now moving into better paid jobs in manufacturing.[65] Since the government refused to invest in modernizing non-Jewish neighborhoods and imposed rigid restrictions on building any new structures in Arab-majority towns and villages, Israeli Palestinian construction workers had no choice but to make the arduous commute to Jewish urban centers, where their participation was still strictly controlled (martial law would not be officially lifted until 1966) and was limited to low-skill jobs that no Jews could be found to do.

Another reason for the shift in policy was that the government was still struggling to house the post-1948 immigrant wave, which had doubled Israel's Jewish population. After the *Nakba*, the authorities took over a massive amount of Palestinian housing stock—from property forcibly vacated between November 29, 1947, and September 1, 1948—as a fixed asset of the State of Israel and placed it under control of the Custodian of Absentee Property. An estimated 124,000 immigrants, mostly Holocaust refugees from Eastern Europe, were permitted to possess the houses, along with the contents that had not been looted. By the time this stockpile was exhausted, nearly 200,000 Jews had occupied Arab homes.[66] These houses now functioned as stony, Zionist "facts on the ground," whose ownership was considered beyond dispute. Their renovation, often by Israeli Palestinian masons familiar with their construction and maintenance, formed a further layer of immunity against the right to return of their pre-1948 occupants.

In contrast with the housing offered to Ashkenazi refugees, the immigration authorities offered less preferential treatment to the next wave of immigrants—Mizrahi Jews, extracted from other Arab countries through "rescue" operations (like the Magic Carpet and Ali Baba campaigns that brought Yemenites in 1949–50 and Iraqis in 1950–51) in hopes that they would fill the low-skill jobs formerly allotted to Palestinians. Imported as "coolie labor"[67] and housed on arrival in the wretched conditions of "reception" (*ma'abarot*) camps, they were then transferred to *moshavim* agricultural settlements erected on "wilderness" land seized near the Green Line, or to work villages, provided by the JNF or the state, located close enough to urban employment markets for residents to earn a livelihood.[68]

Building Out

Across the Green Line, a stark counterpart to the transit camps and villages could be found in the establishment of refugee camps by UNRWA, the relief agency set up by the UN in 1949 to assist Palestinians who had been "swept away." Constructed from 1952 onward, the camps replaced the tent cities and other shelters that refugees had improvised, not too far from their former residences, in the West Bank, the Gaza Strip, Lebanon, Syria, and Jordan.[69] Designed as provisional solutions to a humanitarian crisis, these fifty-eight UNRWA camps were destined to be forever "temporary." Descendants of the original residents, overwhelmingly from peasant backgrounds, were so committed to their UN-sanctioned right to return to their pre-1948 homes that they strongly resisted any efforts to regard the camps as permanent settlements. Today, the camps house 1.5 million individuals, less than one-third of the 5.6 million Palestinian refugees worldwide who are registered with UNRWA.

Initially, the forms of shelter in the camps were thrown together from locally available materials (mud, cane, plywood, hollow bricks, asbestos, and corrugated iron) in order to deflect any appearance of housing imposed from elsewhere. Even though UNRWA had no official position on the right to return (the result of strenuous Israeli lobbying in 1949), its staff, many of them refugees themselves, were also under pressure from residents not to construct anything that resembled former dwellings or villages. In many camps, the agreed-upon policy was self-help, and so UNRWA provided materials with which residents could build their own shelters.[70] By the late 1950s, prefabricated shelters with zinc and corrugated tin roofs had replaced the first wave of improvised huts, and, after 1967, when Nesher's cement became more readily available, concrete structures would follow.[71]

But in the ensuing decades, camp residents viewed any effort to more substantially "improve" the physical stock as undermining the right to return, and, for a long time, they imposed their own moratorium on building any new homes. This communal will to preserve the provisional nature of the camps has more recently been balanced against the pressing need to safeguard public health and better the physical circumstances of residents and their families. Today, densely populated, multistory buildings loom over the original, narrow alleyways and rudimentary sewage and drainage lines installed in the 1950s. Yet many resident families are still wary of UNRWA's latest Infrastructure and Camp Improvement program, launched in 2007 to upgrade these facilities. Although rehabilitation and planning are no longer taboo, there is still a strong degree of community pushback against any sign of normalization of the camps' status as places of settled residence.[72]

Inside the Green Line, the new Mizrahi Jewish immigrants had quite a different response to being herded from tents in the *ma'abarot* transit camps to the self-help environment of the work villages. Unlike the Palestinians refugees, who stoically embraced what they saw as the reflection of their plight in the ad hoc conditions of the UNRWA camps, these settlers—many of them from countries like Morocco, Iraq, Yemen, and Egypt, which had afforded Jews protection and co-existence for centuries—resented the substandard communal housing on offer. Many had been lured by promises of the Zionist Dream, which included permanent single-family housing akin to that enjoyed by Ashkenazi settlers in the better appointed Garden City labor towns (*krayot amal*) of the 1930s and 1940s. Nor would they get to "enjoy" the benefits, bestowed on post-1948 Ashkenazi, of moving into cleansed Palestinian houses. Though the Green Line separated these two types of refugees by only a few kilometers in some cases, their rights were interpreted altogether differently.

In 1950, a team of Israeli architects under Arieh Sharon (a Bauhaus graduate appointed to head the government's new planning department) unveiled a national master plan, which included a permanent successor to the *ma'abarot* reception camps and work villages in the form of "development towns," located on the periphery of what was now Israeli territory.[73] At the same time, the government launched a new program of agricultural villages (*moshvei olim*) to offset the overconcentration of Jews in the large coastal cities.[74] As with previous forms of settlement, these towns and villages were strategically situated in "frontier zones" in order to fortify the 1948 armistice lines, or were part of the Judaization of Arab-majority regions: Galilee, Northern Negev, and Jerusalem itself. Officially designated as part of the plan for "population dispersal," they were informally regarded as colonial outposts.

A similar colonial attitude applied to the Mizrahi Jewish settlers who were assigned to these remote locations. Since they were Arabs by culture and language, the authorities decided they should be distanced from Israeli Palestinians, with whom they might have forged social, political, or romantic connections, and also from Ashkenazi populations, whose purity of culture they might taint with their "Levantine" ways and standards of hygiene.[75] They seemed to have little in common with the tutored idealism of earlier generations of settlers, and they were routinely derided by Ashkenazi elites.[76] Judged to be "backward" in mentality by immigration officials and depicted as "human dust" by Ben-Gurion himself, they were brusquely transferred, sometimes by truck in the middle of the night, in line with the state policy of "from ship to village."

The neglect continued as they struggled to move out of economic deprivation in their soulless new living quarters. Scant government resources were put into the development of these anonymous outposts (critics labeled them "underdevelopment towns"). As a result, the industries that gravitated toward them were looking for the cheapest labor and the most vulnerable workforces.[77] As they were built out, they relied more and more on a standard public housing type—cheap, uniform apartment blocks (*shikunim*)—which quickly became stigmatized as a low-income residential marker, reinforcing the second-class status of their occupants. When residents voiced discontent with their involuntary role in this centrally planned project, it fell on deaf ears, and when rebellious youth answered the more radical call of the Israeli Black Panthers in the early 1970s, the Mizrahi insurgency was met with clumsy efforts at cooptation by Golda Meir's administration. They would return the disregard at the ballot box by helping to drive the Ashkenazi-led Labor establishment from power in the watershed 1977 elections.

The building of the development towns in the late 1950s coincided with the unrestricted re-entry of Israeli Palestinians into the construction sector. Their rapid expansion helped absorb the Mizrahi immigrants in immediate need of employment, but the construction also required the labor of local Palestinians, recruited to participate in large-scale building that was on formerly Arab land. In many cases, the town plans were drawn to obliterate the evidence of prior Arab residence (and prevent the "infiltration" of refugees back into the area) just as surely as the JNF forests that were planted over ruined Arab villages. Of the thirty new towns that were built, "eleven had an old Arab core," according to Arnon Golan:

> another seven were established near the sites of demolished former large Arab villages that had been regional centers for surrounding Arab popula tions before being uprooted, and another two were established near existing Arab towns.[78]

In some cases, the existing Israeli Palestinian population presented an obstacle to development, so they were declared to be a security threat and evicted. The cleansing of al-Majdal, for example, now the location of the Israeli city of Ashkelon, was requested by Yigal Allon. "The transfer began at the beginning of 1950," according to Gideon Levy,

> although the "official operation" took off in June. There were still those who spoke of dispersing the Arabs around the country; in the end, they were deported to Gaza. They were loaded onto trucks and dropped off at the border—"deliveries," as they were termed. Just to remind you again, the state already existed. The last delivery of 229 people left for Gaza on October 21.[79]

From the construction of the development towns, and especially after 1967, when employers were able to tap the manpower supply from the Occupied Territories, Palestinians were always fully engaged in building the houses of Zion. With brief periods of exception, due to the mass permit cancellations after the first and second intifadas, they would be the dominant ethnic group working in the manual sectors of construction.[80] Their mass re-entry into the Israeli labor market at a time of near-full employment in the late 1950s meant they would no longer be in direct competition with the Arab Jewish immigrants. By then, the majority of Mizrahi *olim* had moved into factory employment, where they were assigned the least skilled "Jewish jobs," with pay levels well below the Ashkenazi rates. Nor have they gained much ground in the intervening decades. A recent study of 2012 data showed Ashkenazi earnings at 42 percent higher than the national average, with Mizrahi income at only 9 percent above. The same study showed Israeli Palestinians earning 34 percent below the national average, reflecting their many disadvantages.[81]

After 1967, the occupying power was in a position to integrate the economies of Israel, Gaza, and the West Bank, and so Israeli Palestinians (who now enjoyed union protection and social insurance) now had to compete for construction jobs with the Palestinian workers streaming across the Green Line.[82] By 1987, roughly 40 percent of the Palestinian workforce (almost 109,000) in the Occupied Territories were legally working inside Israel, while more than 30,000 were crossing the Green Line illegally.[83] They built and renovated houses in existing Israeli towns and cities; they constructed Jerusalem's spreading suburban satellites and expansions of the development towns; and then they built settlements in the Occupied Territories. Over time, they would be joined by migrant workers, imported in large numbers (from Romania, Thailand, Poland, Turkey, China, Nigeria, and Ukraine) in the course of the 1990s in an effort to replace them. Yet industry employers, when they were not under government pressure, continued to prefer Arab labor.

From time to time, Histadrut officials launched recruitment and training drives aimed at encouraging Jews to re-enter the "pioneer" builder occupations. These campaigns, which largely failed, were ostensibly sparked by the need for additional manpower at a time of chronic housing shortages. But the offer of higher wages to those who took job training placements was also laced with guilt about modern Jewish disdain for the once hallowed work of building Zion.[84] After all, the original Labor Zionists set out to upend the historically inverted occupational pyramid and fill every level with Jewish workers. Yet within the space of two generations, almost none could be found in the broadest levels of the pyramid base.

These earlier Zionist doctrines have long lost their hold on the national sense of purpose. Even the West Bank settler credo, which still appeals to an active version of *self-made* nationalism, depends on the low-cost utility of Palestinian labor. It is one thing to be reminded that your towns, cities, and farms sit on occupied land: people in settler colonial nations are occasionally forced to reconcile their denial of this history with the democratic self-image of their liberal societies. By contrast, most Israelis do not seem to lose much sleep over the knowledge that occupied and conquered peoples have built their houses, towns and suburbs, prisons, border walls, and shopping malls and are still doing so.

2

From *Kurkar* to Concrete and Back

Why had something of the living past remained? Would it not have been easier if it had all gone, better still all crumbled and buried in the ground? Why this half reality, neither fully there nor fully gone?

—Raja Shehadeh, *Strangers in the House*

Among the abiding staples of Zionist history is the image of a pioneer (*halutz*) portrayed as a construction worker, balancing bricks awkwardly but stoically on his shoulders or putting his back behind a shovel to dig a ditch. Perhaps this New Jew would be a philosopher, unused to manual labor, and he would have learned overnight how to mix sand, gravel, and cement to create the nation-making concrete that would soon be glorified as Hebrew wonderstuff.[1] In the iconic scenario, the backdrop to his sweat might be the swelling patriotic poetry of Natan Alterman's 1934 "Morning Song of the Homeland," which imagines the land of Palestine as a vacant space ("we shall paint and build upon your wasteland") and also as a woman ("we shall dress you with a gown made of concrete and cement"). The worker might even be a woman herself, trained in construction skills by the Histadrut's Council of Women Workers and hustling for employment in an overwhelmingly male trade.[2]

The typical counterpoint to these heroic profiles was the depiction of the Arab hill peasant fellah, scouring the stony fields with a hoe in hand and with an ox-drawn scratch-plough by his side. The point of such comparisons was usually to illustrate how a backward, feudal civilization was destined to give way before the dynamism of the industrious settlers, bent on modernizing the rural and the urban landscape. Yet the true analogue of the Jewish greenhorn, unsure of his or her new dusty vocation, would have been the ubiquitous Arab mason, quarryman, or builder, skilled in the arts of extracting and dressing local stone and constructing climate-appropriate buildings. He was the master of the built environment in towns, villages, and cities, and he was neither duty-bound by tradition nor closed off to modernity. But for the Zionist picture of the diligent pioneer to hold its own, the centrality of these stone men would have to be sidelined and relegated to the rubble of the Ottoman past. As we have seen, settlers could not achieve this feat of exclusion openly through the labor market—Palestinian workers were cheaper, more skilled, and more available than their would-be Jewish competitors. Nor could the Conquest of Labor in the long term be wholly reliant on world Zionist subsidies to make up a "European wage." To elevate and protect the Jewish worker, it proved necessary to introduce construction techniques and building materials that were not dependent on, and could bypass, Arab know-how and manpower.

Herein lies the story of how concrete came to play such a revered role in the building of the Israeli state. In the years before 1948, the adoption of this construction material was seen as emblematic of the forward-looking spirit of the new Hebrew civilization. In the decades after independence, the indelible association of concrete with large state-sponsored building projects prompted many enthusiasts to regard exposed concrete as a metaphor for the tough fortitude of the Israeli national character. Typical of the overriding retro interest in concrete as the "stuff of Zionism" was *The Song of Concrete,* a major 2008 exhibition, curated by Yehudit Matzkel, at the Eretz Israel Museum in Tel Aviv. Featuring a vintage concrete mixer and images and films of buildings and pioneer workers, it was "devoted to the cultural history of concrete and its use in the Land of Israel."[3]

Yet the bow to modernity was not the only reason why concrete became the preferred building block of the Zionist state. The story of the founding of Tel Aviv, intended to be the "first Hebrew city" and demonstrably modern in comparison with the ancient city of Jaffa from which it seceded, illustrates why the selection of concrete was largely determined by the labor conflicts generated by Jewish settlement.

Greater Jaffa?

As Palestine's principal city of commerce and culture, and one of the Mediterranean's oldest *entrepôt* ports, Jaffa was open in every sense, even to the influence of international architectural styles. Indeed, by the end of Ottoman rule, many of its more notable villas, in upscale neighborhoods adjacent to the antique central core, were Arab-European hybrids, and the Mandate would bring another wave of cultural fusion, in line with the preferences of British colonial planning. Notwithstanding this cosmopolitanism, most of Jaffa's buildings were constructed from local *kurkar*, the calcareous quartz sandstone deposits that lined the coastal plain of Palestine. The stone from these lithified sand dunes was cheap and readily available, and its cutting and dressing were central to

Photo by author

Picture of Jaffa and Tel Aviv shorelines on an Old Jaffa wall.

the Jaffa stonemason's craft. Jaffa itself was built on a tell on top of a *kurkar* ridge, and, over thousands of years of habitation, the city had drawn on this local supply, or from quarries to the north (up to Caesarea) and in Gaza (which had the softest stone), to replenish and expand.

Before Ashkenazi settlers arrived in larger numbers at the turn of the twentieth century, Jaffa was home to a significant, and largely assimilated, population of Sephardim, or "Ottoman Jews." By 1914, 30 percent of the residents would be Jewish, most of them renters, but the established business class owned and built houses and were long accustomed to employ Arab craftsmen for construction and maintenance work. When the plan for a new Jewish suburb to the north of Jaffa was drawn up in 1906, the Zionist preference for Hebrew Labor was still in its infancy. Shortly after this district—Ahuzat Bayit (literally "Building Houses")—was established as a town in 1909, and before it was renamed Tel Aviv, Aryeh Weiss, chairman of the planning committee, called for the exclusive employment of Jewish workers. The housing scheme was being underwritten by a commercial loan from the JNF, backed by the Zionist Organization, and so the credit came with the understanding that the settlement should be raised, stone by stone, by Jewish hands.[4]

In practice, this stipulation was unlikely to be observed. The new Jewish settlers were unfamiliar with local stone or building techniques, and, because of their ethnicity and European background, they were in a position to demand higher wages from Jewish employers. The well-to-do members of Ahuzat Bayit's organizing committee were swayed by estimates of the savings to be gotten from using the cheaper and more capable Arab workers. After all, most were cost-conscious businessmen, and Ahuzat Bayit was a private development that would see its share of landlord profiteering in the 1920s. But their commercial instincts met with fierce challenges both from world Zionist backers and from a cadre of Russian Jews petitioning for gainful employment in the wake of the failed Rothschild agricultural colonies.

These socialist-minded workers used the language of class conflict to confront the prosperous burghers over wage rates. But instead of arguing for the equalization of wages for Arab workers, they made nationalist appeals to persuade these employers of the virtues of a Jewish-only workforce, even if it meant stretching the available funds. Arab workers, riled by the prospect of their exclusion, were equally vehement about the injustice of cutting them out of the labor pool for constructing the town. A compromise was reached. The Hebrew Labor requirement would not be written into Ahuzat Bayit's bylaws, but it would be informally encouraged. In practice, this meant that the founders would employ Arab masons to build most of the villas in the new settlement (officially renamed Tel Aviv in 1910),[5] and they would employ the Russian Jews on the more public buildings, such as the landmark Herzliya Gymnasium, Ahuzat Bayit's first Hebrew school.[6]

Yosef Eliyahu Chelouche, one of the most prominent Sephardic businessmen in Jaffa and a key intermediary between the city's Arab and Jewish communities, was contracted to build many of these homes, and he was fully aware of the advantages of employing the skilled Arabs. Commissioned in 1909 to construct the Herzliya Gymnasium, he was pressured to fall in line with the preference for Jewish labor, especially since this would be a public building with a high profile. But Chelouche showed his colors by advertising for Jewish workers willing to work at "market rates." Not surprisingly, there were few takers for what were considered "Arab wages," though a team eventually came all the way from Jerusalem to take on the jobs. Chelouche also resented having to pay wage supplements for each design modification ordered by Joseph Barsky, the fanciful architect who had designed the building façade to evoke the Temple of Solomon in accord with "Hebrew aesthetics."[7] His general disaffection with the Hebrew Labor policy was boosted by the results of an inquiry into the collapse, during a storm, of the roof of the Yechiely Girls School in Jaffa's Jewish proto-suburb of Neve Tzedek. The investigating committee found that the fault lay with the poor quality of the Jewish roofers, who were hired against Chelouche's own assessment of their shortcomings.[8]

Like other Sephardic Jews comfortably assimilated within Jaffa's Arab-majority population, Chelouche was increasingly critical of policies adopted by the new Ashkenazi settlers, whose Zionist separatism and indifference to native Palestinians introduced conflicts where co-existence had been the norm. Indeed, his memoirs, published in 1931, included a scathing attack on the "builders of the Yishuv who came from the diaspora" and who disseminated "Zionist propaganda" that depicted Palestine "as a wasted, ruined, desolate country, with no inhabitants." Chelouche pointed out that this myth of a "virgin land" had preconditioned the settlers' disdainful attitude toward "those inhabitants that had been living here."[9]

Not surprisingly, the growing conflict over Tel Aviv's construction led to clashes between Jewish and Arab workers. How did the Zionist settlers try to resolve the "Battle of Tel Aviv"? Not through negotiation or joint organizing, but by introducing new technologies. According to Or Aleksandrowicz, an early solution presented itself in the establishment of a cement brick factory by David Arber, a flour merchant who promoted his product as cheaper and more durable than the local *kurkar* stone.[10] Two other firms, one belonging to the Chelouche family, were already making prefabricated hollow concrete bricks, which offered better thermal insulation than Arber's. These brick variants were soon in competition for the heavily politicized prize of adoption as a *kurkar* substitute. Such products were becoming industry standards in Europe and the United States, and so the molds were cheap to import.

But the primary advantage was that the process of production and the practice of building with the finished materials was no longer dependent on *kurkar* quarrying or on Arab workers skilled in sandstone construction. This switch in technology meant that the factories and construction sites would potentially be freed from any reliance on local Arab labor. Although most of the raw materials would still be coming from overseas and would undoubtedly be handled by non-Jews, the bricks still offered the prospect that the Conquest of Labor could be brought about, not by fractious, and racist, hiring decisions, but on the basis of technical efficiency.

The fabrication of Arber's product proved too labor intensive to penetrate the market, however, and Chelouche was initially reluctant to stir up labor trouble by supplanting the time-honored *kurkar* standard with a brick that depended on imported material. In addition, an alternative proposal by Alexander Levy, founder of the Association of the Builders of the Land of Israel, to utilize wire mesh and loam (a traditional construction material in the Middle East and North Africa) foundered on the lack of local supplies.[11] Ultimately, Chelouche would introduce a more lasting technical solution in the form of a silicate brick, made from a mix of locally available sand and lime and molded into shape by machines.[12] Allegedly, he walked off with the trade recipe for the brick after enlisting in the workforce of an Egyptian factory.[13]

After delays from the war, a silicate brick factory was finally opened by Joseph Ziedner (a close friend of Herzl) in 1922, launching its career as the new Zionist construction standard.[14] Whether applied in its exposed form or plastered over with stucco, its white appearance—one of the origins of Tel Aviv's "White City" moniker—presented a stark contrast with the yellow and tan *kurkar* hues of old Jaffa, and, most important to Zionist sponsors, its use in construction could now be done more practically by unskilled Jewish hands. Members of the Building Group, an Ashkenazi workers' organization formed to train its members in the building trades, learned how to use the silicate bricks and also the craft of stucco plastering from Yemenite Jews.[15] Other cooperatives followed suit, and by 1925, an estimated 45 percent of the Tel Aviv workforce (the town then had a population of 35,000) was engaged in construction, much of it under the auspices of Solel Boneh's Public Works unit, which actively tried to enforce Jewish-only employment.[16] Before long, a reliable supply of local cement would be available from the new Nesher plant in Haifa, offering a cheaper source of "Hebrew" materials. As the use of concrete became more prevalent, the established reliance on Arab skills decreased.

By the end of the decade, discontent with this form of *technological disemployment* became a factor in Arab–Jewish conflicts like the 1929 Buraq Uprising, sparked by clashes over access to Jerusalem's Western Wall. The ensuing 1930 Hope Simpson Report, commissioned by Mandate authorities to analyze the causes of the uprising, was sharply critical of both the Hebrew Labor policy and the JNF's exclusivist land purchasing policies. The combination of the two, according to the report, was yielding an "extra-territorialized enclave in Palestine from which the Arabs are excluded," from any "advantage" or "employment."[17] In their attention to Arab disemployment, the commission members took particular note of the discontent over the new technologies:

> The increased use of cement, reinforced concrete and silicate brick, all manufactured by Jews, is replacing dressed stone for constructional purposes, and so displacing a large number of stone dressers and stonemasons, nearly all of whom are Arabs. The Arab quarrymen are also being displaced.[18]

The uptake of the new materials mentioned in the report was accompanied by a more philosophical debate among Yishuv leaders and their backers about whether Tel Aviv should pioneer a new kind of low-density "Zionist" urbanism, distinct from existing congested Jewish neighborhoods like New York's Lower East Side, London's Whitechapel, or any of the Levantine quarters densely populated by the region's Arab Jews, including, of course, Jaffa itself.[19] After all, the founders of Ahuzat Bayit had envisaged a

> *Jewish urban center in a healthy locality,* laid out in a most comely manner and in observance of the laws of hygiene, so that instead of the filth and excrement in the present Jaffa houses, we will find a resting place amidst gardens and fresh air.[20]

After a series of violent Arab–Jewish clashes in 1921, an influx of Jews moving out of Jaffa put pressure on Tel Aviv land prices. Those who fled (to live in shacks and tents around the new town) were generally poor renters, and so profiteers rushed to take advantage of their predicament by building the kind of multiunit tenements more reminiscent of the clogged districts of the Jewish urban diaspora. The resulting real estate speculation yielded a mishmash of multifamily structures with a higher density feel that no longer corresponded to the ordered, semipastoral vision of the founders.

City officials saw the need for a plan to regulate future development. Patrick Geddes, the much-lauded Scottish town planner who had already produced a master plan for Jerusalem, was duly commissioned to do the same for Tel Aviv, with the goal of developing areas to the north in the form of Garden City suburbs. As a champion of organic, regional planning, Geddes was especially keen on nurturing connectivity between new urban forms and the older cities from which they would grow. Building on his efforts to reconcile the gulf between Edinburgh's medieval Old Town and the methodical Enlightenment grids of its New Town, his overall approach in Tel Aviv was to preserve its lines of continuity with Jaffa, envisaging the result as a unified conurbation, or region-city. His report called for a joint-planning commission for the two cities, described by him as a "Greater Jaffa." Needless to say, this was not a label that endeared him to Zionist powerbrokers like Meir Dizengoff, Tel Aviv's first mayor, who had in mind a "greater Tel Aviv" that did not include Jaffa at all.[21] Moreover, Geddes's emphasis on regional planning did not lend itself to the mythmaking already underway that Tel Aviv was created ex nihilo and owed nothing to the great Arab city from which it had broken away.

In the course of his earlier visits to Palestine, Geddes had expressed an appreciation for the traditions of Arab building:

> Look at any good photograph of an Arab hillside village. See the plain walls, but wall above wall; the flat roofs, but roof above roof. See how these contrast and compare with one another; see the bright walls, and brighter dome-roofs in the sunshine, and how, as it were, they chime together, with the dark walls and masses in shadow giving deeper notes. These simple houses and small domes make up the essential picture, ranging from sunrise joy to sunset glory ... Here is architecture in its very essence.[22]

Geddes was not the first, and certainly not the last, foreigner to romanticize the hill-country Palestinian village in this way—today's West Bank settlers prize their top-down views of such picturesque towns—but his warm assessment was quite at odds with the preferred Zionist perception that Jaffa and its surrounding villages were "filthy" and "backward," while Tel Aviv would be a fresh start, with no precedents and with all the healthy arcadian attributes of a Garden City. Geddes's master plan for Tel Aviv was for a city quite removed in form from the villages he had idealized, but he took pains to include his prior opinion within the text of his report:

> Without recommending any more adoption of Arab Architecture ... it is important to realize that this [Arab] architecture and decorative art, at her best, are second to none in the world.[23]

Geddes included no style prescriptions in his master plan, but, in line with his affection for traditional local architecture, he was a known advocate for a mixed, or integrated, style of building that blended European and Arab influences. Fusion architecture of this sort certainly had its adherents in Tel Aviv in the 1920s (and in Jaffa's bourgeois quarters), where individual housing commissions led to an often flamboyant mix of historical facades known as the *eclectic style*.[24] But the city's Zionist managers were ultimately bent on making a clean break with anything that smacked of regional architecture. While Geddes's master plan for a city of 100,000 inhabitants was partially adopted from 1929, his regard for stylistic integration was increasingly out of official favor, making way for the stripped-down Bauhaus modernism of the 1930s around which the city would much later come to be branded.

The Arab–Jewish clashes of 1929 were arguably one factor that gave birth to this shift in mentality. The conflict stiffened the Zionist will for separation and reinforced the desire for this break to be reflected in the physical appearance of the city's buildings. In line with the asceticism of the modernist movement, ornamentation was out, including details that evoked historical references, and especially anything Ottoman. The clean lines and the white plaster facades of Bauhaus functionalism (hailed today as Tel Aviv's signature mark) were in. While it was typically promoted as egalitarian and universal, the stark introduction of this International Style had a local connotation wherever it landed in the world, but nowhere was this more conspicuous than in Tel Aviv. The adoption of the style in the course of the 1930s was hailed as another fresh start, but the White City (as its central core would later be labeled) could also be described as the architectural equivalent of ethnic cleansing because it expunged all visual references to the surrounding Arab habitat.

The underlying principle of erasure also applied to the use of building materials and the composition of the workforce. Unlike the eclectic stone or brick villas of the 1920s, the blocky Bauhaus units were more likely to be constructed from concrete, with a plaster finish on top, which made it even easier (at least in principle) to employ the less skilled Jewish laborer. By the time that the effort to build out Geddes's master plan was launched in 1929, concrete had begun to supplant silicate brick, which required more labor-intensive skills in fabrication. Concrete was also adopted as the construction material of choice for two of the city workers' cooperative housing schemes: the workers neighborhoods of self-built, single-family housing, initiated by the socialist administration of 1925–27, and the collectivist housing estates of *meonot ovdim* (laborers' dormitories) designed by Arieh Sharon in 1931.

As Yael Allweil has shown, Geddes had selected the self-housing model of the former as the driving concept behind his master plan, and it was informed by his anarchist vision of a bottom-up city, built on the sweat equity of homesteaders.[75] This model was a riposte to Tel Aviv's profiteers, who, by the mid-1920s were throwing up apartment housing to squeeze ever-higher rents out of the town's working class. From 1925 to 1927, a socialist faction wrested control of the municipal government from Meir Dizengoff and launched the regulatory framework for implementing Geddes's program. In the Geddes plan, self-built houses, each with a lot portion for subsistence farming, would be dropped into what he called "home-blocks," on land purchased beyond the speculators' ring of high-rent tenements. While most historians have concluded that these ideas were shelved after the socialists were quickly edged out, Allweil found that some parts of Geddes's vision were successfully realized. Within the "Geddes area," she discovered that as many as sixteen workers' neighborhoods of home-block housing had been initiated on land purchased by cooperatives (including one set up by the Camel Drivers Union).

Indeed, one of the residents was Ben-Gurion himself, and his position at the time as general secretary of the Histadrut is a clue to how the scheme operated. The basic housing designs were provided by the chief engineer of Solel Boneh, and financing for the self-built housing came through loans from Bank Hapoalim or Shikun Ovdim, the Histadrut's workers bank and housing arm, respectively. In one case that Allweil researched (and which may have been typical), the new owners transferred the title to the JNF, pledging the land to the Jewish nation and foreclosing its purchase from either Arabs or land speculators.[26] So was this self-housing an anarchist example of workers' self-governance, as she argues?[27] If so, it was far from autonomous, or even self-organized, in the way that most anarchists would recognize. Indeed, it was only feasible because of the Histadrut's capacity to control and combine financing, land acquisition, and infrastructure services and to place unionized members and their families in residences they built for themselves. Above all, the model presented a comprehensive version of the Histadrut's policy of Hebrew Labor; finally, Jewish workers were building Jewish houses on Jewish-owned land with Jewish financing.[28]

The Histadrut wrapped a similar package of support around the construction of the collective workers' housing (*meonot ovdim*). Unlike the self-housing model, these were multi-unit garden estates with communal facilities and were built in the Soviet style on a modular pattern. Because they were a direct response to the housing needs of immigrants recruited into construction jobs through Solel Boneh's Shikun Company, they could provide a guaranteed version of Hebrew Labor, withdrawn and protected from the marketplace, in much the same way that the kibbutzim did for agricultural production during the same period.

This all-round formula would soon be scaled up, sans the cooperatives, in the labor towns (*krayot amal*) built as garden suburbs on the urban periphery, and later in the much larger "development towns" of the 1950s when the Labor establishment of Israel exercised maximal control over building projects. By then, the use of concrete was no longer the calling card of Hebrew Labor, since the "threat" of Arab labor had been all but eliminated. Instead, concrete took on a fresh significance. The plaster facades of Tel Aviv's White City were rejected by the native-born, or *sabra,* generation in favor of the exposed concrete of Brutalist style. This shift in taste away from the International Style—now spurned as an inauthentic European import—toward the Brutalism of the large-scale state-sponsored projects was embraced as the expression of a more rugged and resolute way of being (even though Brutalist style itself was just as derivative).[29]

The adoption of Brutalism coincided with the growth of a full-blown patriotic cult of concrete. The formidable compressive strength of the material was a good fit for a new nation that saw itself as yielding to no one. Its plasticity and ready availability, combined with the convenience of fast casting, made it a serviceable solution for the expansionary needs of a state struggling to absorb successive waves of new immigrants. From a Zionist perspective, concrete was portable and durable, and so it was well-suited to become the hard, immovable edge of settler colonialism, metastasizing aggressively over former Palestinian land and across the Green Line itself, onto the hilltops and through the valleys of the West Bank. Selected, initially, as a technical solution for enforcing Hebrew Labor, its smooth surface, cracked and discolored over time, would become the repellent brand-mark of the Occupation, scarring serene hill-country landscapes with its widening realm of precast walls, checkpoints, road blocks, watchtowers, settler-only bypass roads, and residential colonies.[30]

Who Will Build Tel Aviv?

Unlike the workers' housing schemes of the 1930s, most of the 4,000 buildings grouped in Tel Aviv's much-lionized White City cluster were privately built, and therefore it proved much more difficult to shut out the cheaper, more proficient Arab labor. This turned out to be the case even after the use of silicate brick had largely been supplanted by concrete. Arab workers continued to build core sectors of "the city that begat a state," despite strong-arm efforts by Histadrut officials to blackball them. Indeed, in 1935 the federation's executive committee had to go so far as to declare a "public war" against contractors who hired Arabs, deploying the same shaming tactics as the Jewish zealots in the Product Loyalist Alliance who used intimidation to enforce the boycott of Arab goods.[31] Flying pickets were sent from site to site, Arab workers were assaulted, and their Jewish employers were libeled.

Much of the strident campaigning was for Zionist propaganda purposes, since the 1930s economic boom and the investments from overseas had all but eradicated Jewish unemployment. But the economic incentive to prefer Arab labor was long-standing and could not be dislodged. The British authorities had instituted a lower Arab minimum wage, in part to minimize the costs of their own public works and those of companies sheltered by the colonial presence. Jews working in construction commanded double the pay of Arabs, and Zionist donors had become less inclined, over time, to make up the gap between them.[32]

Under such circumstances, any efforts to insulate a self-segregated Jewish sector from Arab labor were partial at best, and mostly aspirational. In a building boom, the ready availability of cheaper Arab workers, especially the landless fellahin streaming in from rural areas and finding housing in Jaffa's northern suburb of al-Manshiyya adjacent to Tel Aviv construction sites, was irresistible to contractors. Since Ashkenazi settlers, especially those who came with resources, were disinclined to accept "Arab jobs," their loud tributes to the pioneer spirit of Zionist nation-making were haunted by lingering doubts about who would respond in kind to the call to hard labor. The title and leading question of Yemenite singer-dancer Bracha Tsfira's well-known 1930s song, "Who Will Build a House?" (*Mi Yiveneh Bayit*), captures some of this uncertainty:

> Who will build, will build a house in Tel Aviv?
> Who will build, will build a house in Tel Aviv?
> We the pioneers will build Tel Aviv!
> Give us the clay and bricks—and we'll build Tel Aviv!

So, too, the more recent efforts to champion the White City as an expression of Jewish modernity have concealed much more than the inconvenient role played by Arabs in its construction. Designated by UNESCO as a World Cultural Heritage site in 2003, this clustering of Bauhaus-style buildings immediately became a prime draw for the city's tourist profile and a reliable driver for the local real estate industry. Even when its promoters are marketing Tel Aviv to visitors as "the city that never stops," they are still able to spice up the appeal of its architectural landmark, as seen in this tourist website pitch: "Tel Aviv's *White City* might be a UNESCO World Heritage Site, but the words boring, historic, or ageing do not describe it at all!"[33]

In a landmark 2010 book, architect Sharon Rotbard debunked the White City's lustrous mythology, noting that the actual Bauhaus input was minimal; Tel Aviv had very few Dessau-trained architects, and their work in the city postdated the period associated with Bauhaus style. So, too, the vast majority of the units included in the White City cluster were private apartment buildings and had nothing in common with the utopian social housing espoused in Bauhaus ideology. To cap it all, he argues that the White City was only "discovered" after Michael Levin, the curator of a 1984 architecture exhibition (entitled *White City, International Style Architecture in Israel, Portrait of an Era*) at the Tel Aviv Museum of Art, suggested that these otherwise disparate buildings be grouped together under a common label.[34]

In Rotbard's alternative account, promotion of the White City emerged as Tel Aviv's calling card on the international circuit of urban prestige largely because it served as a nostalgic cover for a city built on violent dispossession. The real "white city" was a racially separationist Ashkenazi *flight* from the "black city" of Jaffa, and the demarcation between the two cities echoed the spatial segregation found in other colonial cities (Dakar, Algiers, Casablanca), where a planned European enclave developed apart from the indigenous one. According to this view, the mythmaking about Tel Aviv's architecture was necessary in order to sideline, if not entirely erase, the urban scale and sophistication of Jaffa (where, as Rotbard points out, there were many International Style buildings constructed in the 1930s).[35]

Rotbard's own Shapira neighborhood, where I visited him in South Tel Aviv, has long served as a gateway to generations of Jewish immigrants and migrant workers. Developed by Meir Getzl Shapira, an American immigrant in the early 1920s, its lots were advertised as situated in a no-man's-land, "neither in Jaffa nor Tel Aviv," and therefore subject to no burdensome regulations, though the district was subsequently annexed by Jaffa.[36] Shapira's population mix and location placed it within Rotbard's boundaries of the modern Black City, a conglomeration of neighborhoods that grew up under Jaffa's jurisdiction and which today are still under-serviced by the Tel Aviv municipality and unconnected to its go-go identity. After 1967, construction workers from the West Bank rented rooms in South Tel Aviv neighborhoods like Shapira to limit the time they spent on commutes from home. Today, these areas play host, not only to the bulk of migrant workers recruited to replace Palestinians after the first intifada, but also to the more recent Sudanese and Eritrean refugees. Due to its marginal location, and because of the city's skyrocketing land prices, the Shapira I visited was in the initial throes of gentrification, readying for the entry of big money.[37]

As we walked to his home, Rotbard pointed out a sprinkling of tar paper shacks left over from the neighborhood's origins as an isolated Jewish pocket surrounded by Arab orchards. In his elegant memoir on the construction of his own home ("the cheapest house in the whole of Israel"), Rotbard mused on the experience of "employing work crews from the West Bank": "When I look at my house ... I see the fingerprints of all the people who had built it, most of them Palestinians.... I see their labor, their efforts and their endeavors, and sometimes their mistakes, their omissions and their sabotage as well."[38] The memoir is a rare reflection, by an architect, on the ethical dilemmas faced by design professionals typically employed in land development. His personal commitment not to work on land cleansed in 1948, or with the Israel Land Authority (which owns and leases 93 percent of all Israeli land) has drastically minimized what he can do with his own practice. His only recent design work, he told me, was for al-Araqib, a Bedouin village in the Northern Negev/ Naqab that has been demolished by Israeli forces almost a hundred times.[39]

On his neighborhood tour, Rotbard was able to show me how the construction of Tel Aviv literally sliced into the preexisting landscape. By long-standing custom, Arab houses with *kurkar* walls were built directly on top of the natural, sandstone surface layer. But in order for the new "Hebrew housing" to be constructed with cement and concrete, the sandstone had to be excavated and cleared away to provide a solid foundation.

Sharon Rotbard, showing the gap between the old kurkar *surface grade and Tel Aviv's street grade below.*

Photo by author

As a result, much of Tel Aviv was constructed at a meter or two lower than the surface grade of the land. This is readily apparent in vertical sections in the pavement, below which houses and sidewalks were constructed. "It is one of the materializations of the border between Tel Aviv and Jaffa," he explained, "a frontier zone between these two cities." Or, as he put it in his book, in reference to Tel Aviv's origin myth, "the city was not really built on dunes at all, but instead of them."[40] When his tour took us to the remnants of Sheikh Murad cemetery, which once belonged to the village of Abu Kabir,

and which serves today as the final resting place of Palestinian collaborators with the Israeli military, he explained why the cemetery
lies a full three meters above the road and 1950s public housing
blocks below. "Tel Avivians call this a *kurkar* hill," Rotbard pointed
out, "as if it were artificially raised up, but the reality is the opposite—the surface ground of this cemetery used to be the natural
level of the landscape."

Rotbard's book helped to further erode the city's origin myth
about arising *ex nihilo* from the sand dunes, or, even more ethereally,
as Naomi Shemer's 1958 tribute song "The White Town" (*Ha'ir
Hal'vanah*), puts it, "out of foam, wave and clouds." Generations
of writers and homegrown boosters have embellished this founding
fantasy about building on the sandy wilderness of untouched land.
It is the kind of fable that is fundamental to the imagination of settler
colonists, and, in this case, it dovetails neatly with the bromide about
pre-Zionist Palestine as a "land without people."[41] Yet historians
have shown that, contrary to the iconic tableau of the "virgin dunes"
(Abraham Soskin's disputed photograph of the founding families,
gathered on a sandy area to cast lots for land parcels),[42] the majority
of Tel Aviv's land, even the Karm al-Jabali lot purchased for the
initial Ahuzat Bayit settlement, was far from vacant; it had been
occupied by vineyards and well-managed citrus groves, interspersed
with well-houses and other agricultural structures. Indeed, the right
to the original Jabali parcel was so heavily contested that Bedouins
with grazing and ownership claims on the land had to be forcibly
evicted by Ottoman troops to clear the way for building.[43]

The wide swathe of land cultivation for fruit orchards was the
basis of Jaffa's thriving pre-1948 economy, driven by overseas
demand for the Shamouti orange, which attained international
cachet in the course of the 1800s and early 1900s as the region's major
export.[44] By the mid-1930s, citrus accounted for some 60 percent of
the customs revenues of Palestine as a whole.[45] The expansion of the
industry made Jaffa a major regional employment center, drawing
workers from Egypt, Lebanon, and other Mediterranean countries.
It was a catalyst for the growth of related sectors—banks, land and
sea transportation companies, import and export firms, and a variety

of industrial enterprises—and it underpinned the city's preeminent position as the cultural center of Palestine.

From the turn of the century, the industry also attracted Jewish growers, who purchased large acreages from absentee effendi landowners and then were pressured over time to adopt Hebrew Labor policies. The Histadrut's efforts to shut out Arabs, which included pickets, defamation, and other strong-arm tactics, led to violent conflicts, as they had done in the construction sector.[46] After the *Nakba*, most of the remaining Arab-owned groves were seized under the 1950 Absentee Property Law. In some cases, Palestinian residents who were not expelled across the Green Line were hired to work as day laborers in orchards they once owned. With each new wave of Jewish immigration, the groves fell under the spreading realm of urban development. Only a handful remain today.

Jaffa/Tel Aviv and orange groves circa 1923.

Map compiled by Tyler Bray

A brand with this kind of widespread international recognition could not be wasted, and so Jaffa citrus, though no longer grown in the Tel Aviv–Jaffa region, has had a second career as a premium Israeli product. It was promoted by association with pioneer myths about "making the desert bloom" or through the socialist romance of the kibbutzim, which won Israel many left-wing admirers during the Cold War. By the time I worked in Kibbutz Ginosar's orchards in the late 1970s, the Shamouti orange had been replaced by more durable varieties and was fast disappearing from the commercial markets. But the Jaffa name itself had been transformed into a full-blown umbrella brand, covering as many as twenty citrus products, including the pink grapefruit, promoted overseas as "Jaffa Sunrise," that I was tasked with treating for disease in Ginosar. In 1965, JAFFA was registered as Israel's first Appellation of Origin under the Lisbon Agreement that protects regional products like Champagne, Cognac, Roquefort, Chianti, Porto, Tequila, and Darjeeling.[47]

By then, the fruit products no longer had any *terroir* association with the real soil and climate of Jaffa, yet the brand was carefully protected by the Citrus Marketing Board of Israel (CMBI) and zealously promoted as part of the nationalist campaign to market Israel itself. The fledgling "cultural diplomacy" (*hasbara*) campaign to enhance Israel's international image was boosted in part by the commercial success of JAFFA in the course of the 1970s. In Eyal Sivan's 2010 film, *Jaffa: The Orange's Clockwork*, about the industry's history, Zvi Kenan, former CMBI chair, recalled: "We knew we were promoting Israel's cause to the public.... In 1976, we learned it (JAFFA) was second only to Coca-Cola in public awareness." Overseas visitors to Israel are greeted by an orange orchard (planted in the early 2000s) outside the terminal at Ben Gurion International Airport, presumably to echo global recognition of the brand.

Marketers like Kenan learned that international consumers were willing to pay a high premium (10–20 percent) just for the perceived quality of a JAFFA brand.[48] The value that JAFFA added to the national brand was so great that, in the late 1990s, the CMBI decided to license its use to growers in other countries. Under this arrangement, royalties flow to the CMBI, while foreigners promote the number one Israeli brand for free. But the prominence of the brand proved to be a double-edged sword. When large agribusiness firms like Mehadrin and Carmel Agrexco began to export JAFFA fruit sourced from West Bank settlements, the brand (along with the companies) was placed on the boycott list of the international Boycott, Divestment, and Sanctions movement. High consumer awareness of JAFFA has amplified the economic power of the boycott, which is beginning to eat into sales and profits in the same way as the anti-apartheid consumer boycott campaign took its toll on South Africa's Outspan orange producers from the 1960s onwards.

The Hebrew Bulldozer

The orchards were not the only feature of the regional landscape to disappear after 1948. Along with all of the twenty-four surrounding villages, entire urban neighborhoods of Jaffa were wiped out. Indeed, the physical making of Tel Aviv is as much a story about mass, targeted demolition as it is about the construction of the new.[49] Shutting Palestinians out of construction work was one thing; it was quite another to bulldoze away all evidence that they had ever built houses, let alone large towns and cities. Israeli authorities took their cue from the British before them and used some of the same wrecking tactics. As one of the many brutal acts of retribution for the Arab Revolt, which began with a strike at the Jaffa port, the Royal Air Force initiated the attacks on Jaffa's urban fabric by bombing parts of the city in 1936.[50] In June of that year, as part of Operation Anchor (officially, and cynically, labeled as "urban improvement"), combat engineers blasted apart the old core with gelignite to make way for two wide military roads. House demolition as a form of collective punishment thereby began its long career on Palestinian lands.

Worse would follow in 1948 when Irgun bombers targeted and flattened Jaffa homes, and the Haganah's demolition squads moved from house to house during their invasion of the city as part of Plan Dalet's Operation Chametz. In the aftermath, Israeli forces used parts of the old city as a military testing ground to determine how demolitions could be carried out without harming the soldiers handling the dynamite. As for the inhabitants, the Jewish military factions drove out 97 percent of the city's 1948 Arab population of 100,000 residents (in the city and in surrounding villages) and barred them from return. They rounded up most of the 4,000 who managed to stay, or who filtered back in, and forced them inside the Ajami neighborhood (unofficially referred to as "Ghetto Ajami") in conditions reminiscent of the recently liquidated ghettos of Polish, Hungarian, and Soviet Belarus cities. In other sizable Arab cities, like Acre, al-Ramla, Haifa, and Lydda, occupying forces staged the same roundup and corralling. As in Haifa's Wadi Nisnas district, they sealed off Ajami's one square mile enclosure with barbed wire, and soldiers guarded the only two entrances, enforcing a curfew, from 5 p.m. to 6 a.m., that endured for a full three years after the creation of the state.

Children in ruins of Jaffa, 1948.

Photo by Herbert Sonnenfeld. Courtesy Beit Hatfutsot/The Museum of the Jewish People

The Arab state proposed by the 1947 UN Partition plan was supposed to include Jaffa, but within a year, and even before the Mandate forces withdrew, the city's complex social and cultural life had been torn to shreds and tossed to the winds by Zionist invasion forces.

Jaffa's entire middle class of notables, merchants, and profession-als, including engineers, teachers, lawyers, and intellectuals, either fled or were literally forced into the sea (to escape by boat), and the headquarters of Palestine's cultural and commercial life ceased to exist. For this cosmopolitan class, the fall of the "Bride of the Sea" (also known as "Mother of the Stranger"—*umm al-gharib*—on account of its openness to newcomers) was the most grievous outcome of the *Nakba*. In decades to come, the "tragic nostalgia" of Jaffa's bourgeoisie for their lost urban paradise left little room, as Salim Tamari observed, for those who managed to stay on and whose efforts to eke out a livelihood were deemed tawdry in comparison with the perfumed past.[51]

Lacking any resources to flee, few of those who were subse-quently quarantined in Ajami's open-air prison had any prior attachment to the homes to which they were allocated. They would soon be forced to share apartment units with new Jewish immigrants who could not be accommodated in other occupied neighborhoods. After they were ransacked and looted, Ajami's ornate villas, built by the city's well-to-do, were subdivided among the immigrant Jews and the Palestinian remnant. By 1960, Jaffa hosted as many as 10,000 Bulgarian Jews (and was known as Little Bulgaria) before their outmigration in subsequent decades to the relative privacy of state-sponsored apartment block housing (*shikun*). While city officials preserved some of Jaffa's old housing stock for this temporary use as an immigrant way station, they consigned portions of the remainder to the bulldozer. To scrub away all physical proof of its Arab past, they slated large parts of the city for demolition and renamed most of the remaining streets.

In 1949, the military authorities had decided to entirely eradi-cate the old, and badly damaged, Jaffan core, and this new wave of destruction was only stopped in 1951 after a spirited coalition of artists and archaeologists made the case for cultural preservation on the grounds of protecting religious and archaeological Jewish sites.[52] But the domicides continued in other locations for the next three decades: city planners cleared away al-Manshiyya to the north, which had the highest Arab density in the coastal region, to make way for a seaside park and the development of South Tel Aviv, while authorizing widespread demolitions in Ajami and Jabaliya to the south. Internationally, the 1950s and 1960s were the decades of "urban renewal," when war-damaged neighborhoods in Western Europe and designated "slums" in North America were condemned for clearance, making way for new residential quarters and business centers. In the United States, urban renewal was nicknamed "Negro removal," because of the high volume of displaced African American residents. But in Israeli cities, the razing of neighborhoods like al-Manshiyya had an additional racial edge, since it was largely driven by the Zionist goal of erasing any evidence that Arabs themselves had once built a thriving urban center on this land.

The Judaization of Jaffa was further hastened by the 1960s reconstruction of the ruined core (only two blocks were still standing out of the original walled twenty-one acres) by a newly created public firm, the Company for the Development of Ancient Jaffa. The result was branded "Old Jaffa," an intentional tourist destination that highlights the Crusader and Jewish histories of the site, boasts a Jewish "artisans' village," and, through its curation and signage, blatantly disregards centuries of Arab presence. Architects and engineers who worked on this project were subsequently employed, after 1967, on the reconstruction of the Jewish Quarter in East Jerusalem's Old City.[53] The Old Jaffa initiative may have been undertaken in a secular, commercial spirit, but it became a prototype for the controversial archaeological excavations of ancient Jewish settlement that followed the Israeli occupation of East Jerusalem.

In that other city, state archaeologists were guided by religious Zionist goals, and they crossed many of the red lines established in the heritage conservation field by neglecting (or in many cases, bulldozing through) the ample physical record of the last two millennia in order to reach the sought-after artifacts of archaic Jewish kingdoms. Other violations occurred when land was seized and residents were expelled in order to redesign the Jewish Quarter, much enlarged and with a Jewish-only population, while the rest of Jerusalem's Old City was left to decay. The neglect was so blatant that UNESCO repeatedly condemned, and eventually expelled,

Israel from the organization in 1974 for abdicating its responsibility to protect the cultural heritage of occupied territory. Further conflicts with UNESCO followed after Jordan successfully nominated the Old City for inscription on the list of World Heritage Sites in 1981 and on the list of World Heritage in Danger in 1982.[54] The 1974 UNESCO resolutions and the later inscriptions were vigorously opposed by the United States in support of Israel. Washington's heavy-handed diplomatic pressure resumed in 2011, after Palestine became a full UNESCO member, and again, in 2017, when Hebron's Old City was included on both lists.

The more commercial model set by the Old Jaffa reconstruction initially took the form of an artists' colony. In an overt form of "artwashing," the development company evicted the remaining Palestinian residents from the ruins—by then the "poorest of the poor"—and invited select artists to take up residence in the reimagined urban village on condition that their studios were open to passers-by. Needless to say, the art on display is tailored to tourist fantasies about the quaint alleyways and arches that were entirely reshaped to evoke the antique core of the city. Although the comparison is often made, it is a far cry from Disney. Unlike Walt's idealized Main Street, the real Jaffa existed quite recently on the actual tourist site, and still lies underneath it, like a vandalized cemetery.

On my first visit to Old Jaffa, I asked a guide at the central information booth why none of the zone's signage informed tourists that this place had been a major Arab city.

Art gallery in an alley of reconstructed Old Jaffa.

Photo by author

He smiled awkwardly, but also sheepishly, as if to convey that he was obliged to stick to his script. "Jews have always lived here," he replied, "at different points of Jaffa's history." On subsequent visits, I always made a point of interrogating the young men staffing the booth. One of them pointed defensively to the presence of minarets (the extant mosques of Mahmoudiya and Masjid al-Bahr), but advised me that "no Arabs live here anymore, because times have changed. If you want to see how they live," he advised, "go to the hood [of Ajami]." Another took the time to explain his defensiveness—"things happened here, it is not our job to judge the past"—and to expound his geopolitical view of the world: "Look!" he proclaimed, signaling to the east, "over there is ISIS, and over there [to the west] is Miami and extreme capitalism. We are in a sweet spot, where there is still some idealism." On a later visit, I found a staffer on duty who was openly apologetic: "I am sorry, it is true you will not find that part of Arab history here in the Visitors Center or anywhere in Old Jaffa. I wish it were otherwise, but the people who designed this space—it is reinvented—clearly wanted it that way." Pressed on details about the *Nakba*, he reverted to script: "there are two sides to that story."

The solitary wall plaque in the tourist zone that does mention the "Arabs of Jaffa" records that the city "sheltered strikers, rioters, and snipers" during the 1936 Arab Revolt and that "two broad streets were blasted through the center in order to suppress the revolt and improve access" to the overcrowded quarter. "Many ancient houses were demolished," according to the plaque, and "residents were left homeless." For the tourist, drawn by the visual appeal of the vintage stone houses, the plaque reinforces the association of Arabs with violence, and, of course, the British, not the Jewish forces, can be blamed for the sin of demolishing the quaint housing.

Visitors will look in vain for information about how this densely populated urban center was bombed and devastated by Irgun and Haganah forces in 1948. But if they venture past the parking lots and parkland that spread out north of the old center on the former location of al-Manshiyya neighborhood, they will find, on a prominent spot by the seashore, a small boxy museum devoted to the Irgun's

(Etzel) "liberation of Jaffa." The Etzel museum is built on top of one of the neighborhood's few remaining Arab houses, and its glass and steel walls rise up from the old stonework.

A veteran mortar cannon, aimed at Jaffa, guards the entrance to Etzel Museum.

Photo by author

Because the taking of al-Manshiyya was accomplished solely by Irgun forces, engaged in direct combat with British troops and artillery, the site holds particular significance for Zionist militarists. Palestinians, on the other hand, will recall how the Irgun moved on Jaffa shortly after the massacre of villagers in Deir Yassin, on April 9, 1948, a horrifying pogrom of violence (even for the ruthless Irgun) that triggered a wave of fear throughout Palestine's Arab population. In the wake of the attacks, Ben-Gurion confided to his diary that "Jaffa will be a Jewish city.... War is war," upping the ante on what he had written during the 1936 revolt: "If Jaffa went to hell, I would not count myself among the mourners."[55]

After 1950, the destruction proceeded under the legal cover of the Absentee Property Law, which permitted state seizure of all Palestinian houses whose residents had left home between November 29, 1947, and September 1, 1948 (or, in some cases, were simply not at home when the registrars came calling). Many of these homes were condemned in preparation for the rehabilitation of South Jaffa as an upmarket residential location. Planners proposed replacing the old port with a yacht marina, backdropped by hotels and upscale condo units arrayed along the Jaffa Slope. From the mid-1970s to the mid-1980s as many as 1,347 residential buildings (amounting to 41.4 percent of the total number of residential units in Ajami and Jabaliya) were bulldozed to make way for the redevelopment, and the rubble was piled up on South Jaffa's main beach.[56]

Soon, outsiders were dumping their garbage on this site, much of it industrial waste, including asbestos and other toxic materials, generating illnesses among the Ajami residents living adjacent to the dump. When chemically triggered explosions occurred inside the garbage mountain, by then fifteen meters high, a public petition helped push the Supreme Court to issue a stop to the demolitions in 1987 on the grounds that the redevelopment master plan had never been legally authorized at the national level. The garbage, which included the remains of much of Ajami's housing stock, was ground down and returned to the sand from whence the *kurkar* originally came. The authorities converted the mountain, reduced in size, into a seashore park.

Even before the dumping was terminated, the tide was already turning against the Zionist version of urban renewal. In 1979, a group of Jaffan intellectuals formed an advocacy committee, *al-rabita li-ri'ayat shu'un 'arab yafa* (League for the Arabs of Jaffa) and mounted a vigorous defense of their right to remain in the city. Their stance echoed with the spirit of *sumud*, or steadfastness, that had become a Palestinian pillar after the 1967 war. Unlike the 1948 Palestinians who had fled for fear of their lives, the new generation pledged to resist by remaining in place. The Rabita League's expression of Jaffan values spoke directly to the Arab heritage of the neighborhoods, under existential threat of being swept away entirely. The campaign attracted a Jewish ally in the form of *Yafo Mamat Yamin* (Jaffa, Belle of the Sea), a pressure group of upper bohemian settlers from Tel Aviv who wanted to preserve the old housing stock as a quality-of-life issue.

In response to the agitation, Jaffa's Palestinian residents were promised alternative, affordable housing under the state's Project Renewal for neighborhood rehabilitation. But the housing did not materialize, and the offer of rehabilitation was short-lived. The real estate market was about to call the shots. Land prices had begun to shoot up, and the juggernaut of gentrification began its steady march down the coast. The ancient city's human and physical remnants would no longer be an expensive problem for City Hall to pretend to fix. The old Bride of the Sea was now a big money-spinner, enticing a new generation of Israeli Jews with a craving for the heritage real estate, gastronomic authenticity, and ethnic coexistence of a mixed city.[57]

During the postwar decades of Tel Aviv's modernist growth, Jaffa's antique style was unloved and retrograde, tainted by its association with the Ottoman past. In the course of the 1980s, the taste of the new would-be gentry underwent a sea change, and the evolving public appetite for historical preservation came to the fore. This neotraditionalist shift in mentality occurred in many industrialized countries, when a younger generation developed a new appreciation of heirloom buildings and rejected the modernist planning doctrine of slum clearance and urban renewal through concrete. In Israel, this generational conversion got a boost after the occupation of the West Bank in 1967 from the newfound nationalist zeal for recovering and restoring the artifacts of ancient Jewish life. Old stones were no longer an obstacle to be bulldozed in the name of Zionist progress. Now they needed to be preserved as proof of the antiquity of the Jewish nation, and sometimes, at least to the undiscerning eye, anything old would do.

Jaffa was not Jerusalem, however, and its old stones would be reassessed for different reasons. With unequaled views of the sea, unobstructed by high-rise condos, Jaffa's remaining *kurkar* buildings fell under realtors' close scrutiny. However dilapidated and, in many cases, drastically altered from their pre-1948 forms, this housing stock would increasingly be coveted for its upmarket realty value. From the mid-1990s, a major stimulus for this heritage-oriented market was the sell-off of homes from the inventory of Amidar and Halamish, two public housing companies with absentee property holdings. But stepped-up government revenue was not the only factor driving the Amidar and Halamish sales. The 1993 Oslo Accords, and the prospect of Palestinian refugees somehow making good on their claims to their pre-1948 property, had also motivated the authorities to offload these homes to private buyers, in apparent violation of the custodial trust.

In 1995, the city finally approved the Jaffa Slope redevelopment master plan, which had first been drafted in the 1960s. Planners revised the original to incorporate the preservationist features deemed attractive to the incoming wave of settlers. In particular, they made sure that the desirable sea views were protected by restrictions on building heights. That same year, Jaffa's Palestinians— an expanding population threatened by rising prices and realty speculation—went public with their dissent when thirty families decided to squat in empty houses in what came to be known as the "housing intifada" (*intifadat al-sakan*).[58] Grassroots activists re-issued a longstanding demand for affordable housing.[59] By the mid-2000s, as many as 500 Palestinian families (one in four of Jaffa's Arab population) in the 2,000 Amidar-owned houses found themselves under threat of eviction, charged with technical violations that had gone unenforced before Oslo and the housing boom. Many of the residents were legally exposed because they had undertaken renovations or had added rooms in spite of the postwar embargo against any construction or housing upgrades in Arab-majority areas.

To make matters worse, Amidar, the absentee property agency, had issued rental contracts after 1950 that only guaranteed protective tenancy to the next generation, and now the agency was looking to take advantage of this lack of long-term security. Among those being forced out of their homes were residents still within the generational limits of their protective tenancy. Some even had legal title to the homes but faced an uphill legal struggle to prove their claims, since they were registered in Ottoman-era archives in Turkey that were difficult to access and which Israeli courts were wont to dismiss in any event. Others were simply deemed to be illegal squatters of absentee property under the 1950 act. These evictions generated a new wave of homegrown activism, this time on behalf of families beaten down by decades of blatant discrimination, and with few resources to defend their right to remain in Jaffa.

In 2006, Esther Saba was one of those residents served with an eviction notice. In her case, it was thrown over her fence into the backyard. The order had been triggered by the failure of her husband (incarcerated at the time) to respond to the rent notices. Traumatized by the prospect of losing her house, she contacted some Jaffan arts activists who called on community members to gather and greet the demolition crew. They constructed a barricade around the house, and more than a hundred locals who responded to the call massed on her roof and in her yard, along with a throng of media. The five police who showed up with a solitary bulldozer were turned away, and Darna: The Popular Committee for Land Protection and Housing Rights in Jaffa was born. In the years that followed, Darna members waged a gutsy battle in the streets and the courts to save housing for those at the heart of Jaffa's Palestinian community. In recognition of their efforts, in 2008, the central events of Land Day (the annual commemoration of the watershed 1976 uprising against land expropriation in the Galilee) were held in Jaffa, the first urban community to claim the honor.

Happily, Saba was still in her home when I visited her in the fall of 2016. "No one had the courage to speak up before I did," she told me, "and I did it because I really had no choices left." The authorities were singling out families, and "most of them were too ashamed" to reveal their plight. She recounted why she became active and went on to help organize others with the basic resources provided by the Popular Committee: "I was always a strong individual, but this fight to stay here made me feel much stronger." In the years that followed, she survived many obstacles thrown in her path—a bout of cancer, the municipality's punitive efforts to cut off her electricity and water, and a long, grueling season in the courts to assert her right to retain the house. Invoking her own version of *sumud*, she explained: "I decided that I really needed to stay in this place, and now, having fought so long for it, I would not exchange it for a palace." Indeed, her modest dwelling was now surrounded by newly constructed four-story buildings, occupied by affluent Jewish tenants and owners, who she reported had "disrespected" her when they offered her "high price items they did not like as castoffs." Nor did she spare the wealthy Palestinian investors and real estate professionals who had bought Ajami property from Amidar and leased it exclusively to Jewish tenants: "they are part of the problem," she added, because they are "contributing to the Judaization of the neighborhood."

As for the impoverished Jews who had stayed on in Ajami, they were just as vulnerable to Amidar's demolition threats. After leaving Saba, I visited a Jewish couple who had recently won a court case to hold on to their house. Forced out initially, they had erected a tent around the entrance to prevent access to realtors seeking to enter the property. Who were the prospective new owners? "Distant relatives of ours," they said, scornfully, "they faked an Amidar claim to the house, and set up their son to find financing to buy it." As we were celebrating their victory, Sami Nada, a longtime Palestinian activist who won his own case a few weeks earlier, dropped by to join the celebration. Here was a scene, not simply of coexistence, but of Palestinian–Jewish solidarity.

For Yudit Ilany, who co-founded Darna and ran the legal unit until recently, these victories were especially sweet. The committee had lost its funding two years before, so it no longer had the resources to mount legal challenges. As she took me on her tour of Ajami, she pointed to the failures along the way—the crumbled foundations of walls in the red dirt where her clients' houses once stood and generic condo blocks being built in place of demolished houses. The committee had been tenacious, even to the point of tracking down hoary title claims in Ottoman Turkish that had been transcribed in Arabic script. With no resources left for the legal fight, she feared that formerly winnable cases would almost certainly now result in evictions, demolitions, and new condos. Over the years, she had learned some things about the institutional goals of Amidar and was comfortable in summarizing them: "to get rid of as much Palestinian property as possible and to extract maximum profit in the process."

One rundown and isolated building that we passed drew her contempt. It was rumored to be haunted—a previous Christian owner had never been properly buried—and also to be earmarked for sale to the US-backed Garin Torani community, a militarist settler group that had established colonies in Jaffa and South Tel Aviv in order to amplify the religious Jewish presence. The original Torani group were settlers who had been "withdrawn" from Gaza in 2005 by Ariel Sharon and had decided to pursue their territorial ambitions, not in the West Bank, but in Israel's "mixed cities" in order to combat secular drift and intermarriage between Jews and Palestinians. Ilany reported that a community action was being planned to block acquisition of this particular building. Previous tactics employed by her activist team to scare away potential buyers included the display of Hezbollah paraphernalia and loud Arabic chanting.

The ethnic profile of gentrification, she reported, was also being shaped by the master plan's restrictions on new construction, further reducing the pool of affordable housing for the expanding Palestinian population. New buildings were now subject to codes that regulated apartment unit sizes (a minimum of 120 square meters) in ways that effectively excluded Palestinian families with limited means, while the protection of sea views imposed a cap on building heights to four floors. These codes had helped boost Jaffa's skyrocketing land values but were further narrowing access on the part of low-income Palestinians with traditionally large families.

So, too, the new historical preservation codes laid out strict compliance requirements for construction and renovation. To restore older buildings, the regulations stipulated the use of *kurkar* stone, which was an expensive undertaking (at $120 per meter), requiring the attention of skilled masons who no longer existed among the general population. For new buildings, developers could choose to clad the ground-level facades with synthetic stone bricks that passed the *kurkar* test. Alternately, they could apply a stucco finish from a palette of prescribed colors. Since the intent was to curate the aesthetic appearance of Jaffa as a quaint Mediterranean haven, planners also placed an embargo on building with the "Jerusalem stone" of Tel Aviv's rival to the east. Indeed, the local flavor of this coastal refuge was now enforced by rules about construction materials in much the same way that the integrity of Jerusalem's signature architecture was protected by a 1918 ordinance (intro-duced by British governor Ronald Storrs) that mandated the use of local dolomitic limestone within city limits. While the new Jaffa regulations had not resulted in a revival of *kurkar* quarrying, the long-lived Jerusalem rules were a mainstay of the West Bank stone industry.

Preserving What?

I n the West Bank, as we shall see in the next chapter, the restora-tion of traditional masonry skills and construction materials has become a nationalist initiative, aimed at building up Palestinian pride and heritage and protecting village lands from seizure by set-tlers. In Jaffa, the craft of restoring homes is catering to different kinds of settlers: bohemian Tel Avivians with a taste for urban soul and "edge," and prosperous professionals who see rapidly rising land values and a short commute to the city. Some of the most pas-sionate amateur historians of old Jaffa are youngish Jewish hipsters (and not a few like-minded Palestinians) looking to do their thing in a multi-ethnic setting. Architects commissioned to design new villas and three-story buildings have learned how to incorporate arches, arabesques, and other Arab features that were unwelcome during the decades of Tel Aviv's modernist growth.

As for the workers who are busy on construction sites on almost every other Jaffa block, they hail from West Bank villages near cities like Hebron or Nablus. Between 1967 and 2008, a goodly number were Gazans, many of whose families had fled after 1948 to the refugee camps of Jabaliya, al-Shati, or Rafah. During that period, some of these workers were hired to demolish and rebuild on sites close to their old family domiciles or those of their relatives, while others labored in the remaining citrus orchards. Less than twenty years after their forced removal, their forefathers' trade was being deployed again in Jaffa, this time to obliterate all signs of their prior residence.

Unless they were from refugee camps, the new generation of West Bank Palestinian workers with whom I spoke were less likely to feel the pain and were more focused on the uncertainties of the present day. "There are more people here from Nablus than there are Arab residents of Jaffa," joked Ramy, a worker I interviewed who hailed from the village of Jama'in. Along with his brother and cousin, all in their twenties, they formed a work crew that had been coming to Tel Aviv, without permits, for the past eight years. Pay was good—400 shekels ($111) a day—and their rooms and board were covered by a friendly Palestinian contractor during the ten-day to two-week spells they spent away from their families. The only other expense was the 300 shekels for the fixer who helped them across the Wall and into Israel. Jama'in was well-known for its limestone quarries, and one of the three workers, who had been trained as a school teacher, had an uncle who owned a stone factory in the village. None of them had worked there for more than a week, however. The factory pay was only one-fourth of what they could get in Jaffa, nor could Jama'in compare with the perks of being able to enjoy a largely Palestinian urban culture inside Israel where they could walk the streets and shop without attracting unwanted attention. "It's actually a paradise for us" confessed Ramy. "Most of all," he added, "we have the beautiful sea"—which most West Bankers could only dream of, and which those with work permits had no time to enjoy, since their working hours and travel regime were so rigid.

Had they any reservations about building Israeli houses on former Palestinian land? "Maybe if we were working in a wholly Jewish city," mused his brother. "But we cannot allow ourselves to think about such things. If we did, we might have to stop doing this work, which puts food on the family table and which has allowed us to build our own houses in Jama'in." They could see that there was some kind of connection to be made between the antiquity of their West Bank village and the rage for preserving the old stones of Jaffa, but they seemed much more caught up in the pace of change in both places. In Jama'in, almost everyone was dependent on the Israeli demand for their limestone, and so "the landscape was constantly changing," as hills were leveled and ground gouged out to carve out the "white oil." They all knew of families "who suffered because they lived near the stone quarries and factories and who had to be 'compensated' for the noise and pollution." The most profitable stone, they said, was quarried from as deep as fifty meters below the surface. Here, in Jaffa, they found themselves employed in a different kind of extractive industry—by contractors and developers bent on quarrying profit from the upland views of the Mediterranean Sea.

The new taste for historic preservation was an especially bitter pill to swallow for longtime Ajami residents like Sami Abu Shehadeh, another Darna founder. A Palestinian historian, Balad Party activist, and director of a youth empowerment NGO, he explained that "when the authorities finally got around to talking about planning for preservation in the 1990s, there was nothing left to preserve. None of the things that relate to preserving our cultural identity existed any longer, so the planners didn't have us in their mind when they talked about preservation. We had gotten used to the fact that someone else was planning our life, and so this was normal for us. And since we [Israeli Palestinians] were not recognized as indigenous, we don't exist as a people with collective rights, only as a handful of religious minorities." Abu Shehadeh dismissed the idea that Ajami residents had any kind of deep ancestral connection to the buildings. "Very few here live in a Palestinian house the way they used to." Nor, he took pains to point out, did the Rabita League and other activist groups prioritize "building preservation"; "they were more focused on the survival of a community that no one in power ever took into consideration."

Above all, Abu Shehadeh took issue with the much-cited "Judaization of Jaffa." Dismissing the dire warnings about this tendency, he noted that "if you look at the actual numbers, the Arab population here has increased from 4,000 to 20,000 since 1948," and that, "over the same period of time, the Jewish population has decreased from 70,000 to about 30,000." Judaization, he added, "is actually wishful thinking, because there is nothing more to Judaize in Jaffa." Quality of life was another matter. "Jews have other urban centers to go to," he observed, "while we do not," and "so the rise in Jaffan house values has squeezed us badly. Our professionals here are doing well, but 50 percent of the Palestinians in Jaffa are living under the poverty line."

Ajami was once notorious for its high crime rates and drug economy, and it is still demonized by Tel Avivians as a place of low "Arab morals," but Abu Shehadeh had an alternative explanation for the cycles of violence within the community: "The government has long used Jaffa as a hiding place for Israeli collaborators (*umala*) from the West Bank. When they lost their cover over there, they were brought here to protect them from recriminations, and the state knew how destructive and divisive their presence would be." "They were weak and desperate and self-hating," he added, "and so they became the most violent criminals. Everyone knows who they are—their family names are not from anywhere around here."

In recent years, Abu Shehadeh had turned his historian's knowledge of Jaffa into a livelihood, working as an alternative tourist guide out of an office on Yefet Street. He was able to customize a tour for me, focusing on particular buildings and land parcels with a ghostly political history. On these streetscapes, where multimillion-dollar residences are sprouting alongside tumbledown stone cottages, Abu Shehadeh was a sure-footed, though hardly dispassionate guide. Along the way, he made light of my interest in *kurkar* stone. "*Kurkar* has its problems with humidity and water penetration" he pointed out, "and it does not insulate so well against winter cold." "Palestinians," he pleaded, "have modern needs and deserve modern buildings," and added, with good reason, "we have not exactly benefited from being associated with antiquity."

We ended up at the house of Ismail, his grandfather, who before the *Nakba* had harbored dreams of studying Islamic law in Cairo and who had stories to tell about the stonemasons of the city when he was employed as a young water engineer. He got quite animated by the technical talk about stone and recalled that some of the masons with whom he worked had developed an unusual blend of materials —eggs, crushed roof tiles, and lime-based mortar (*sid*)—to bind and seal the surface of water wells. Their work took them to Tel Aviv on occasion, where he said he only ever saw Arabs on construction sites. "Arabs built Tel Aviv," he insisted, "I never saw Jews doing that kind of work, not even when they were building with concrete. The Arabs were always cheaper, and they knew what they

Photo by author

Restored kurkar *wall, Jaffa.*

were doing, so the contractors preferred us." His tone was more sober when the topic turned to the period of military rule in post-1948 Jaffa. Unable to obtain a travel permit, he was one of the many who risked arrest (and he was caught more than once) by migrating to find work outside the Ajami ghetto.[60]

Unable to find anyone else in Jaffa who was old enough to have pre-1948 stories about construction, I paid a visit to Balata refugee camp in Nablus a few months later, where many Jaffans had wound up after the *Nakba*. Each of the three camp elders I separately interviewed, all of whom had grown up in villages on Jaffa's outskirts, had a similar recollection of Arabs working on Tel Aviv's construction sites. Omar Abu Shahid, whose family owned orchards to the east of Tel Aviv, recalled the conflicts over building materials: "Jews didn't know how to use *kurkar* and traditional mortar, so they needed Arabs, but even when they used concrete, and even when Histadrut started a boycott, there were still mostly Arabs employed there." His memory of Tel Aviv's Jewish community, like that of the others I spoke to, was not a threatening one: "They were a poor minority at the time, and they depended on us for everything—water, electricity, food. We would sell fruit at the Hatikva market, and visit their city—no one said anything—but at that time Tel Aviv was nothing compared to Jaffa."

By 1945, Tel Aviv's population had surpassed 150,000, and it was considerably larger than Jaffa, so it was odd to hear their perceptions of the Jewish community as small and under-resourced. Abu Shahid's grandson, who joined us, told me he had worked illegally in construction for several years in South Tel Aviv. Did he feel a connection to the place? "It was not a good feeling, I was working for the occupier at the time, and now I no longer have to." During those years, he had been able to visit Jaffa. "I had heard so much from my grandparents about what a great place it was—a real paradise in their stories—but there wasn't much left of the old city... just a few old houses."

Doctor Kurkar

In the last several years, Jaffa's newfound eligibility has caught the attention of brokers in the international real estate market. Ultraluxury realty firms like Sotheby's regularly advertise multi-million dollar listings like this one: "Property of the week: a historic masterpiece in Jaffa, brought gently into the twenty-first century. High domed ceilings and vaulted archways with walls of solid stone. At the heart of Israel's liveliest and most cosmopolitan city, a stroll away from the major hotels, shopping and entertainment centers, while beholding the endless blue of the Mediterranean from one of your many panoramic windows." These properties are marketed to global buyers who want to snap up an antique seaside asset without knowing too much about its history. Large-scale luxury housing projects have quickly sold out, including the especially controversial, gated community of Andromeda Hill, designed, in broker parlance, in the "romantic Jaffa style" and generously fitted with "Oriental" details.[61]

During my visits, the most visible restoration work was being executed by the Starwood group's W Hotel brand, pioneer of the concept of the "lifestyle hotel" that had become a symbol of gentrification in many cities worldwide. At the southern perimeter of Old Jaffa, the W builders were busy retrofitting two nineteenth-century landmark sites, the School of the Sisterhood of Saint Joseph of the Apparition, and the French Hospital, into an ultra-luxury complex advertised as the *W Tel Aviv–Jaffa Hotel and Residences*. Built as a gift to the nuns who had tended to its malaria-stricken donor, the French Hospital opened in 1885 to provide medical services free of charge to all Jaffans, regardless of nationality, gender, or religion. Constructed in a French style, with imported European materials, but on lots bounded by *kurkar* walls, the compound (housing a church, hospital, and a hostel for the needy) had been a vital part of Jaffa's public health infrastructure. It maintained operations after the *Nakba* as a state psychiatric hospital but was sold to developers in the late 1990s. Even though there had been no free services offered on this site since then, the price tags on the W's extravagant condo residences were an obscene upgrade.

The renovated property hosted what its owner called "the most expensive penthouse for sale in Israel," designed by "London-based master of minimalism John Pawson." It would go on the market for 60 million shekels ($17.6 million). Shahar Perry, the CEO of RFR, the American real estate investment firm behind the venture, imagined how the hotel would suit the urban appetite of his classy clients: "This place is undergoing a transformation from sleepy and quiet Jaffa to something far more bustling and vibrant. A younger and more dynamic population has moved here." In a promotional video for the development, Mark Trehame, the project architect, spoke in ethereal terms about the architectural qualities of the renovation, while displaying a casual attitude toward its recent Jaffan past: "When we found this place in 2006, it was completely overgrown, it was as if the door had been shut on it for 120 years."[62]

The historical details of the hospital building—Roman columns, Corinthian cornices, and vintage metal fixtures—were being restored, and the pre-French remnants include thirteenth century stonework from the city's southern wall, which would now surround the lounge/lobby, the signature of W's lifestyle branding. W officials reported that the fabric was being restored by experts from Europe, but all the workers I questioned on site were either Palestinians from the West Bank or Eastern European migrant workers. Across the street, at 27 Yefet, I found Abed Dajani, from Hebron, repointing the facing on the entrance to the palatial two-turreted building of the former Saint Joseph's Girls School that would house the W offices and meeting rooms. The facing was built from limestone blocks, and he felt confident in placing their point of geographic origin in the Hebron area. "We are both from the same place," he joked. The stone, if he was correct, would have made the trip sometime in the late nineteenth century, quite possibly by camel, and accompanied by masons who dressed it on site. He had crossed the Green Line that morning and would return the next day before Shabbat.

He told me he had not worked with the local sandstone and directed me to some workers across the road. They were building up a wall with *kurkar* blocks, piled high in crates by the roadside. It was the south-facing wall of the old hospital grounds, shielding the hotel's swimming pool from the street, and it was adjacent to the six-story condo wing. When questioned, the foreman of the work crew—all of his workers were from the West Bank—reported that the stones came from fallen-down houses in Ajami. On a later visit, I found a mason from Carrara, in Italy, applying the finishing touches to the wall. He was proud of his town of origin, a place long exalted for its stone and masons, and he expressed suitable disdain for modern building techniques: "I never use cement-based mortar, only the traditional kinds." As for the *kurkar*, he reported that it had been procured from old buildings knocked down in a coastal town in the north.

Looking for further clarification, I tracked down Fayez Abu Nasser, a local stonework specialist who referred to himself as "Doctor Kurkar" and who had overseen much of the stone restoration work in the older parts of the city. The family company, Old Doors, was operating out of a storefront located across Yefet Street from the W. From that location, his son sold well-weathered doors, shipped from Morocco, Egypt, and Turkey, and gussied up to satisfy the hankering of Jaffa's new money class for Ottoman shabby chic. Abu Nasser's father and grandfather had both worked in the French

Hospital, maintaining the infrastructure, and so "stone care" was a family tradition.

Corroborating what I had been initially told, he reported that he and his father started collecting *kurkar* in the wake of the Ajami demolitions, and he had amassed one of the very few sources of the original stone available today. Employed as a youth on rebuilding the houses on the Old Jaffa project, he had learned from the Nazareth builders employed by the company charged with the reconstruction, and soon became the town's go-to local specialist. Tel Aviv engineers, he told me, had tried to train Jewish workers in the mason craft, but they didn't stick with it for long. He took some pleasure in being regarded as the "Arab without a degree" who knew more than the Jewish professionals about how to breathe life back into an old stone building. Mostly everyone in Jaffa over a certain age had something to say about *kurkar*, but no one spoke about it like Abu Nasser, with authority and an abiding passion. Like Ismail Abu Shehadeh, he insisted that mostly Arab workers had built Tel Aviv during the Mandate period; "yes, we were cheaper but we were also better."

His own workers were West Bank Palestinians and Sudanese, and he was doing his best to train them as *kurkar* masons. One of the former was Mohammed Dahbour, from Nablus, who later told me he got Abu Nasser's call only when specialist work was needed. Otherwise, he went out on conventional construction jobs, which were more straightforward and less time-consuming. "I get paid 120 shekels a meter for *kurkar* work, and 100 for the other, but it takes me longer to do the *kurkar* stuff, so it evens out." As for Abu Nasser's son, an onlooker in our conversation, it appeared as if he would not be learning his father's craft. There was too much profit, and much less physical stress, he told me, in buying and selling the old doors that had become more central to the family business. The father might turn out to be the last of Jaffa's stone men.

The only others I could find in town were the Abu Talebs, who cut and sold stone for kitchen countertops, sinks, and other interior fixtures. Salim Abu Taleb and his brother said they were the last Jaffan Palestinians still doing business in the stone sector. Only a small portion of their customers still want natural stone from the West Bank, and Salim explained that the market is increasingly dominated by engineered stone, branded as Caesarstone. Originating in Sdot Yam kibbutz near Caesarea, this product is based on an Italian industrial process that molds quartz aggregate, sand, glue, and resin into slabs. Though the Israeli labor costs make it more expensive than natural stone from the West Bank, the product's popularity derives from the broad palette of colors that customers can choose from. However, since the product contains a high percentage of crystalline silica, it poses a severe health risk to workers who cut, size, grind, and polish the stone. Silicosis, cancer, tuberculosis, and lung and kidney diseases have been linked to this kind of engineered quartz.[63] Salim himself had been a casualty. He pointed to the side of his abdomen, where a tumor had been extracted. In the factory yard, the Sudanese workers who labored at lathes were wearing face masks, albeit flimsy ones.

Salim did not expect his sons to take over the factory, as he himself had done from his father, and he could only stay in business by offering an "Arab price" that attracted Jewish customers. "This is how it has always been here," he reported with a shrug that summoned more than a hundred years of Jaffan history. "They come to me because I am less expensive, it's the only reason." In the case of his own commercial niche, the lower price had a tangible human cost. In the Muslim cemetery adjacent to the factory lay the gravestones (including new ones sculpted from Caesarstone itself) of several Jaffan workers who had succumbed to the industry cancer.

3

Old and New Facts

Figuratively, a person with good character is compared to good mortar, *fintuh mnihah,* "his origin (lit. his mortar, i.e. parentage) is good." In the place of *fineh,* one may hear *djableh* (mixture), *djabeltuh 'atleh,* "his mixture (parentage) is bad."

—Tawfik Canaan, *The Palestinian Arab House,* 1933

I. Restoring the West Bank

In the years after 1948, the fate of occupied Palestinian houses was decided by the Custodian of Absentee Properties, an Orwellian title for an office that obscured a crime scene with layers of legal sophistry and skullduggery. For Israeli Jews who took over other people's homes, the subsequent re-appearance of the "absentee," whether in the form of a ghostly visitor, a petitioner to a land title in court,[1] or as a key-holder insisting on the right of return, was an inconvenient reminder that they had acquired an ample share of settler colonial guilt (or denial) along with newly cut keys to the house.[2] In recent years, as the taste for antiquity filtered into the upper tiers of the real estate industry, the vogue for acquiring newly valuable remnants of the Ottoman past has washed over this bedrock of residual shame. The procurement of old stone and interior craftwork is now in great demand, and anything that looks local and dated is grist for the mill. Jews in West Jerusalem will pay top dollar for well-preserved floor tiles and carved wood from Palestinian houses in East Jerusalem, and what cannot be bought might be expropriated as the Judaization of the city steadily proceeds.

In Jaffa, the vintage texture of the city's Palestinian remnants is driving gentrification at a fast clip. Just twenty-five kilometers away, on the other side of the Green Line, the quest to restore and preserve traditional stone-and-mortar buildings has quite a different meaning and function. In the West Bank, the rehabilitation of old houses and historic centers has little pull in the real estate market— at least not yet—but it has been feeding into a reevaluation of national heritage that might yet affect how Palestinian people can survive on their land. In territories where every building, ruin, or buried artifact is a potential fact on the ground, to be coveted or seized by the occupier, the task of conserving evidence of the long history of settled Palestinian residence has become an urgent political need. In most urban centers of the world, rehabbing period homes and dilapidated interior detail has long been a routine feature of the real estate industry. But in the Occupied Territories, restoration has only recently become a source of patriotic pride. In some cases, it has been undertaken to protect villages and land against theft by settlers who have already designated Hebrew names for them and whose claim of right rests on archaeological evidence of an ancient Jewish presence on these sites. So, too, the traditional craft of dressing stone, assembling cross-vaulted walls, and mixing lime and clay mortar to bind them has become a sustainable niche livelihood, if not the key occupation it once was.

The Palestinian Bulldozer

Over the last two decades, efforts at breathing new life into old, and often abandoned, stone structures have surged under the auspices of several cultural heritage organizations: Riwaq (in Ramallah), the Center for Cultural Heritage Preservation (in Bethlehem), the Hebron Rehabilitation Committee, and two branches of Taawon: the Nablus Restoration Unit and the Old City of Jerusalem Revitalization Program. After their initial fight for official recognition by the Palestinian Authority (PA) as

NGOs and then again for cooperation or support from government sources and donors, these organizations drafted historic preservation plans and strengthened building codes as they set about restoring run-down urban neighborhoods and village centers, stone by stone.[3] As late as the 1990s, the conservation of cultural heritage was far from a national priority. Ordinary Palestinians as well as PA officials had to be dissuaded from viewing old buildings as decaying reminders of a feudal past, to be swept aside on the road to a cleaner, postcolonial future. In the intervening years, restoration has become a more acceptable component of nation-building, an addition to the proud record of *sumud*, and maybe also a vehicle for economic development in communities starved of employment.

It was not always thus. Waves of eviction and flight in 1948 and 1967, and then again (though to a lesser extent) after the two intifadas (1987 and 2000), saw the steady depopulation of many Palestinian towns and villages. Due to the ongoing shift away from the land to wage labor on Israeli construction sites, the agricultural economy that once bound together the settled social life of the villages rapidly eroded. Residents moved out of their compact, stone-built cores— which hosted communal resources like the olive press, the flour mill, oven (*tahoun*), and guest house. With post-1967 earnings from working inside the Green Line (or in the Gulf states), they erected concrete houses on the fringe of these villages or in new clusters closer to commuter roads. From the mid-1990s, the Oslo Accords made it easier to build, resulting in a construction free-for-all. Diasporic Palestinians of means threw up outsized villas—McMansions with Arab hallmarks—on high ground adjacent to their villages of origin.

In larger towns and cities, and especially in Ramallah, the real estate boom was debt-fueled and turbo-driven by the determination to give Palestinians a contemporary Arab profile, in sync with the profile of modernity set by the Gulf states. This took the form of high-rise hotels, glass-walled banks and condos, shiny shopping malls, and a street retail landscape ruled by brand name consumerism. By contrast, residence in the West Bank's decaying town centers, now the preserve of the poorest in the community, took on a kind of stigma.

To make matters worse, the Oslo Accords' allocation of Palestinian civil and military authority over the urbanized Area A resulted not in the protection of historic buildings but in their endangerment. Since the territory designated as Area A (18 percent of the West Bank) was already densely populated, every quarter-acre would be in high demand from land developers, with speculators in close pursuit. Pressure to demolish the old urban cores and build concrete high-rises followed suit. The realty boom in Ramallah, superheated by the influx of well-resourced NGOs, elevated land prices to unimaginable heights and resulted in a catastrophic frenzy of building sprawl out to the boundaries of Area B. Compounding the loss of heritage buildings to the "Palestinian bulldozer" was the destruction wreaked on the ancient urban centers of Nablus, Hebron, and Bethlehem in 2001 when Israeli tanks and bulldozers were dispatched to put down and exact collective punishment for the al-Aqsa intifada.

Sadly, there were no regulatory protections on the books to help stave off the neglect and developers' brisk destruction of old buildings. The Palestinian Antiquities Law of 1929, re-adopted under the 1966 Jordanian Law of Antiquities and then largely preserved under the Oslo Accords, protected only Palestine's pre-1700 structures and therefore excluded most of the Ottoman era. British Mandate laws against new building and rezoning were maintained under Jordanian rule, after 1948, as a way of promoting Amman as the regional Arab capital.[4] Under the Occupation, Israeli authorities upgraded these laws in order to restrict residents' claims on the land, but the PA's subsequent deregulation unloosed the haphazard beast of sprawl on existing population centers. In this way, the decay and demolition of the old town centers were all but ordained by a succession of ruling authorities: British, Jordanian, Israeli, and Palestinian. A revised conservation bill was drafted in 2004, but it awaits the signature of an elected president who can claim authority over a unified Palestinian population. More nefariously, as Riwaq's director, Khaldun Bshara, reported, "The Israeli occupation also encouraged drug trafficking and other antisocial activities, which accelerated the process of desertification and the classification of the old town centers as unsafe and dangerous."[5]

Riwaq was founded in 1991 by virtuoso architect and writer Suad Amiry to halt the decay and remedy the neglect, and it has played a key role in jump-starting the renaissance of attention to Palestinian traditional, or vernacular, architecture. Born in Damascus after her parents fled from Jaffa, Amiry studied in Beirut and set her sights on Ramallah, where she would eventually become a deputy minister of culture in the PA's first administration. She began her work at Riwaq by compiling a registry of all buildings on the West Bank and Gaza Strip with significant historical value. Since the majority of these buildings had no legal protection, many were under immediate threat of demolition from developers, and, in locations in Hebron and East Jerusalem, where Jewish settlers were encroaching, the case for preservation was especially urgent.

Completed in 2004, the registry listed more than 50,000 buildings (half of them abandoned) in Palestinian localities, including sixteen cities and 406 villages. As it happens, roughly the same number of villages were ethnically cleansed during the *Nakba* and were either demolished or underwent a Zionist makeover in the aftermath. Almost as if in response to the physical liquidation of Palestinian heritage, and in the spirit of saving what was left, Riwaq singled out fifty strategic centers in the West Bank, and with the help of foreign donors, set about the task of safeguarding and restoring them.

To accomplish this task, the Riwaq team had to research and collect information and know-how about stonemasonry and materials and then pass it on to engineers, contractors, and workers. Much of this knowledge had been forgotten or could not be located easily within the skilled workforce. In his meticulously compiled 1933 inventory of traditional building tools and techniques, Tawfik Canaan had lamented:

The Europeanization of Palestine is certainly proceeding so quickly that in most villages western architectural methods are being introduced and the old oriental ways gradually abandoned; a few years more and the Palestinian methods will probably be forgotten, and the specific terms for material, work, and tools will be lost.[6]

Canaan's documentation of these methods in the 1930s proved to be invaluable while other resources were sought out. But government officials were not convinced, initially at least, that historic restoration was a priority or even a worthwhile endeavor. Nor was there a readily available workforce to recruit to the task. By the late 1990s, and in the spirit of the Oslo Accords, Israel had allowed the flow of construction workers across the Green Line to regain its strength, and the wages on offer were more than double the size of a West Bank pay packet.

But after 2000, Israeli retribution for the al-Aqsa intifada took the form of further border closures, and the commuter flow from the West Bank was sharply reduced. All of a sudden, there was a large surplus of skilled Palestinian builders, unable to secure Israeli work permits or employment at home. Riwaq responded by launching a program of "job creation [*tashgheel*] through conservation" and devised workshops for the unemployed about how to handle traditional materials, as well as appropriate techniques. Buildings in communities with high unemployment were targeted for selection from the registry, and the most labor-intensive restoration methods were favored in order to keep workers employed for as long as possible. Eschewing factory-processed products and even the use of mechanical mixers, the *tashgheel* approach entailed re-using the stone found on site and manually preparing all materials. Wherever they were available, regional lime, clay, and straw were preferred, and metallic fixtures and tiles were fabricated locally.

Even though these make-work measures made the outcome less efficient in places, one of the overall goals was to show that restoration through traditional craft was no more costly than modern industrial techniques. Riwaq claimed that some commissions were completed for 40 percent of the estimated cost of new construction.[7] But there were also outcomes that could not be assigned a cost—the value of preserving national heritage or reintroducing craft pride in stonemasonry. Then there were the benefits of job creation, however temporary, in locations no longer associated with gainful employment and in a construction sector that might generate many more jobs if a profitable growth trend for conservation projects took hold.

Long accustomed to filling construction jobs across the Green Line, in Israeli settlements, or in the high-income precincts of Ramallah's real estate bubble, Riwaq's Palestinian workers found themselves, for once, in the more gratifying position of laboring for their own class rather than for their Israeli oppressors or for Palestinian elites.

Riwaq's ten-year *Tashgheel* program (2001–11) did provide many jobs, though workers subsequently struggled to find employment that called on their new skills. A few urban architecture firms began to move into the conservation field, but their demand for skilled workers was sporadic and minimal. On the other hand, the buildings restored during the Riwaq project helped to revitalize civic life, since the majority were commissioned for public or communal use as centers for children, youth, women, and senior citizens or as libraries, schools, computer centers, and guest houses. Yet one of the lessons learned from the program, as a Riwaq team member put it, was that "community participation in the formulation and implementation of projects is critical to project success."[8] Delivering a restored building to a single beneficiary, however grateful, did not guarantee it would be fully used, let alone feed into the life of the community as a whole.

With this caveat in mind, Amiry and Bshara launched the *50 Villages* project in 2005 with the explicit aim of triggering community participation as an integral part of the process of restoring public space.[9] Their goal was not just to save a strategic or "architecturally important" building but to revitalize the entire area of a neglected village center and renew its use by the population that had abandoned it. In this approach, reviving the commons would be more important than the adaptive reuse of stand-alone buildings.

Even so, the Riwaq team had to select some buildings initially for emergency treatment, or "preventive restoration," in order to anchor the target area. In their subsequent meetings with village groups, they focused on encouraging the community's re-occupation of the old common space, while their studies of foot traffic helped in curating the rehabilitation of the village core. This kind of attention piqued community interest. Villagers soon began to imagine new uses for their ancestral homes or even decided to move back into the old houses themselves. To meet the first kind of demand, Riwaq struck a leasing arrangement that allowed rehabbed buildings to be purposed by an NGO for ten to fifteen years before reverting to the owner. For others, bent on returning to their homes more rapidly, a housing incentive scheme allowed them to occupy their home if they provided the labor to restore it through sweat equity.

Tour of Inspection

I n the winter and spring of 2017, I set out to meet some of the workers who had been employed on the *Tashgheel* and *50 Villages* projects. My visits took me to sites in the central highlands of the West Bank—to regions east of Jerusalem and north of Ramallah—where the landscape of hilltop villages comes closest to matching the picture-book iconography of the Holy Land. The hills are well-rounded, and limestone outcroppings are exposed at every elevation; dry stone walls and mule paths wind around their contours, protecting the terraces where olive and fruit trees used to grow in greater abundance than they now do. These walls and terraces, and the landed economy they still keep in place, are hundreds, if not thousands, of years old, but their chief (agricultural) purpose has been gradually sidelined over the last half-century. Some of the highest hilltops overlooking the villages are occupied by strategically placed Israeli settlements, their uniform red-tile roofs and defensive architectural orientation declaring their alien, quasi-military presence on the land.[10]

In their old family home in Jaba village, just to the north of Jerusalem and east of the mammoth Qalandia quarry, I sat down with two brothers who had worked on Riwaq projects for three and a half years. Formerly employed in a cake factory at a meager 30 shekels a day, and with no prior construction experience, they had been hired by a Riwaq project contractor on a 90 shekel per day rate (eventually earning 120). After learning many skills on the job from a master mason, Mohammed (the elder brother) noticed a change in his social status in the village. "When people saw me consulting with the architect or engineer, I was seen as someone important." Looking around at the family home he had helped to rebuild, Mohammed drew attention to the craftwork that sealed the stones in the walls, and the dark grout (*kuhla*) used for pointing. Underneath was a traditional lime-based (*sid*) mortar that had seen centuries of usage by Palestinians—the stone facing itself was from Birzeit, to the north, famous for its gray colors. "My children and grandchildren," he said proudly, "will know who did this and why."

Nor did he think his restoration labor was merely a family matter. "When I work on this," he asserted, knocking on the walls of his home, "I am working for my people, for Palestine. Sure, I could earn more money in Israel, but you are working for the oppressor there." His brother chimed in, as if to soften any suggestion of militancy: "We don't throw stones, we build with them." Geva Binyamin, the nearest Israeli settlement, was visible just across the highway, and given how fast "Greater Jerusalem" was expanding its suburban orbit in their direction, it was easy to see how vulnerable Jaba could be. The Riwaq project to reconnect community ties between the old center and the more recently built part of the village was supposed to firm up the lines of defense, in anticipation of worst-case eviction scenarios.

Even more precarious was the village of Beit Iksa, sitting just outside the boundary line of the Jerusalem municipality. The Israeli

Old Jaba, before restoration.

Courtesy of Riwaq. Photo by Tanya Habjouqa

Photo by author

Jaba core, after restoration.

authorities had already seized most of the town's agricultural land in the 1970s to build the surrounding settlements of Ramot and Har Shmuel, and, more recently, for a high-speed train line to Tel Aviv. Even more acreage is under threat from an impending confiscation order by the military authorities. These steady encroachments are in keeping with Israel's policy of expropriating land but not people, in order to preserve the demographic balance favoring the Jewish majority. Of its pre-1948 property of 16,000 dunums, a mere 680 remain in Beit Iksa hands. Portions of the Separation Wall now encircle the village and its 1,600 inhabitants, and a military check-point straddles the only entrance. All the visible evidence suggests that Beit Iksa has been earmarked for incorporation into Jerusalem. Ahmed, a painter and draughtsman formerly employed by Riwaq, told me that the checkpoint was intended to prevent nearby villagers from establishing residence in hopes of securing one of Jerusalem's much sought-after blue identity cards. "Some people made up rental contracts, and others fabricated village IDs to stake a claim."

Beit Iksa also seems to offer easy access across the Green Line. "You can see why," Ahmed pointed out, gesturing to the valley below the southern edge of the village, "walk from here and you will be on Jaffa Road [in Jerusalem] in twenty minutes." Such a journey would take more than two hours to go by car, through secondary roads now lined with concrete, military walls topped with razor wire, and then through Ramallah and the heavily congested Qalandia checkpoint. Those who risk the twenty minute (illegal) journey by foot through the valley below would have to pass by the foreboding sites of two former Palestinian villages, Lifta and Deir Yassin.

Lifta is the only pre-1948 Palestinian village in Israel that was cleansed of people but not razed or repopulated by Jews, and it is a rich heritage site, with buildings dating to Hellenic and Roman eras. A joint Israeli–Palestinian coalition recently sprang up to save the village from being redeveloped for luxury housing. Little remains of Deir Yassin, a former town known worldwide for the 1948 massacre (and rumored rape) of as many as two hundred residents by the Irgun and Lehi paramilitaries. Before it was decimated, Deir Yassin had been famous for its quarry and stonemasons and for a variant of *mizzi yahudi* (Jewish stone) limestone named for the town itself (*hajjar yassini*). The quarry, which had sustained so many livelihoods, became a dumping ground for the massacre victims.

News about the Deir Yassin massacre travelled all across Palestine, prompting mass flight. A Beit Iksa village councilor told me that "most of our residents fled to the east, across the River Jordan, and today as many as 37,000 of our refugees have been identified in Jordan." He also recounted how the village center was almost destroyed during the Haganah occupation from 1948 to 1953, after which it was exchanged for another village south of Jerusalem in a deal with the Jordanians ("but we only got half our land back"). The 1967 invasion saw additional damage and another wave of evictions. Most of the refugees, he admitted, especially the ones with money and education, had stayed on in Jordan because of the better opportunities there. The family of Ahmed the painter was one of those who never left, and he continued to reside in the ancestral home until it began to crumble. Earnings from working stints in Jordan and in the nearby Ramot settlement eventually allowed him to build a new home further down the hill, but when Riwaq offered him a job, the convenience of working in his own village was sufficiently appealing, even though the wages (90 to 100 shekels per day) were less satisfactory to him.

On a return visit to the village a few months later, I interviewed Abdu, a contractor—and veteran of more than ten Riwaq projects— and one of his crew. Both confirmed that the compensation for the restoration work was lower than the going rate for conventional construction jobs. Abdu took on both kinds of work, but he preferred the restoration, even though it was more dangerous (falling walls, snakebites, unexploded bombs), more onerous (lifting stones that weighed 180 kilos), and more of a technical challenge by far. Because of his expertise, he said that Israelis had approached him, offering to double his salary to work on old Jerusalem buildings. Not only had he refused, but he was also vigilant about fending off the not infrequent efforts of settlers to steal old stones and tiles from Riwaq project sites. "This kind of restoration is important if only to protect the stones lying around on the ground from being carted off," he insisted, recalling his role in one such operation: "they came to al-Tayba during the night, with a large truck, to try to steal an entire well, but we were alerted and rushed there and managed to save it." Ibrahim, his crew worker, also spoke of the value, to himself and to Palestinians, of protecting the stones. He had an Israeli work permit and had worked in Tel Aviv and Beit Shemesh in the past, but preferred the Riwaq projects, even though they paid less. "Going inside '48 is too humiliating for me," he insisted, "and I discovered that this is what I really want to do."

Even so, it was not so easy to find, let alone retain, local workers like him. Beit Iksa's population was quite well-educated, thanks to funds sent by the Jordanian refugees, and so many villagers were employed in white-collar jobs in Ramallah. Moreover, Shatha Safi, the Riwaq architect who supervised the Beit Iksa project, found that the logistics of getting workers into Beit Iksa from nearby villages was a daily headache; depending on the soldiers' whim, materials and manpower were frequently held up or denied entry, even though the restoration project and its supply needs were well known to those staffing the checkpoint. She acknowledged the challenges of keeping the trained workforce needed for this kind of work, especially when better pay was available to those who crossed over to Israel or who worked in settlements. "We may reach the point where we have to offer much higher wages," she conceded.

Ahmed the painter showed me how his ancestral house in the old center had been stabilized, but it still had no roof, and he expressed regret that Riwaq's investment had not brought what he believed the villagers really wanted—a medical clinic and new, modern houses. "Riwaq only restores the old houses, but that's not real progress," he opined. As we spoke, high-spirited children ran around us, clambering over newly installed play-sets in the refurbished commons at the center of the old village. This commons (which attracted a throng of picnickers on Thursdays and Fridays) and the adjoining Women's Center, retrofitted as a sustainable facility for cooking with locally grown food, had won an international prize (the Holcim Award) for adaptive reuse. There were also plans for an Eco Kitchen, aimed at generating income for Beit Iksa's women, arguably an example of "progress," though perhaps not what Ahmed had in mind.[11] Palestinian women have one of the lowest labor force participation rates in the world and have few outlets for earning an independent income, so the opportunity to eke out a livelihood in their own backyards was an obvious stab at economic development. Riwaq had helped the villagers reclaim fifty acres for crop-growing with the goal of supplying the women's activities. Showing some real economic value would help break the patriarchal taboo against their working outside the home. Yet, as Safi reported, the military isolation of the village had placed limits on the potential market for the women's products, and there had also been a backlash from male elders.

Nonetheless, in several sites on the *50 Villages* project, Riwaq had been trying to promote heritage conservation as an economic stimulant in its own right. This new emphasis chimed with international efforts to move the field beyond its reputation as an aesthetic passion pursued only by well-heeled enthusiasts. It also helped to combat the routine disparagement by developers and their allied elected officials who saw restoration as an irksome obstacle in the way of modernization. To dispel those perceptions, heritage conservation had to be redefined as a better pathway to economic growth. UNESCO's 2011 Paris Declaration made a point of highlighting the concept of "heritage as a driver of development." Subsequently, international bodies including the International Council on Monuments and Sites (ICOMOS) began to push the cause of cultural "uniqueness" toward the forefront of global accords on sustainable development goals. They have touted heritage in urban planning, for example, as promoting social cohesion, mobility, equity, and inclusion; resilience in the face of climate change and disaster risk; ecosystem conservation; and sustainable tourism, among other benefits.[12]

How did this new emphasis on sustainable development fare in the Occupied Territories? People struggling against colonial rule often rely on a revival of folk customs and other forms of cultural heritage to boost nationalist sentiment. In the past few decades, the political awakening among Palestinians has benefited from renewed attention to traditional arts and crafts like *dabkeh* dancing, costume embroidery, olive wood and mother-of-pearl carving, bamboo furniture, hand-painted ceramics, and soap-making, not to mention stonemasonry itself. Some of these, like the embrace of the kaffiyeh headdress, came under assault from authorities when associated too closely with overt acts of militant resistance. Others, especially in the lore of refugees, are pathways to remembered life in their former villages, where highly local variants of custom and language were very common.[13] Reinforcing a people's sense of durable cultural belonging and identity enhances their ethnic pride, self-esteem, and well-being. In the case of Palestinians in particular, these expressions of heritage also helped to offset the repeated Zionist claim that they were not even a recognizable people with a would-be national history: as Golda Meir notoriously said, "There is no Palestinian people."[14]

But looking at heritage activities through the lens of economic development is much more of a challenge for people living under a military occupier who stifles every attempt at independent economic life. In addition, this approach to heritage has often led to unwelcome outcomes elsewhere in the world. Neoliberal policymakers, for example, have been quick to exploit the commercial potential of heritage promotion as a crude vehicle for tourist marketing or to label neighborhoods as "historical" or "cultural districts" in order to inflate land values. Adaptive reuse of old commercial buildings typically opens the door to upmarket real estate or, relatedly, incubation facilities for new private enterprise, while business owners will emphasize the historical "uniqueness" of their cities for branding purposes, as a way to attract investment.

Riwaq's conservation efforts in the rural West Bank are clearly not aimed at providing such frankly entrepreneurial opportunities. While some villages might attract "alternative tourists," there is little expectation of luring investors or homebuyers on the basis of historical place-making, let alone branding. Nor is anyone predicting more than a slight growth in the labor market for upskilled restorers, since architecture firms in the historical renovation business are few and far between in the West Bank. Whatever economic benefits there may be, they are not the kind that can be measured in the short term or registered in GDP growth data. But restoring the civic resiliency of Palestinian villages could well be a "driver of development" for other reasons. For example, food insecurity, aggravated by Palestinian dependency on Israeli imports, is widespread, and so the revival of village-based, traditional agriculture could boost efforts at a more sustainable economy in the West Bank. In this regard, land retention is key to developing a long-term, local food supply for Palestinians.

In the short term, holding on to agricultural land is also a bulwark against the settler movement, and it is most effective when a community is close-knit enough for its members to act in solidarity with each other. When networks of mutual aid erode, as they have done under a wage labor economy, individuals and their families are all too easily isolated and persuaded to sell land to settlers. The guilt generated by such sales (not uncommon in many West Bank towns, including some I visited) is a social poison that further weakens the fortitude of the community. It remains to be seen whether the *50 Villages* goal of restoring common space and the communal use of it will help serve as an antidote. In its next phase of innovation, Riwaq is moving to a "cluster" model, aimed at reviving the networks and markets that traditionally bound together a group of villages. The first two clusters—east and west of Jerusalem—were chosen to help buttress regional defenses against the invasive spread of the settlement grid.

In Beit Iksa, as elsewhere, it was not difficult to find generational differences of opinion about this kind of resistance. Ahmed the painter's new hillside house afforded a panoramic view of the Ramot settlement across the valley. "Quite frankly," he confessed, "it gives me an ulcer to wake up to that view every morning, but I have gotten used to it." He seemed even more resigned about the imminent fate of the village. "Our future here," he darkly warned, "is very uncertain." Safi confirmed that this sentiment was shared by many. "They are demoralized and have given up," she reported, "and some are already leaving." Yet, not that long before, Beit Iksa youth, in league with those from other villages, showed some grit by erecting a tent encampment down in the valley. The camp site was on an Area C parcel under threat of Israeli confiscation for an extension of the Separation Wall. Named Bab al-Karama (or Dignity Gate), the encampment was inspired by Bab al-Shams (or Gate of the Sun), a similar effort in January 2013 to draw international attention to Israeli plans for settlement building in the area east of Jerusalem known as E1. Like Bab al-Shams, the youth's camp was destroyed within days by Israeli soldiers but its mere existence suggested that the record of land loss attached to Beit Iksa's name could be defied, even halted, if residents were willing to take a stand.

After my time there, I drove north to Abwein, twenty kilometers above Ramallah. Like Beit Iksa, it used to be a "throne village" (*qura karasi*), designated as a regional center for tax collection by the Ottoman authorities. Architecturally, Abwein is dominated, as were most of the twenty-seven throne villages, by an ornate palace called Suhweil Castle, this one named for the powerful clan that ruled over the district.[15] Like Jaba and Birzeit (the highly praised pilot site for the *50 Villages* project), Abwein has hatched a satellite village further up the hill, where many of the concrete-built homes and new cars in the driveways are secured by post-Oslo loans from Palestinian banks. Like their fellahin sharecropper grandparents who eked out their living on credit extended by landlords or moneylenders, these residents are also in a debt trap, albeit one set for them by a finance elite, and not the old effendi class of absentee owners. The approach road took us through Jiljilya, where million-dollar villas sit on hillside perches. These are the ostentatious trophy homes of expatriates in North America or the homegrown beneficiaries of the West Bank's new capitalist order. Boarded up for most of the year, the jumbo mansions sport built-in Arab features—domes or arches—as a reminder of the owner's origin, but the overall design mixture is wildly eclectic, communicating the message that prosperity, like their owners, is located elsewhere.

Abu Azzam, a middle-aged bus driver who also maintains his family's allotment of olive trees, welcomed me to his new domicile, now cleanly refurbished and in a central part of Abwein's restored core. His personal return to the core came at an intermediate stage of Riwaq's engagement with the village. "At first, I thought they were crazy," he admitted, "this whole area was abandoned and falling down, it really was like a cemetery. But when I saw the initial results of their plan, it all made sense to me." The neglected center had too many historical buildings to restore as a whole; more than 200 were listed in the Riwaq national registry, and some were rudimentary peasant dwellings in an advanced state of ruin. As such, they did not meet Riwaq's standards of architectural value; the more "important" listed buildings generally had stone cross-vaulted or barrel-vaulted roofs and sturdy crescent-shaped walls. Instead of a comprehensive physical reconstruction, the architects decided to approach the village core in the spirit of an "archaeological park," landscaping the open spaces between the buildings for public uses like picnicking, art displays, or celebratory feasts. The guiding aim, as in Jaba, was to connect this restored commons with the new settlement further up the hill. As in Beit Iksa, women's groups were invited to return and set up culinary facilities as a community and commercial operation. So, too, the Riwaq team tried to revive the custom of mutual aid in the village—individuals, like the blacksmith, with serviceable skills for everyone were encouraged to swap their labor in return for a home improvement, such as a green roof or a grey-water treatment system.

Abu Azzam was persuaded, over time, of the benefits these improvements brought to the community, and he subsequently expressed interest in moving back into the old village. He applied to the housing incentive program to work on a home for himself, committing his labor to the restoration in return for the right to the house, which had been acquired by Riwaq. As part of this swap, materials were provided to him and he put in the work, learning the building skills along the way. Had he done a good job? "If I did," he laughed, "then this house will be here for another 200 years." But there was also a larger purpose: "Buildings like this show that we were here and still are," he pointed out. "These are our facts on the ground."

II. City on a Hilltop

As Abu Azzam was telling his story, Friday prayers at the mosque had ended, and a throng of Abwein villagers who had heard about my visit joined us in the elevated living room of his home. Almost all of them were employed in the construction of Rawabi city, which was stretching its broad wings on a commanding hilltop directly above Abwein, and it was their day off work. Rawabi is the first planned city to be built in the West Bank, and its high-rise modernity is a stark contrast to the traditional buildings being restored in villages like Abwein and Beit Iksa. Even the nearby Jewish hilltop settlements of clustered single-family homes are miniscule in comparison with Rawabi's dizzying array of apartment towers. Given the scale of the city plan, the construction jobs created in Rawabi far outnumber the combined employment pools provided by Riwaq and the other restoration organizations in Jerusalem, Bethlehem, Nablus, and Hebron. With a tight labor market on the West Bank, and employment in the settlements and inside the Green Line officially restricted to a quota of permit-holders, the fact that a homegrown Palestinian initiative is generating so many livelihoods ought to be a source of pride, if not appreciation.

But pride was not what these workers communicated. The stories they told were mostly about exploitative, and often dangerous, labor conditions on site. Rawabi's bidding system for contractors was highly competitive, they reported, and so workers were squeezed hard on wages and hours, often waiting for weeks for paychecks when payments to their subcontractors were held back. Temporary three-month labor contracts were common, enabling employers to avoid paying benefits. Injured employees were simply laid off—the on-site medical center was basic—and some of those in the room recalled workers who had died on Phase I of the project. Average pay was around 100 shekels a day for unskilled work, rising to 120 a day for more skilled jobs. While this was roughly one-third of what they could earn inside the Green Line, it was a much shorter and simpler commute to Rawabi, and jobs had been promised to inhabitants of Abwein and the neighboring villages as partial compensation for the 1,750 dunums (432 acres) of land parcels taken by eminent domain for the project by the PA.

None of the villagers in the room—plumbers, metalworkers, and laborers—expressed any support for the view, held by Bashar Masri, its primary developer, that Rawabi was a "national achievement" that advanced the Palestinian cause. First and foremost, they saw it as an economic scheme, of interest primarily to the Bayti Real Estate Investment Company, which is a joint venture between Qatari investors (Qatari Diar) and Masri, the Palestinian tycoon who owns the land development firm of Massar International. Compared to the favorable changes wrought in Abwein by the Riwaq project, about which they did show some pride, they could see little overall benefit from Rawabi other than their fitful employment. By contrast, there was a vigorous discussion in the room about whether the city deserved to be labeled as a "Palestinian settlement" and also about whether Israeli Jews were buying apartments there. Two of the workers claimed to have seen buses of Jewish settlers come in for tours, and security, they reported, was beefed up on these days. Another pointed out that a settler occupation of the city could not be ruled out in the long term. No one could stop the Israeli military moving on Rawabi, and settlers on neighboring hilltops who had tried to stop the project also coveted it. As one of the workers in the room put it, "if that happens, it might turn out that we were really building a Jewish settlement all along."

Rawabi is a topic of conversation guaranteed to polarize Palestinians. When I moved on to visit Ajjul, a nearby village, I heard a stiff defense of the fledgling city from Bawadi, a tiler who had been personally recruited by Masri to lay the floors of the showpiece sales building. Well-known for his work in Ramallah, he brought his brothers onto the team, and they pulled additional night shifts to complete the job. "Bashar [Masri] is a hands-on guy," he assured me, "especially when he is dealing with the highly skilled workers, and he made a point of showcasing my work as an example of the high level of craft that is going into the city." Openly expressing his loyalties, he continued: "He is diplomatic and strategic, and he has always said that he is doing this for Palestine. Rawabi, to me, is a fact of progress—a modern Arab city, in Palestine." Bawadi was part owner of land that the PA had taken by eminent domain for the city, and the compensation had been far below the price it was worth to the developer. This use of eminent domain (*istimlak*) for a private development was highly unusual, and unprecedented in the West Bank, and it had been strongly resisted by many of the residents of the three villages in question. In return, Ajjul had been promised a community center, but it had not yet been delivered. So, too, much of the acreage uphill from the village was being sold in anticipation of further development. Bawadi was not vexed: "The land wasn't being used for much anyway, it's not good for growing. The olive tree may have a sacred significance for us, but the stone used to build the city has much more economic value."

Yet his distinction, however neat, between these two natural resources did not explain why Rawabi whips up such strong sentiments. For many Palestinians, Rawabi represents an unacceptable rendition of the country's future. Versions of this future have sprung up in other planned and gated residential communities in the northern suburbs of Ramallah, prompting resentment but usually not full-throated criticism, and least of all from the white-collar urbanites driving the construction boom.[16] Yet its appearance here, among these idyllic villages, was more of a stark violation of the pastoral spirit of the rural West Bank, officially cherished by Palestinians, even the most urbanized, as the national *sumud* heartland. Hard-nosed villagers like Badawi, however, were devotees of the neoliberal mindset introduced to Palestinians in the wake of the Oslo Accords and were therefore more inclined to accept the dollarization of every dunum of land. In their eyes, the loss of an orchard or farmhouse to a Palestinian bulldozer was the price of national progress, especially if it was also a passport to prosperity for themselves and their families.

Views of Rawabi

There is nothing even remotely like Rawabi on the West Bank. First-time viewers of the site could be excused for mistaking this soaring city on a giddy hill for a CGI effect, superimposed on stock footage of a rolling, rural landscape. It might be part of a video game, and that airy citadel a defensive stronghold either to lay siege to or to protect from assault. Rawabi's nine-story towers stand in formation, even as they march down the hill, and the stone

Rendering of Rawabi buildout, on wall of sales center.

Photo by author

massing presents a formidable face to the world below. Depending on your standpoint, many messages are being communicated,
ranging from "these buildings are indisputable Palestinian facts on
the ground" to "Arab capital can deliver big things, even here in the
West Bank."

As a physical development, Rawabi, whose municipal boundaries
cover more than 6,500 dunums (1,600 acres, or two and a half square
miles), can be seen as a natural extension of the post-Oslo construction boom. When pressure from urban overcrowding became
unsustainable, and as real estate loans became more widely available,
developers gobbled up and subdivided land in Areas A and B located
north of Ramallah for planned communities; Al-Ghadeer (Brook)
and Al-Reehan (the Neighborhood) Suburb, both developed by
arms of the PA's Palestine Investment Fund; Reef (Countryside), a
compound of luxury villas developed by Baidar; and the Diplomatic
Neighborhood, built for senior PA officials. Those with insufficient
income to secure mortgages had to settle for cheaper alternatives,
like the more informal urban build-up of Kafr Aqab to the south.
The northern suburban communities were clearly earmarked for
Ramallah's new middle class and were priced accordingly. They
occupied high ground, like Israeli settlements, and offered a range of
housing—from upscale apartments in multifamily blocks to custom
villas. But none came close to the scale and master-planned ambition
of Rawabi, initially designed to house 40,000 residents, nor did they
attract the same kind of flak.

From the outset, Rawabi aroused suspicion because of the high
degree of cooperation between developer Bashar Masri and Israeli
enterprises. Though the city's master plan was drawn up by EDAW,
a British subsidiary of the international firm AECOM, Masri con-
sulted closely with Israeli urban planners and engineers in the course
of its evolution, including Moshe Safdie, the architect who designed
Modi'in, the controversial hilltop city west of Jerusalem. With no
comparable expertise available on the West Bank, Masri insisted
he had no choice but to turn to the Israelis. In accord with the
Oslo agreement's Paris Protocol, he was also obliged to use Israeli
cement and to rely on Israeli permissions to build the access road

and connect Rawabi with the water grid. In spite of the obstacles that Israeli authorities threw in his path—water was delayed for four years, and the single access road, which lies in Area C, has only a temporary permit—critics were quick to brand the project as an act of collaboration with the occupier. Others decried it as a Palestinian–Israeli joint venture, if not a project masterminded by the Israeli government itself. An early gift of 3,000 pine trees, for use in landscaping, from the Jewish National Fund (reviled for planting forests where Palestinian villages had once existed) added fuel to the fire.

In October 2012, in a rare condemnation of a fellow Palestinian, the Boycott, Divestment, and Sanctions (BDS) National Committee, which represents a broad cross-section of civic society groups, called out Masri for "normalizing the Occupation" and accused him of advancing "personal interests and profit making at the expense of Palestinian rights."[17] This early criticism (which issued from many quarters of Palestinian society, and which resulted, at the very least, in the replacement of the JNF's non-native pines with olive trees) was barely tempered by Masri's widely publicized refusal to use

any services or products from Israeli settlements. His stance meant that Israeli suppliers were also contractually barred from sourcing any settlement products for use in materials sold to Rawabi—an action that prompted right-wingers in the Knesset to draft anti-boycott legislation in 2011, containing a "Rawabi clause" that punished the companies in question.

By the time I interviewed him in spring 2017 in Rawabi's newly opened

Photo by author

Portrait of Bashar Masri and dog, hanging in Rawabi sales center.

commercial center, Masri was comfortable enough to wisecrack about the backlash. "Don't be too harsh on us," he quipped, "we had a lot of criticism in the past, but now it's dying down, the suffering is over." With his tall, slight build, fast talk, constant phone interruptions, and the very late breakfast he was taking in his office, he was the epitome of the fastidious businessman who curated his life and investments from minute to minute. "Rawabi has happened in spite of the Occupation, and in defiance of the Occupation," he explained, "the whole world knows we are victims, but this city is about empowerment for Palestinians, and is sending a strong message to the international community that says—'Look, we built a whole city in spite of the Occupation, so of course we can build a state, we who have helped build other peoples' states.'"

Masri has some nationalist credentials of his own. As a Nablus teenager, he was jailed several times for throwing rocks and organizing demonstrations, and he played a role in maintaining lines of communication between the exiled PLO and the grassroots leadership of the first intifada. From the outset, he promoted Rawabi as a Palestinian city for Palestinians, and the giant national flag that flies outside its sales showroom is such a provocation to the settlers in Ateret on the facing hillside that they have stolen it on occasion. Elsewhere, he has described the city as a nation-building project that represents freedom from philanthropic reliance on the "donor community, which remains focused on a welfare society in Palestine." Palestinians, he insisted, "need to generate long-lasting jobs rather than wait on handouts every month."[18]

As it happens, Masri had little choice but to go it alone. Aside from his partner, a real estate arm of the Qatari government, which was financing two-thirds of the venture, overseas government donors had shown scant interest, and there had been next to no support from the financially strapped PA. After the construction of the city was declared a top-level national priority, the PA issued the compulsory purchase order (in November 2009) to acquire land parcels from surrounding villages.[19] The PA also pledged to provide the off-site infrastructure such as the approach road and electricity and water networks, in addition to wastewater treatment and sewage. But there was no follow-through on these commitments and so most had to be privately funded, including schools, which the PA, at the very least, was still expected to staff and maintain. "To my knowledge," he lamented, "not another city in the world has been financed completely privately—every single thing from A to Z: sewage, water, schools, telecoms, electricity, roads, religious places. Everything is paid for by us."[20] No doubt this was only partly true, since other sources reported that USAID funds paid for the approach road and retaining walls.[21]

But for many of Rawabi's critics, Masri's rhetoric of nation-building is a cover for the privatized underwriting of the city. Commenting, for example, on the seizure of land by eminent domain, Ali Abunimah, a prominent early proponent of the "one-state solution," argued that it was only "because they framed it as … part of national development and building up the Palestinian state" that they were able "to market it as being public use. But there's nothing public about it … It is a private, for-profit real estate venture."[22] Yet, when viewed in the context of the West Bank's heavily neoliberalized economy, the exploitation of Rawabi's nationalist credentials to promote private profits is less of an exception than the rule. Much of the post-Oslo business of providing basic services and infrastructural needs to the Palestinian people has been just that—a business, and a highly lucrative one for the circle of well-connected tycoons who reap the benefits.

Palestine's Capitalists

After the 1993 Oslo Accords, Yasser Arafat's PLO leadership embraced the Washington Consensus promoted by the World Bank and IMF, and it called on wealthy expatriate Palestinians, as well as international donors, to invest in the new national cause. These diaspora capitalists were viewed as essential to the developmental process that would eventually give birth to a Palestinian state.[23] Masri's tycoon uncle, Munib (alternately dubbed the Duke of Nablus and the Godfather of Palestine), was one of those who responded, not just with capital but by returning in person to

build the family's business network throughout the West Bank and
Gaza. On a Nablus mountaintop, using local stone, he also built the
largest villa in the West Bank: a copy of La Rotonda, Palladio's six-
teenth century masterpiece. Two hundred of Masri's wealthy peers
poured start-up money into PADICO, the investment conglomerate
that he chairs and that comprises thirty-five companies operating
across the entire range of industrial sectors vital to the national interest, including the Palestinian Stock Exchange. Their alliance with
the PA leadership offers these "crony capitalists" trade monopolies
over key Israeli imports (telecommunications, electricity, cement,
and fuel), a wide range of commodity goods, and internationally
vested sectors like finance, hotels, and real estate development.[24]

The intimacy between the government and business elites began
in the years before Oslo, when Arafat, eager to facilitate openings
with foreign governments, turned to business acquaintances of his
among the Palestinian entrepreneurs in the diaspora who had established a niche as trusted brokers between the Gulf monarchies and
international capital. Some had built huge companies in construction, banking, and services. (Arafat himself owned contractor firms
in Kuwait.)[25] Aside from facilitating their investments, the PLO
groomed these diasporic capitalists (Arafat called them "the tigers
of the Palestinian economy") as a responsible national bourgeoisie,
a more worldly cohort, it was assumed, than their *ayan* predecessors who had failed the Palestinian people in 1948. So when Arafat
"froze" class struggle—national unity was needed for the anti-
colonial struggle—he gave them a central role in the PA's newly
assumed oversight of primary economic sectors. Joint (profit-
sharing) partnerships were set up between the PA and the investors'
conglomerates, and, since very little business could be done without
Israeli approvals and material supplies, Israeli firms were dealt a
hand in the proceeds.

The capitalists' influence increased after Arafat's death in 2004
and Mahmoud Abbas's assumption of power at the head of the PLO.
Their standing was further boosted after 2007 when former IMF
technocrat Salam Fayyad was appointed as prime minister with a
mandate to promote the future Palestinian state to international

investors as an open marketplace.[26] Fayyad was put in place after combined pressure from the Israeli, Fatah, and US leaderships led to the overthrow of a Hamas government, democratically elected in 2006 on the back of widespread anger at PA corruption and upward wealth redistribution. Under Fayyad, government and consumer spending would be fueled by open credit lines, through banking reforms that set the country and its people on a debt-dependent path. The result generated additional wealth for this monopolistic class, along with rewards for smaller, indigenous capitalists who had been sidelined in the first post-Oslo "Marshall Plan" but who were able to establish a stable position as subcontractors for the Israeli textile and footwear industries or as dealers for Israeli commodity imports.[27]

Though Fayyad campaigned to reduce corruption in the patronage network of the PA's upper hierarchy, by then the capitalists' alliance with the leadership and with Israeli say-so lay at the structural heart of the economy, and it continued to oil the engine of profit-taking. Indeed, it was in response to an earlier 1997 report on corruption by the Palestinian legislative council that Arafat had notoriously declared: "We will worry about our internal problems—the questions of social justice within Palestine—after we fight colonialism, our common enemy."[28] Ultimately, if there was any doubt about the PA's commitment to neoliberal policies, Article 21 of Palestine's Basic Law was unique among nations in specifying that "the economic system in Palestine shall be based on the principles of a *free market economy*."[29]

Bashar Masri himself was among the returnee capitalists of the mid-1990s (in his case, returning from Washington, DC, where he had attended college). Unlike his uncle, however, Masri's fortune was created after his return, and much of it from real estate ventures in the Gulf and the Maghreb that were facilitated by family connections. His new Ramallah base placed him at the nucleus of the "national capitalists" who had solidified their influence over PA policies. What role were they playing in the Occupation? In a typical colonial arrangement, the colonizer needs willing (*comprador*) partners among the occupied population in order to extract wealth and resources without stirring up too much domestic unrest or resistance. Palestinian subcontracting or other forms of joint ventures with Israeli firms and entrepreneurs fit this pattern. The relationships cannot be too overt, and, insofar as they are transparent to the public, they need to be presented as an unavoidable consequence of the colonial economy within which the Israelis call all the shots and have forced Palestinians into dependency.

For example, with the exception of stone, which was extracted from on-site quarries, Rawabi's construction materials were primarily purchased from Israeli firms. Forced to publicly defend this trade, Masri pointed out that most of the cement used for construction in the West Bank had to be bought from Nesher, the Israeli monopoly.[30] He presented this outcome as the result of a normative, if unfair, business practice. But Rawabi's operations were always guaranteed to attract other interpretations. During one of my visits to Ramallah, I met with Ali Husseini, an engineer who had been handpicked to manage the supply line of materials in the early phase of Rawabi's construction. After a few months on the job, he noticed that, regardless of the price or quality, Israeli companies kept winning the open bids, for foam blocks, gypsum boards, and the other finishing materials. "I also noticed that Israeli professionals, soldiers, and high-ranking officers kept coming around. What were they doing in a supposedly Palestinian city?" Initially, Husseini concluded, in line with other critics, that Rawabi was really more like an "Israeli joint-venture, and that it was only allowed to exist in order to reinforce Palestinian dependency and create profits for Israelis."

Husseini corroborated some of the complaints registered by workers I had interviewed—wage delays and lack of benefits and workplace safety. But he also acknowledged that Rawabi was providing decent jobs at wages comparable or superior to those on offer at Ramallah's other large masterplanned developments where he was now employed after being fired by Masri ("He did not like that I took issue with some racist comments made by an Israeli supplier of wood products"). But in his time at Rawabi, he had also came to suspect that profits were being extracted from the price differential of materials on either side of the Green Line. The conditions of the Occupation invited such opportunities; connected companies, for example, could purchase products from Israel and sell them to others that could not, at a substantial markup. It was because of this suspected profiteering, and not the sellout of the Palestinian national interest, or even the circumstances under which he had been fired, that Husseini seemed to have soured on Rawabi.

Rawabi was not the only joint venture to attract this kind of conjecture. According to one study, Palestinian capitalists invested in Israeli enterprises at a far greater rate and volume than indigenous ones.[31] Many of these investments were in the industrial zones attached to Israeli settlements in the West Bank. Registration under an Israeli name provided cover for the investors, expedited the approval process, and obstructed legal exposure of these arrangements.[32] In 2004, the PA faced down a major corruption scandal when it was revealed that businessmen had obtained an export license (from the Ministry of National Economy, run by a Masri family member at the time) to sell 360,000 tons of high-quality cement to an Israeli importer. As a goodwill gesture, Egypt had offered the cement at a large discount to help rebuild housing in Gaza after Israeli forces inflicted widespread destruction during the al-Aqsa intifada. Most of the cement that was sold ended up being used to build the Separation Wall in the northern West Bank.[33] Revelations like this sharpened popular distrust of the capitalist circle around the PA. While the Palestinian people were putting their lives on the line opposing the Occupation, the business class was profiting from the very instruments of the Occupation: the Separation Wall, the settlements, and the asymmetrical trade rules set up under Oslo's Paris Protocol, the customs union agreement that allowed Israel to effectively control imports and exports of goods, market access, tax collection, and other key aspects of the Palestinian economy.

The high visibility of Rawabi, its connections to Israel, and the prominence of the Masri family made the city an obvious target for criticism in the media and on the street. Masri and the Bayti staff members I interviewed on the hilltop had heard them all. In fact, Jack Nassar, director of the Rawabi Foundation, had written his master's thesis at the University of London's Goldsmith's College on this very topic. Partly based on a survey of popular opinion,

Nassar had looked at both sides of the debate on whether Rawabi was an example of Palestinian nation-making or a vehicle for the normalization of the Occupation. For the most part, his analysis of the results followed a middle path. In one telling example, he pointed out that while the city planners had indeed mimicked the form and many of the infrastructural lessons of Israeli hilltop settlements, they had also built in recognizably Arab elements through the use of local limestone, architectural features like arches, and neighborhood clusters, of fifteen to twenty buildings, that emulated traditional village neighborhoods.

In his interview with me, Nassar argued that Rawabi gets labeled as a settlement because the only examples of modernity his generation have ever seen are Israeli ones, and they are built, like Rawabi, on West Bank hilltops. Israeli strictures against new housing, and the resulting embargo against Palestinian development, have forestalled the growth of any home-grown modernity. "We should not automatically associate planned cities with Israeli settlements," he cautioned. "Besides, if Rawabi were not here, the settlers would probably have taken over this hill." Nassar's job at the foundation was to seed cultural and educational initiatives for residents (a library, lectures series, sports center) and also to create enough of a vibrant cultural scene to attract tourists for three-night stays. "I want Rawabi to be like London," he said wistfully. The roster of attractions under consideration was a fairly conventional list: museums; hotels; petting zoos; a botanical garden; a convention center; a recreational safari park with bungee jumps, zip lines, horse-riding, and an all-terrain vehicle track. But some more avant-garde amenities were also in the running: a Mindfulness Center, a Relationship Museum, a children's Innovation Museum, and a Samaritan study center. For the commercial center, dozens of middle-market brands were being courted to attract shoppers from Ramallah and Jerusalem, and the city, which boasted the only fiber-optic network in the West Bank, would also be luring high-tech companies to locate a branch or to incubate a start-up.

However improbable, Nassar's vision of Rawabi as a lively tourist destination was consistent with the lifestyle environment conjured up for would-be residents by the sales team: a place that is privileged, unharried, well-serviced, and self-assured that its location matters in the world. "Many Palestinians emigrated for this way of life," he pointed out, "now they can stay in Palestine and enjoy it, because we need to show the world it can be done here." Like other staff, he had been encouraged to buy into the development; his three-bedroom apartment, on a rent-to-own scheme, was $700 per month, about 20 percent below Ramallah prices. In Phase One, he told me, the first two neighborhoods were occupied, with 2,500 residents, and 90 percent of the third were sold out. (One year later, Rawabi's population had increased by more than a thousand, and was growing fast.) The PA had appointed a mayor, and homeowner associations were being set up to enforce regulations in each neighborhood. For the time being, the sales force was targeting middle- and upper middle-class professionals, from Ramallah, Jerusalem, and the overseas Palestinian population. As the development gets built out, Nasser speculated that "castles for the rich would be built at the top of the hill, and efforts, maybe through these sales and other subsidies, would be made to incorporate lower-income residents."

Two decades ago, I spent a year in residence in Disney's new town of Celebration in Central Florida, writing a book about similar efforts to build a city from scratch.[34] Relying on the deep pockets of its developer, the Celebration team labored hard to launch the town as a destination, with its own commercial town center up and running even before a fraction of the residents had moved in. This decision went directly against the grain of conventional real estate development, though it had become more common in themed master-planned developments since then. By contrast, it took more than twenty years for the 1960s' planned city of Reston, which had drawn Masri's attention while he was a student in Virginia, to generate its own town center.

Masri mulled over the lessons from these two examples when I brought them up in our conversation. "If our town center had been built much earlier," he told me, "we would have brought people in, built confidence, and sold apartments for higher prices, but we always had a developmental, not a commercial, goal to offer

affordable income housing." Plus, he admitted, "we did not have
enough money to do it, and now we are looking for capital to fully
complete the retail area." The town center officially opened for
business in May 2017, populated by brand names—Mango, North
Face, MaxMara, Steve Madden, Lacoste, Timberland—that were
licensed by Masri to lure shoppers. Nowhere in the West Bank,
he assured me, was there anything like this array of stores and
merchandise, and he expected people from a fifty-mile radius (1.1
million potential consumers) to flock to buy goods and to consume
other recreational amenities on offer.

A week before the official opening of the commercial center, I
quizzed some of the youthful retail assistants about their prospects.
Several had college degrees, but their salaries—$450 a month, plus
one percent commission on sales, for an estimated $600 overall—
meant that none of them could really afford the New York prices
($40 T-shirts, $500 dresses) of the merchandise they were selling
in the stores. At least they were actually living in Rawabi, renting a
shared room for $90 a month, though I learned that this was primar-
ily because they were expected to work until the stores closed at 10
p.m. They may have been educated, but, like the laborers who were
being driven hard to complete the central mall in time, none of them
earned enough to qualify for Rawabi homeownership. This was true
even of the skilled tilers, plasterers, and painters whom I interviewed
on their lunch break and who were earning twice as much (4,000
shekels, or $1,110) as the retail assistants. The tradesmen were all
keenly aware of this irony, though those who hailed from villages
had their mode of oneupmanship. "Rawabi is for people without any
land to build their own house on," sniffed a Birzeit installer who was
sweeping clean a wooden floor he had just laid.

Makers, Buyers, and Debtors

Early on, Masri decided that Bayti employees would enjoy a
starting salary of $600 (or 2,150 shekels)—a cut above the PA's
minimum wage of 1,400 shekels ($390)—rising to $650 after
six probationary months on payroll. Since the firm was playing the

combined role of investor, developer, and general contractor, this wage floor was consistent across as many as 2,000 direct employ-ees. The other 2,000 subcontracted workers, and the 3,000–4,000 offsite, were another matter. "I cannot force the contractors to pay this wage—I'm not in a good bargaining position with them," he conceded, "but the market forces them to do so because their $400 workers will see my $600 workers and they will want more." Even at the higher wage, workforce turnover was brisk, and Masri com-plained to me about a labor shortage stemming from the recent increase in Israeli work permits. As for workplace safety, he acknowledged that there were "serious accidents" in the past, but the firm had "put their foot down," and things were now shipshape. For the record, very few of the workers I saw during several visits to the Rawabi site were wearing safety helmets as required.

Masri's definition of affordable housing was pegged to the Rawabi business plan, not to national income data. Rawabi's $1,400 monthly household income threshold for qualifying for a twenty-five-year mortgage (with a 10 percent down payment) was far above that of the median Palestinian family ($600). But he insisted that it was within reach of a family with two members earning Bayti's $650 basic wage: "With a spouse, or a brother earning the same, you are almost there," he pointed out, "and 80 percent of employees in the Ramallah area are earning this kind of money." However, he admit-ted, "if you are below or have no spouse, Rawabi is not for you." Could he foresee being able to subsidize lower income housing in Rawabi? "That is not the job of the private sector," he replied, "we have to be careful not to distort the market." But his firm already did low-income housing in Morocco, where, he said, the "govern-ment gives you everything—infrastructure, tax and VAT waivers," so he was familiar with the necessary financing models, and indeed went so far as to predict that "sooner or later, we will convince the PA they need to do the same." But "it is wrong," he cautioned, "for the private sector to lead on its own—they can get greedy, we have to remember that." Palestine cannot be a "private sector nation," he said, "we have to be a public–private partnership, and the PA is beginning to take notice of our achievement here." Why now? I asked. "Because now there are voters and taxpayers living here, and politicians respond to such things."

"Our original plan for the cheapest apartments was for 160 square meters," explained Ibrahim Natour, one of Rawabi's chief architects, responsible now for managing contracts, bids, and material delivery, "but we scaled down, according to sales feedback, and ninety-two square meters is now the standard, especially for new couples buying a first home." The price tag for these was $65,000, rising to $200,000 for the largest 340 square meter apartments. Rawabi's residential density, he pointed out, is "moderate, much less than where I live, in Kafr Aqab" (he was born and raised in a Jericho refugee camp), and "40 percent of the total area in Rawabi is public space." Nor was there any danger in his mind that Rawabi would end up as a bedroom community for urban commuters. To minimize the restrictions on mobility imposed by military checkpoints, Rawabi's planners were building in shared workspace and remote offices for telecommuters, and hoping for call center–type jobs to move from Ramallah.[35] By the end of 2017, ASAL Technologies, a subsidiary of Masri's Massar International, had moved its headquarters to Rawabi, employing as many as 200 software engineers. The Tech Hub itself was almost up and running, prepped to incubate information and communication technology start-ups, and more than a dozen companies had set up in the commercial office center. Internship and entrepreneurial fellowship programs were strongly oriented toward female participation, in line with Masri's own prescriptions.

Like other ranking employees I interviewed, Natour was openly nationalist. Part of his job involved the frustrating task of petitioning Israeli authorities over the permits for the access road and also in fending off claims from nearby settlers over Rawabi's authorized use of Area C land. "Over our dead bodies will they take Rawabi," he declared, "we are more likely to take their settlements." "There is nothing good about this Occupation," he continued, "but we do need to change the profile of Palestinians always living in misery. We need to move beyond *sumud* and start living in the future," by which he meant in the world imagined by and for Rawabi. Part of the challenge, according to Natour, was to "get over our fear of order, which is bad for our mentality." The example at hand was "planned cities," which Palestinians tend to only associate with Israel and violent land theft.

Natour shared my own growing passion for stone, and his tour of the site and of the production sheds was punctuated by praise for textural details and craftsmanship. Good quality stone had been found in the vicinity of Rawabi, and the quarry had produced an ample local supply—in three different hues—that was cut and dressed on site. Even so, most buildings were constructed from concrete with a thin five-centimeter stone cladding on top. Sidewalk surfaces, he acknowledged, were weathered to simulate age, and the dry stone walls in each neighborhood echoed the crumbling remains of those on the terraced hills surrounding the city. "But nothing is really local anymore," he conceded, "and so we don't 'pretend' to be local, we are innovating here on behalf of Palestinian architecture." His own pride and joy was the 15,000-seat amphitheater (the largest in the Middle East), intended for concerts and marquee events.

Gesturing at the epic scale of the stadium, with its semi-circular colonnaded Roman stage and stepped seating, he asked expectantly: "Well, what do you see?" "Classicism?" I replied tentatively. "It's actually Mediterranean," he explained, "a potpourri of all the

Rawabi amphitheater.

Photo by author

civilizations that were here before," pointing toward the ring of three-story buildings on the top tier, with their architectural references to Crusader and Ottoman styles. Blown-up portraits of Arab film stars and singers (selected by Masri himself) were featured on the walls, adding a different kind of kitsch grandiosity to the site.

In the production sheds, we inspected the stone cutting machinery. A manager showed me a mechanized hand tool, developed on site to render the finer markings (*msamsam* and the less coarse forms of *taltis*) on the surfaces of stone slabs. Moving past the cement silos we reached the open-air chiseling shed, where machines had no dominion. Fifteen masons from Bethlehem and Hebron, wielding their hammers and chisels, were chipping away methodically at the sections intended for surface cladding. They were being paid by the meter, on piecework rates, and so they rested at will, downing tools regularly for cigarette breaks. The stones that were piling up beside their stations had a roughly hewn texture (the rusticated finish known as *tubẓeh*) and would end up as ground-level facing for the last buildings in Phase One.

How many jobs had Rawabi created? "We have filled 10,000 job openings over the last six years," Masri told me. Next to the PA, whose mass provision of public sector jobs in administration, police, and the military sustained almost 22 percent of the Palestinian population in 2017 (38.1 percent in Gaza and 15.4 percent in the West Bank, according to the Palestinian Central Bureau of Statistics), Rawabi has been the single largest source of West Bank employment, and it is the one achievement that the city's critics do not disparage. As for the next phase of nation-making, Masri predicted that future cities would follow on the success of Rawabi by building around a job cluster, in "tech or car assembly, for example." Indeed, he imagined the next new city would be located in the triangle between Nablus, Jenin, and Tulkarm, which had seen "the biggest brain drain" of educated, but unemployable, young people. "If others don't do it," he vowed, "then I will."

I did not quiz Masri directly on the vexed question of who could live in Rawabi, though in the press he had been quoted quite clearly on the topic. "Israelis are invited to come and visit any time," he had stated, "and even though our target audience is Palestinian, if Israelis also want to buy apartments there, they're welcome."[36] Like Jack Nassar before him, Natour assured me that Rawabi was an "open city": "Anyone can buy here, in principle, but non-Palestinians have to be vetted by the PA," a requirement for all foreigners intent on buying property in the Occupied Territories. On an earlier visit, however, a company representative insisted that "only Palestinians could buy apartments" and that Rawabi was a "Palestinian city, for Palestinians." She also informed me that homebuyers had to sign a covenant-type agreement not to sell their homes to an Israeli Jew. Clearly, there was some confusion over the official position, and more than enough daylight to fuel the rumors about Jews being bused in to snap up apartments. In truth, it seemed difficult to imagine why they would ever want to live in Rawabi, and, as for housing speculators, they were assured of better returns in Israel, or in the West Bank settlements. The more plausible danger, as Arpan Roy has argued, was that Palestinians from Jerusalem and Israel were buying into Rawabi as an insurance strategy for the impending loss of their homes to seizure, thereby inadvertently "accelerat[ing] the Judaization of parts of Israel/Palestine that as of yet have not succumbed to this fate."[37]

The same employee who had mentioned the covenant acknowledged that because of the Occupation, "it is not easy to sell homes under the current political circumstances," but affirmed that "we are in the business of selling facts, and not simply words." She herself had taken a lot of stick from friends for working at Rawabi and for her loyalty to Masri's can-do nationalism, which she expressed in exactly the same words as he had done: "If you can build a city like this, then you can build a country." As we spoke, young couples strolled around the models in the showroom and watched multimedia displays of the kind of idealized family life they might lead there. The central kiosks in the sales room were occupied by six banks (including Cairo Amman Bank, Arab Islamic Bank, Bank of Palestine, and Arab Bank), where staffers could tell prospective buyers if they qualified for a long-term mortgage.

These mortgages, which were key to the Rawabi Dream—an aspirational lifestyle pursued with borrowed money—were unknown in the Occupied Territories before the US- and PA-sponsored Affordable Mortgage and Loan Corporation was formed to push them in 2008. Indeed, Ottoman laws with strict limits on usurious interest rates had to be invalidated by the PA before this financial product could be offered.[38] Those who signed for a loan would be joining a swelling company of debt-burdened Palestinians, their dreams of national liberation increasingly channeled into the troubled sleep of asset ownership.

The Rawabi Dream, wall poster in sales center.

The spread of debt into almost every household is a corrosive legacy of Salam Fayyad's terms as finance minister (2002–2005) and as prime minister (2007–2013), when he oversaw a program that accelerated the financialization of Palestinian society. After he loosened lending restrictions, credit spread through towns and cities, and personal debt-financing of real estate, automobiles, marriages, education, and other goods and services skyrocketed over this period. According to one estimate, household debt increased sixfold between 2009 and 2014, with the highest concentration among public sector employees (who were able to obtain loans on the basis of their job security). Two-thirds of the credit was held in Ramallah, where borrowers fought to win and maintain a foothold inside the "bubble" economy of the West Bank's most expensive urban center. By 2013, however, only 7.9 percent of the loans were being invested in a productive sector of the economy: short-term financial returns from delivering the promise of the good life through credit were being favored over the long-term business of creating sustainable livelihoods.[39]

Since the state-building effort of Fayyad's caretaker administration was built primarily on borrowed money, national debt also mushroomed, growing by 470 percent from 2007 to 2017 (when the government's internal and external liabilities climbed to a total of more than $8 billion).[40] He promoted his program of "state readiness" to the world's investors by declaring that Palestine was "open for business." Indeed, the announcement of the Qatari investment in Rawabi, at the landmark 2008 Bethlehem conference for foreign investment, was the first fruit of this new orientation.[41] Just as important, preparation for statehood meant being groomed for sovereignty according to the profile favored by multilateral financial institutions. To qualify for entry into the community of nations, a country has to "show" the global markets that it can attract risk-averse investors to its government bonds. Preparing for sovereign debtworthiness typically involves meeting requirements laid down by the IMF and the World Bank: slicing public employment and social programs, deregulating access for foreign investors, and privatizing vital services. Fayyad himself once declared that "everything can be privatized, except security."[42] Also implied in this courtship of global capital is acceptance of the authority of the multilateral institutions to override elected governments and set policy directly, either to ensure that bondholders are paid in full or to quell political instability that threatens the foreign investments.

The economic history of the last fifty years shows how many global South countries were led into this kind of debt trap and how their development aspirations were stymied not long after their first postcolonial run at independence. Palestinians were caught in a debt trap at an earlier stage, before they even got to the starting gate of statehood. Crueler yet, the bonds of debt were not imposed directly by the Israeli occupier, which had many other ways of tightening the screw to discipline Palestinians: tax revenue withholding, road closures, water and energy restrictions, administrative detention, eviction from land and housing deemed vital to Israeli security, restricted speech and movement, curfews, random searches and seizures, peremptory deportation, and the power to shut down any civic institutions at the whim of a district military commander. Palestinian elites were the ones who championed debt financing as the power train of national liberation, and, as the lead players in most enterprises backed by the PA, they would end up among the top beneficiaries.

Most corrosive of all, perhaps, the growth of a personal credit culture has begun to eat away at the cooperative bonds that hold together Palestinian resistance to the Occupation. Solidarity is eroding as the overriding need to make monthly payments and maintain a personal credit score establishes itself at the forefront of people's consciousness. Needless to say, this mentality serves as a brake on the kind of political activity that can lead to a prison sentence or denial of an Israeli work permit. Under such circumstances, the future is no longer measured as an open pathway to national liberation, but as a countdown to paying off the loan. For the supposed small-time beneficiaries of financialization, ready access to loans is a new form of economic pacification—credit for peace—that threatens to prolong the Occupation.

By the time the Rawabi sales team was in full flow, an ever larger share of personal income (and government revenue) in the Occupied Territories was being swallowed up by debt service, while Masri and other members of the capitalist class harvested the proceeds. Palestinians are not alone in this predicament; after a brief decline for five years after the 2008 financial crash, household and public debt has been on the rise all across the industrialized world. Nor is the Masri family singularly responsible for the debt burden weighing down on so many West Bank households. But there is no corner of the Palestinian economy untouched by business empires like theirs, with their deep and broad vested interest in the "coercive, predatory and even cynical arrangement" that Toufic Haddad has called "Palestine Ltd." As part of this arrangement, Haddad argues that "the Western donor community, Israel, Fateh, and Jordan each reap dividends in their currency of preference: power, money, security, and logistical support," and the whole enterprise "relies upon the manipulation and appropriation of the dreams and hopes of an oppressed people for freedom, peace, and justice."[43]

Rawabi is only one example of "Palestine Ltd," but it is a sitting duck for the critics of Palestine's turn toward neoliberalism. Its assertive skyward location dramatizes a widening gap between haves and have-nots that is starkly visible on the landscape of towns and villages, where the spacious villas of the monied command the high ground, lording it over the modest dwellings down below. Even as the gap widens, the language of class resentment is still muted, since all conflicts internal to Palestinian society, such as women's rights, queer liberation, and class de-polarization, have been put on hold until the Occupation is undone. So, too, the emergence of a consumer-based creditor class is relatively recent and has not yet acquired a popular reputation as predatory in nature. During the Ottoman and Mandate eras, moneylenders and land brokers used the instruments of debt to squeeze fellahin who were beholden to the absentee landowning class. The launch of a Palestinian banking sector after Oslo reestablished these burdens, this time through debt-financed consumerism, with a new creditocracy on top.

III. Stones of Bethlehem

Stark inequalities in housing are visible everywhere in the West Bank, even within refugee camps where the long-standing opposition to building permanent housing has eroded over the years and is now crumbling under the gravitational pull of post-Oslo bank loans. On one of my walks around Bethlehem's Aida refugee camp, I was struck by two newly built houses that stood out from the others. They were three stories tall, like others on the alleyway, but their smartly dressed limestone walls exuded prosperity, and they looked like single-family dwellings, unlike the adjoining concrete cast-in-place buildings. I learned that they belonged to Aida members who had amassed enough income to move elsewhere but were still loyal to the old PLO principle that refugees never leave camps except to return to their pre-1948 village homes. In some respects, these buildings were the counterparts, albeit much more modest, of the showy villas in the rural towns.

Population pressure on the limited land available for building has created an extreme housing shortage in the Occupied Territories, but the overcrowding situation in the refugee camps, already among the world's densest urban environments, is in another league. In almost all circumstances, the only solution is to build upwards (which concrete can easily facilitate) on structures never designed to bear much additional weight. Self-construction is the norm, and often draws on skills already used by the residents in their day jobs. In the late 1970s, Israeli authorities tried to encourage residents of Gaza's refugee camps to disperse, by subsidizing "build your own" houses outside the camps; more than 10,000 took up the offer, in accord with the condition that their former homes in the camps be demolished. But the program was fiercely opposed by the PLO, and the UN General Assembly went so far as to pass two resolutions of disapproval, demanding that the residents be returned to the camps because the resettlement had constituted "a violation of their inalienable right to return."[44]

Leaving is less of a taboo than it used to be, though those who do move tend to keep addresses in their camps as a registered link to the original 1948 villages of their families. Still, the provisional, or temporary, state of affairs in camps has long been a way of life. So much so that camp archives (other than the official UNRWA ones) have been compiled to record their history of habitation, and efforts are being made to preserve their own "heritage." In 2016, DAAR, the inspirational, Bethlehem-based architectural group, launched an initiative to nominate Dheisheh refugee camp for inscription as a UNESCO World Heritage Site. Undertaken largely as an effort to combat the UN's prevailing definition of camps as "solutions" to humanitarian crises, and thus as places of desperation and poverty, DAAR's heritage designation, by contrast, would try to honor the resilience of the residents—the longevity of their determination both to survive and to insist on return.[45] Under this definition, auto-construction in the camps, far from being a desperate response to a futile situation, could be seen as an example of legacy-building, or, as Marx put it, of people making history under conditions not of their choosing.

If successful, the UN petition would also push the limits of what is considered heritage worthy of conservation in the Bethlehem Governorate, home to Palestine's first two World Heritage Sites— the Nativity Church and Pilgrimage Route (2012) and the village of Battir (2014), renowned for its ancient terraces and irrigation system. The first of these UNESCO nominations was preceded by

The stonemason's handcraft.

West Bank limestone quarry face.

West Bank Palestinians in the Old City of Jerusalem.

Muslim Quarter of Jerusalem's Old City, with Israeli settler flags.

"Orientalized" new condo housing in Ajami, Jaffa.

McMansion on a West Bank hill, near Birzeit.

Time collapse—Dheisheh Camp in 2012 and Doha City in 1955.

Time collapse—Dheisheh Camp in 1955 and Doha City in 2012.

Rawabi city center, under construction.

"Jerusalem Stone," catching sunset light, Ma'ale Adumim.

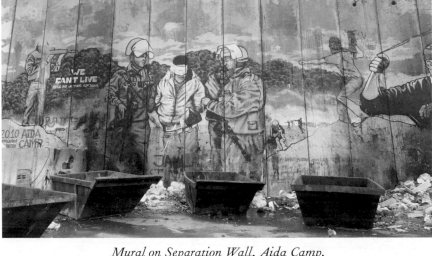

Mural on Separation Wall, Aida Camp.

Har Homa hilltop settlement, overlooking Bethlehem.

Finishing a slab in a Beit Fajjar factory.

From quarry to factory, for cutting and finishing, Beit Fajjar.

Messaging the resistance, Aida Camp, Bethlehem.

Last gate at Al-Tayba checkpoint—going over the top.

a well-funded Millennium campaign of rehabilitation, called Bethlehem 2000; it largely focused on the Christian characteristics of the city and therefore sidelined the predominantly Muslim refugee population. But there were other, more obvious, ways in which the Dheisheh nomination would stretch the city's understanding of heritage far beyond its traditional welcoming role for Christian pilgrims.

Refugees and Pilgrims

Early on, I established a working relationship with the leadership of Aida Youth Center, and Bethlehem became my preferred base for field research in the Occupied Territories. Aida Camp sits on the frontline of the Occupation, directly hemmed in by the Separation Wall, and it is regularly raided by Israeli soldiers on "pacification" forays. According to one University of California report, it is the most tear-gassed place on the planet.[46] Camp youth are exemplary "children of the rocks." Throwing insults, and then stones, at soldiers is an early rite of passage, and, as they grow up, their clashes with the military are almost a weekly recreational activity, following Friday prayers. Children in other countries play at war; in the United States, it used to be Cowboys vs. Indians, but video games now offer more elaborate conflicts. In Aida Camp, the games are ritualized but the conflict is all too real, and young lives and limbs are regularly lost in the process.

In January 2016, Srour Abu Srour, the twenty-one-year-old cousin of Mohammed, one of my translators, was shot and killed by soldiers conducting raids in the adjoining towns of Beit Jala and Beit Sahour. Hearing the news while interviewing workers at the Qalandia checkpoint in Ramallah, Mohammed and I hightailed it back to Bethlehem, noting the stepped-up military presence all along the Wadi Nar road (the only route between the north and south of the West Bank). The killing occurred at the height of the so-called "knife intifada," when soldiers had shoot-to-kill orders. By the time we arrived, crowds had gathered at Beit Jala hospital to prevent the new martyr's body from being taken away. (The Israeli

في فلسطين الصلاة

The cycle of violence against children. Aida Camp mural.

military does not like independent autopsies, and it routinely denies families the right to reclaim victims' bodies for funerals.) Shortly after, Aida youth began to display and honor the body in the court-yard. Lamentations and prayers quickly morphed into protest songs and solidarity chants as the body was carried through the throng to the mortuary. The next day's funeral was preceded by a full-bore procession through Bethlehem's main streets, featuring flags from Fatah, Hamas, the Popular Front for the Liberation of Palestine, and others. The cement had barely been applied to Abu Srour's grave before clouds of tear gas began to drift through the cemetery. Clashes between the camp's more militant youth and Israeli soldiers continued through the evening.

According to Mohammed, his cousin had been "in the wrong place at the wrong time." On his way home from classes at Beth-lehem University he ran into the soldiers carrying out the raids. Bethlehem is in Area A and is ostensibly under the jurisdiction of PA soldiers and police, but that makes little difference. "We can get shot anytime and anywhere, for no reason at all," noted Mohammed, expressing scorn for the PA's weakness, a sentiment that would be echoed by many at the funeral and in the course of the three-day wake that followed. Indeed, it was routinely said that, in the next intifada, Palestinians would have to throw rocks at the PA, as well as the Israeli, soldiers. Over the years, the Abu Srour family had seen its share of martyrs, and because the cousin's own father had been a veteran PLO freedom fighter, the funeral and the wake drew attendees from all over the West Bank, including the Palestinian prime minister. These funerals, which were not only public but also highly political occasions, were coming thick and fast—five youth were killed in the Bethlehem–Hebron corridor the same week—and the time and resources that whole families devoted to attending these events was a massive drain on their limited means.

On the day of the funeral, most of Bethlehem's stores were closed out of respect. By common consent, a few shops around Manger Square, which hosts the Church of the Nativity, were still open to serve the all-important tourist trade. Groups of tourists—Koreans, Indians, Americans, and Russians (who spend the most, according to shopkeepers) shuffled across the square. They were no doubt oblivious to the funeral procession at the other end of town, closest to the Separation Wall, where you can usually find a different kind of traveler—young pro-Palestinian volunteers from overseas, many aligned with the International Solidarity Movement. The presence of both sets of visitors supplies Bethlehem with a cosmopolitan air it has enjoyed since the late nineteenth century when Ottoman authorities first allowed foreign Christian missions to build monasteries, convents, and other sites of residence. Contact with the travelers offers an important window on the world that is typically closed off by the Occupation. When tourist traffic is frozen, as it was for considerable periods during the second intifada, or whenever the checkpoints are closed as punishment for some act of resistance, the city suffers from the loss of vital exchange with internationalists as well as the loss of tourist dollars. Ongoing Israeli efforts to ban tour operators from booking overnight stays in Bethlehem hotels are an especially cruel embargo on one of the city's primary sources of revenue.

For the Christian pilgrims, the violence of the Occupation surely ought to be a desecration of what Bethlehem represents to them: the peace, love, and hope of the virgin birth. But the conventions of religious tourism require the present-day conflict to be seen through the long historical lens of regional strife in the biblical era and after.

There is little room left for understanding Bethlehemites' own, more recent record of proud opposition to military rule. The people of Beit Sahour, an adjoining village, pioneered nonviolent resistance and tax refusal during the first intifada, and Manger Square itself hosted a harsh siege during the al-Aqsa intifada when Palestinian combatants sought sanctuary inside the Church of the Nativity. Residents of the city's main refugee camps, Dheisheh and Aida, are traditionally among the most militant in the West Bank.[47]

Most pilgrims come to sample the feel of the Holy Land, so they want the landscaping that fits their image of biblical antiquity. That includes old stone buildings, views of terraced hillsides and olive trees, and narrow cobblestoned streets and alleyways, all of which are directly threatened by the Occupation. It matters little that most of Bethlehem's supposedly antique buildings date from the eighteenth century, when the city was reconstructed over the remains of the Byzantine-era settlement destroyed by the Mamluks in 1489, or that many of the religious monuments from the late nineteenth century are built in Western architectural styles. Of course, over the course of centuries, many of the older stones were recycled, and traditions of vernacular architecture are continuous from the medieval period through the Ottoman era, but there is no direct link back to biblical times. However, the Oriental imagination of the Holy Land is very powerful; it fills in the gaps and sees what it wants.

Bethlehem's growth as an important center of the heritage conservation movement was foreordained by its status as a Christian tourist site offering abundant historical meaning. But the other factor is its geographic vulnerability. A mere nine kilometers from the Old City's Jaffa Gate, it is almost surrounded by settlements that steadily push the boundaries of Greater Jerusalem outwards. The two road entrances to the city are easily, and not infrequently, closed off by soldiers, whose bellicose forays down the Hebron Road, in the northern part of town, are an ever-present threat. Heritage restoration in this holy place is a line of defense as much as it is an adornment for the pilgrimage economy.

In anticipation of the Christian millennium year, the city launched the Bethlehem 2000 plan in the mid-1990s to rehabilitate the city's infrastructure and dilapidated neighborhoods. This campaign, with heavy PA backing and international donor funding, paved the way for municipal recognition of the value of historical restoration.[48] However, in 2001, violent incursions by the Israeli military, which included shelling and helicopter missile-fire, caused widespread damage to many of these improvements, in addition to heavy civilian fatalities in center city neighborhoods.[49] In the wake of these sorties, and under emergency conditions, the Center for Cultural Heritage Preservation (CCHP) was set up as a government-backed organization. Like Riwaq's post-intifada *Tashgheel* program, the CCHP projects were focused initially on job creation—mass unemployment was one of Israel's punishments for the al-Aqsa intifada. In Bethlehem, however, the CCHP's work of repairing and renovating old buildings, while initially focused on quarters that lay outside the tourist circuit, unavoidably overlapped with the all-important economy of religious pilgrimage.

The damage inflicted by Israeli forces on Bethlehem not only spurred these local efforts but also prompted UNESCO to extend the protective umbrella of preservation to many other endangered heritage sites. A 2002 declaration by the World Heritage Committee encouraged countries to join UNESCO in order to use its protections for sustainable development. In response to the Israeli invasion, a UNESCO team inspected the damage in Hebron, Nablus, and Bethlehem and inventoried other locations in preparation for listing as World Heritage Sites.[50] After Palestine was admitted as a full member to UNESCO in 2011 (the United States pulled its funding in response and strenuously opposed the World Heritage listing of Hebron in 2017), the PA nominated sixteen sites (fourteen cultural and two natural) for inscription: Ancient Jericho—Tell al-Sultan; the Old Town of Hebron al-Khalil and its environs; Mount Gerizim and the Samaritans; Qumran—Caves and Monastery of the Dead Sea Scrolls; al-Bariya—wilderness with monasteries; Wadi Natuf and Shuqba Cave; the Old Town of Nablus and its environs; Tell Umm Amer; the Throne Villages; Sebastia; Anthedon Harbour; Umm al-Rihan forest; Wadi Gaza Coastal Wetlands; Battir, Land of Olives and Vines—Cultural Landscape of Southern Jerusalem; and

Bethlehem, Birthplace of Jesus—Church of the Nativity and the Pilgrimage Route.

Following Jordan's nomination, Jerusalem's Old City had been inscribed on UNESCO's World Heritage List in 1981, and it was added to the List of World Heritage in Danger the following year. These steps generated a strong backlash from Israel and the United States that caused a serious rift in the organization. Over the years, Israeli authorities have all but barred UNESCO from the city and so the protection offered by the listing is precarious. But according to Fida Touma, a key Riwaq member who directed Taawon's Old City Rehabilitation Unit from 2012 to 2016, "the primary threat today is not to the buildings but to the people themselves who are at immediate risk of eviction." Taawon's Jerusalem operation is a mixture of community outreach, technical restoration, and documentation, each aimed at providing protection for residents faced with displacement from their Old City homes. "We tend to prioritize households that are under threat of eviction," she reported, "even when the buildings themselves are not historically significant." With nowhere else to go, as many as 40,000 Palestinians are jam-packed into the Muslim and Christian Quarters, and Israeli authorities, intent on the transfer of as many Palestinians as possible, allow the housing infrastructure in these quarters to deteriorate. Touma explained that "any evidence of structural damage is used to evacuate residents, and after the repairs are done, the settlers move in." Under such emergency circumstances, aesthetics—the driving passion behind most heritage conservation work—take a back seat to humanitarian intervention.

In its conservation work, Taawon's approach is quite at odds with the widely criticized Israeli reconstruction of the city's Jewish Quarter. One exemplary site I visited in that neighborhood with Taawon engineer Bashar al-Husseini was the building that houses the renowned library of the Khalidi family. Constructed during the Crusader rule, it features additions from the later Mamluk and Ottoman periods, and the walls are a patchwork of stones from various eras, not untypical of Old City buildings. Husseini explained that part of the Taawon team's job was to repair the damage caused by the use of cement-based mortar—the stones are corroded by the mortar's salts and cracked by its binding strength. Their work was also being guided by the conservationist's ethos of preserving the legacy of period styles, even when they are a historical mishmash. By contrast, reconstruction efforts visible in the surrounding Jewish Quarter buildings are monocultural; they are primarily aimed at presenting antique facades that highlight their Jewish characteristics. Unlike the exclusively Jewish clients and residents of these buildings, Taawon responds to applications for help from a variety of private and public owners, Arab Muslims and Christians and Armenians. One of the biggest challenges, according to Husseini, is to persuade residents to move out temporarily while the salvage work is being done. "They are afraid," he reported, "of never being able to return."

Although Bethlehemites are increasingly surrounded by settlements (eighteen in total), they are not yet in the same predicament as the Palestinian residents of East Jerusalem or the Old City. By the time of the 2012 UNESCO listing of the Birthplace of Jesus, the CCHP had established itself as more than an emergency organization and was in a position to draft a plan for the management of the site. Significantly, the community surveys conducted in the preparation of the plan demonstrated a desire to rehabilitate Manger Square (which hosts the Church of the Nativity) as a vital center for urban life, rather than simply as a tourist destination.[51] However, this proved to be a challenge, as Faten Lafi, longtime director of the CCHP's Rehabilitation Unit, acknowledged to me: "Palestinians drive everywhere now, and are loath to walk," and "public space," she added, "is still male space," unwelcoming to casual female use. Physical rehabilitation was one thing, but altering mentalities is just as important to creating a vibrant community site.

The Protectors

The CCHP's earliest neighborhood restoration was the Anatreh Quarter, southeast of the Manger Square ridge, and named for one of the seven clans that has dominated Bethlehem life for centuries. Waves of emigration, from 1948, 1967, and after, had left Anatreh in a dilapidated and semi-vacated state, physically worsened by the Israeli bombing raids and demolitions. However, the compact common core (*hosh*) of sprawling family compounds (*harat*) was still intact, as were the peripheral zones, which boasted the more prosperous villas of post-Oslo returnees. The Anatreh restoration, funded by the World Bank, took ten years and set a model for workers and contractors to learn conservation skills in workshops.[52] As with Riwaq's schemes, the CCHP encouraged residents to renovate their own houses and to see their neighborhood with new eyes—not as a broken slum in a spiral of decay but as a proud sanctuary for valued cultural property.

In the wake of the Anatreh project, CCHP staff took on the restoration of singular buildings, as well as entire thoroughfares more integral to the tourist circuit, such as the well-trodden Star Street (alleged pathway of Mary and Joseph, and part of the city's World Heritage Site). In common with Riwaq and Taawon, CCHP's professionals have found it hard to find and retain workers and contractors. Joseph Taqatqa, a regular contractor for CCHP projects, spoke with me about the difficulties. "Typically, the workers I use are the ones denied permits to go to Israel, but I also try to choose the ones with a passion for this kind of work because it's so labor-intensive. Everything has to be done by hand, and never by machine, and the stones are heavier and more irregular."

With twenty-five years of experience under his belt, Taqatqa had developed an eye for what could go wrong (and indeed, what builders from long ago did wrong). "When I look at an old building," he mused, "I think about who built it, and why their knowledge was not always passed on through the generations." "Sometimes," he added, "I see mistakes that were made in construction long ago and that's why this building fell down." In this way, he was able to explain how "a 700-year-old building can survive whereas a 200-year-old one has collapsed." Taqatqa had also come to appreciate the intangible value of preservation. "This is a very important matter for Palestinians," he pointed out, "because we really need to protect our identity, and care for our heritage and our national soul." "Since this area of the Mediterranean is rich in antiquities," he continued, "we are preserving it for all of humankind and not just for Palestinians." Had he seen many private firms develop an interest in restoration? "Not really," he replied, "most of my work has been with nonprofits. As a result, there's not much money in the rehabilitation business, but I can live with that." Taqatqa's family name was well-known in the area's stone industry, and he had a successful career as a factory owner behind him, so perhaps he could afford these less profitable devotions. But there was no mistaking his passion for the politics of conservation. "Rehabilitation," he insisted, "should be an urgent cause for us, and I feel that I am serving our country by doing it."

Taqatqa's crew included Abu Walid, a sixty-year-old mason from Beit Fajjar who had worked with him for almost twenty years. His family history boasted generations of stonemasons, and he was passing on the trade to his three sons, two of whom were also employed on CCHP projects. But Abu Walid's favored protégé seemed to be co-worker Samir, who came from the same kind of family—both his father and grandfather were builders in Jordan in the 1970s. Samir had started his working life in a Beit Fajjar factory before being recruited by the older man, who taught him all his skills on the job. From the outset, he found the restoration work to be at once "more difficult" and "more fulfilling" than what he had been used to doing in the factory. When I interviewed them both they were working in the Beit Sahour village core, on a house with 200-year-old lower floors. Neither of the two were taking home what they considered good wages, and Abu Walid admitted that, in his mind at least, the discount was connected to the gratification he got from working on the old buildings: "It is like an art, so it is OK if I get paid less than I did before, and, besides, this kind of work appeals to me as a Palestinian." Was his age a factor in this preference? "Maybe the younger workers don't feel the same way," he conceded, "they have families to grow and feed, and so maybe they are not in a position to take this discounted work." Indeed, one of his sons, whom I interviewed later in the family home, verified that he could not "afford" his father's views. Besides, he wanted to get out of the building business and start an auto repair company, a desire I heard expressed not infrequently by his generation of stone men.

By now, this kind of discount compensation is familiar to anyone doing "artistic" work, and it has even become a staple feature of labor exploitation in the so-called "creative industries." But it was still a surprise to find the principle being applied here in the tightest of labor markets, where construction workers often measure risks to life and limb against the prospect of a few more shekels. In their case, the sacrifice had an unapologetic nationalist dimension. Both Abu Walid and Samir took pains to describe how they saw themselves as protectors (*hafeth*) of a Palestinian legacy. This was no effort to aggrandize what they did—both men were humble to a fault.

At the time of the interview, I could not help being reminded of the North American indigenous activists who had recently declared themselves "water protectors" during the Standing Rock protests against the Dakota Access oil pipeline. With a long history of seeing their territory and resources taken, members of the Sioux Nation had no difficulty in seeing how the pipeline would desecrate and endanger their lands and their water. But when they took a stand, to be joined by thousands of others in the summer and fall of 2016, it was not to defend their own health or self-interest, but rather to safeguard the water itself as a sacred source of life. The Palestinian BDS national committee found a common cause and issued a statement of solidarity:

> Palestinians understand all too well how settler-colonial authorities use resource extraction and other economic and bureaucratic pretenses as a way to solidify control over indigenous land and dispossess indigenous people. When we look at Standing Rock, we see our indigenous sisters and brothers defending their land, their identity, their dignity and their heritage.[53]

Palestinians are hard-pressed to protect their own water, most of which is systematically diverted for the use of settlers in the West Bank or Israelis elsewhere. But the protection of antique stone is a coherent response to Israeli manipulation of archeological findings to buttress Zionist claims on the Land of Israel (Eretz Israel), the loaded term used to describe all Israeli and Palestinian lands (and, for some zealots, portions of present-day Jordan, too). For the religious nationalist settler in particular, each discovery of the remnant of an ancient home, synagogue, or family tomb is proof of the God-given right to restore the kingdoms of David and Solomon in Judea and Samaria.[54]

So, too, in the battle over the lawful ownership of antiquities found on the West Bank, officials from the Israel Antiquities Authority often argue that Israeli stewardship is needed to protect (Jewish) artifacts from (Arab) robbers. By contrast, when illegal excavations in the West Bank uncover historical artifacts with no particular Jewish significance, these items routinely find their way onto the black market and are lost to Palestinians as a result.[55] In the meantime, and whenever a military opportunity arises, Palestinian built heritage is targeted for deliberate destruction by bulldozers, rockets, and tanks.

In the face of these aggressive settler methods, the protectors and restorers of Palestinian stone are building a different case around the right to remain on their ancestral land, and, for families of refugees, the right to return to theirs. These are rights recognized and upheld by international law and could hardly be clearer. The settlers' claims are based on willful interpretations of a birthright suggested by the Torah, and their only backing comes from the metallic decree of military force.

––––––––––

Just beyond Beit Jala lies the much-cherished Cremisan Valley, one of the last green havens in the Bethlehem Governorate and the home of a monastery and convent of the Salesian Order. In June 2015, and after nine years of strenuous faith-based efforts (including weekly open-air masses and pleas from the Vatican) to block a planned extension of the Separation Wall through the middle of the valley, the Israeli High Court approved the route and the confiscation of 300 hectares of olive orchards and vineyards. Soldiers began to uproot the ancient trees; for centuries, Cremisan had produced some of the most highly valued olive oil in the West Bank along with wine from the famous Cremisan Cellars. In the years to come, it is likely that the valley, long a charismatic destination for walkers, will be filled in with housing designed to connect the settlements of Gilo and Har Gilo.

In February 2018, a free-standing stone structure appeared on some of the remaining hill terraces. It was a version of a traditional Palestinian countryside shelter (*mantour*), offered as a "meditation space" for the monks and other community members to use for contemplating what is being lost. According to Elias and Yousef Anastas, the Bethlehem architects who designed the structure, the latticed, multi-hued stone, quarried from all

Courtesy of Yousef and Elias Anastas

The "little castle," the Cremisan Valley, and the Israeli settlement of Har Gilo.

over the West Bank, was cut and locally crafted to echo the retaining strength of the terrace's dry walls, originally built to capture the available rainfall.

Obviously intended as a quiet counterpoint to the alien invasion of Israel's Separation Wall, this "little castle" keeps company with a man-made topography dating to Roman times. It is also a showpiece for the architects' effort to reinvent the artisanal spirit of the region's stone craft. In their case, the focus is less on masonic skill than on the stereotomic art of cutting stone. The Anastas brothers used advanced computer- and robot-assisted techniques to fashion pieces for their high-concept stone vault installations—the Cremisan project was commissioned by London's Victoria and Albert Museum, and two other freestanding canopies were publicly exhibited in Bethlehem and Jericho—but they were looking for an industrial base to supply custom materials on a regular basis. "We went to factories that do standardized production, mostly of slabs, and they ignored us, as did many small family firms, so we have tried to create a network of makers that can deliver batches of massive stone in different sizes." Their goal, as they explained to me in a Bethlehem café, is to use these "adventurous, local fabricators," to sustain an architectural practice devoted to "building new self-supporting stone structures" that resonated with "the domestic tradition of cross-vaulted dwellings." Although they had done some restoration work, the Anastas brothers were thoroughly modern-minded. Prototypes of a new generation of architects who spurned the concrete-and-cladding formula for sprawl in Ramallah, Hebron, and Jerusalem, they were intent on tapping the creativity of local industry in a land where "no town is more than fifty kilometers from a stone quarry."

4

Extract, Export, and Extort

I am the Michelangelo of Beit Fajjar.

— Kamal, stone industry worker

Some men flirt with women, but sometimes, I feel that I am flirting with the stones.

— Nassar Nassar, stone industry CEO

The Bethlehem district has long been a supplier of accomplished stone masons, and so it was fitting to find craftsmen like Abu Walid and Samir restoring some of its older buildings and architects like Elias and Yousef Anastas devising twenty-first-century applications for these masonic skills. Sepia-tinted pictures of their regional forebears—wielding saws, mallets, chisels, and trowels and accompanied by camels bearing large stone blocks—can be found in archives and memory books or displayed on the walls of antique-themed restaurants. Historians include passing references to the dominance of the masons' influence: according to one source, as many as 1,000 Bethlehem stonemasons were at work during the Jerusalem building boom that began in the late nineteenth century.[1]

Bethlehem's oldest landmarks and public works are a visible testimony to the labor of its stone men: Herod's massive palace and fortress complex (the Herodion); the vast reservoir, known as Solomon's Pools, which served as a central junction for the region's Roman water supply network; and the Bethlehem branch of the Jerusalem aqueduct. Remnants of that aqueduct are exhibited in the bowels of the Bethlehem Museum. Among the displays of embroidery, olive wood, and mother of pearl, the museum also hosts stone artifacts that document the long presence of the city's Arab Christian community, curated, no doubt, with one eye on the city's religious tourist economy. Perhaps these tributes to local craft generate some peace of mind, or reassurance of faith, that visitors can take away from the association of artisanal toil with the builder's trade of Jesus and his father.

According to physician and ethnographer Tawfik Canaan, most Palestinian villages used to boast a mason (m'allim), who, "though lacking any theoretical training in architecture, [had] nevertheless gathered from wide experience much practical knowledge," and who could therefore design and build a wide range of houses.[2] Villages located near quarries usually housed a specialized occupational cluster of stone workers, whose services were always in demand due to Ottoman land codes that specified the use, in construction, of quarried stone that was taxable. But the primary reason for the wealth of local skill in the Bethlehem district is that the city lies at the northern edge of a particularly rich cache of limestone deposits. In fact, the Bethlehem–Hebron highland geological corridor harbors some of the best-quality dolomite limestone in the world. Boasting minimal defects, an attractive color palette, and fairly reliable texture, West Bank stone, quarried from Turonian and Cenomanian geological layers, is relatively easy to hew, and it hardens well after exposure and carving. The color range runs across a geographic spectrum: gray and black from Birzeit; blue from Nablus; cream from Jama'in; beige from Jenin; gold from Tarfur; and yellow and white from Beit Fajjar, Sioukh, Sa'ir, and Bani Na'im.

The mountains between Bethlehem and Hebron host almost 250 quarries, along with hundreds of factories (where the raw blocks are cut into slabs and tiles, dressed, and finished in a range of styles), a variety of smaller artisanal workshops (where custom handwork is done), and crushers (where low-grade stone is pulverized into gravel aggregate). One of the mainstays of this regional economy is the requirement that all buildings in Jerusalem's ever-expanding

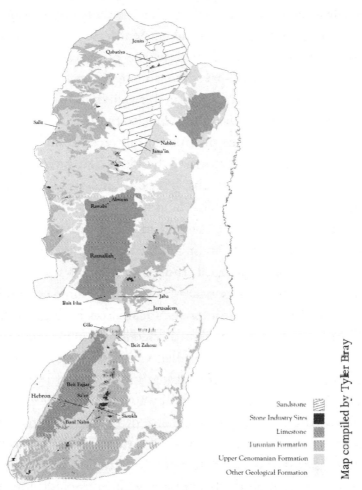

West Bank stone deposits and geological formations.

urban orbit be faced with local limestone, or what is widely referred to as Jerusalem Stone (and more lyrically as Jerusalem Gold). British governor Ronald Storrs, who wanted to preserve the medieval appearance of the old walled city, laid down this stipulation in a 1918 municipal ordinance.

After the 1967 seizure of East Jerusalem and the subsequent Israeli resolve to *unify* all parts of the city, Israeli authorities reinforced Storrs's requirement and applied it not just to the ideology-driven reconstruction of the damaged core but also to areas far beyond the walls of the Old City. In the words of the municipality's 1968 master plan for unification: "The value of the visual impression that is projected by the stone ... [carries] emotional messages that

stimulate other sensations embedded in our collective memory, producing strong associations to the ancient holy city of Jerusalem."[3]
Planners envisaged that, over time, the stone's message would be
transmitted across the spreading metropolitan fringe toward the
"optimal boundaries" of Greater Jerusalem, which reach deeply
into Palestinian territories. But they also made a concession to real
estate developers, whose profiteering interest in building suburbs
dovetailed with Zionist expansion: builders were no longer required
to use expensive stone blocks, but could meet compliance with a
thinner, six-centimeter slab of cladding.

The ungainly result of this pell-mell construction is a form of
sprawl, which architects and planners tend to regard with dismay,
but it is far from haphazard. Indeed, military strategists worked
closely with urban policymakers to establish "ring-neighborhood"
(*Shekhunot ha-Taba'at*) outposts, located on high ground on the
remote periphery of the city's projected limits, in the conviction that
the land in between would be filled with Jewish suburbs over time.
They also chose the land confiscated for these leapfrog settlements
because it was "underpopulated" by Palestinians, thereby preserving the favored demographic balance of the city's Jewish majority,
mandated in the 2000 master plan at a ratio of 70:30 percent.[4] The
year 2017 saw the narrow defeat of a Greater Jerusalem bill to annex
territory enclosed by the Separation Wall (to include 150,000 Jews
in the West Bank settlements of Ma'ale Adumim, Givat Ze'ev, Beitar
Illit, and the Gush Etzion bloc), which would have swung the ratio
to 80:20 percent.[5]

The uniform use of Jerusalem Stone in all of these suburban
developments is supposed to provide visual confirmation that every
square meter of Jerusalem is "unified," even though its ethnic and
religious divisions are deeply etched on the urban geography. So,
too, architects learned how to incorporate Levantine features—
horseshoe arches and domes—as part of the new heritage-oriented
effort to blend into the region's traditional built environment and
to show that Israel's assumed sovereignty is somehow indigenous.
Indeed, the biblical-Oriental aesthetic favored since the 1970s is
almost the opposite of the modernist and secular "Hebrew state"

that was built out with Brutalist concrete in the preceding decades. The smooth surface of the latter was supposed to evoke the *tabula rasa* of a brand-new country, remote in feel and appearance from both the urban quarters of the Jewish diaspora and the stony Arab vernacular of the Ottoman era. By contrast, Israel's contemporary planners, more religiously inclined than their predecessors, strive to make the Jerusalem-centric state look as if it has always belonged to the land, and, by extension, that the land belongs to a Jewish state.

They have applied the same visual formula and architectural code to the construction of settler colonies far beyond the expanded post-1967 municipal boundaries.[6] Perhaps the most prominent example is the suburban hilltop city of Ma'ale Adumim, seven kilometers to the east, and surrounded by the al-Bariya wilderness, known to settlers as the Judean Desert. Ma'ale Adumim's terraced housing, built with concrete blocks and cladded with limestone, gleams at sunset with the fabled hue associated with "Jerusalem of Gold." The radiant effect, which transforms a pale, yellowish daytime appearance into a lustrous glow, is a distinctive quality of much of the stone carved out of hundreds of open-pit quarries that mar the West Bank highlands. But its burnished presence on this particular hilltop is markedly aggressive. The authorities mandated this "instant city," now housing 38,000 residents, to be built precisely at the "end of the desert," and as lead architect-planner Thomas Leitersdorf recalled, to be "as big as possible."[7] Gush Emunim members "founded" it as a pioneer settlement in 1975 near a location earmarked for Jerusalem's new industrial zone. Shortly after, the Israeli government ordered the construction, largely on expropriated land, of a large satellite city. Ma'ale Adumim was planned not only as an outer ring stronghold of Jerusalem, controlling the route to Jericho, but also, quite deliberately, as a means to slice the West Bank almost in two. If the city is annexed as part of the Greater Jerusalem plan, and the connecting corridor filled in with housing colonies (in the controversial E1 zone), then East Jerusalem will be surrounded on all sides by Jewish settlement, and the north and south of the West Bank will be effectively divided from each other.

The profile of many of the world's great cities is linked to the unique character of their dominant building stone: the Carrara marble of Rome, the Portland stone of London, the Lutetian limestone of Paris, the Passaic sandstone of New York's "brownstones," the Craigleith sandstone of Edinburgh, the Berroqueña stone of Madrid, the Roxbury Puddingstone of Boston, the Wicklow granite of Dublin, the Rubislaw granite of Aberdeen, the Porbandar stone of Bombay. But in the case of Jerusalem Stone, communities of faith elsewhere want a piece of it too. Synagogues all over the world try to establish an emotional link with the Western Wall by importing the region's limestone, and increasingly the managers of Christian houses of worship want some Holy Land stone too. Palestinians in the far-off diaspora seek it out for their own suburban homes.

To disguise their origin on Palestinian land and their preparation by Palestinian hands, importers and distributors will typically describe these stones as "quarried in Judea," and in most cases they will have been purchased and repackaged by an Israeli middleman. However offensive, this kind of misrepresentation is nowhere near as galling as the economic double bind that entraps a large part of the Palestinian stone industry and its workforce in the service of Israel's unfaltering expansion into the Occupied Territories.

Outsourcing the Dust

Jerusalem itself sits on top of many ancient quarries. The most well-known are the vast galleries known as Solomon's Quarries, extending for hundreds of meters under the Muslim Quarter, which once supplied *meleke* (the much-prized "royal stone," used for many great public buildings of antiquity) and which can still be visited. The Freemasons of Israel conduct annual rituals in the main cavern, and King Solomon, who allegedly mined the quarries to build the first Jewish temple, is hailed as their first Grand Master. There are still ample limestone deposits in the city's constituent mountains, though the expansion of its suburbs and satellite settlements has taken priority as a land use over the business of stone extraction. For example, developers of the large Jerusalem suburb of Gilo (30,000 population, and squatting on land illegally annexed from Beit Jala in the Bethlehem District) built the settlement directly over the former quarry of al-Slayyeb, which once supplied esteemed, pink-veined stone for the many well-appointed convents, monasteries, and churches in the region.

Above all, Israel's tightened environmental regulations have made the cost of quarrying prohibitive. No one wants to live near an open-air industrial site that generates extractor noise and toxic airborne particulates. The West Bank is another matter, however. Palestinian Authority (PA) regulations are considerably weaker and do not extend to Area C, which harbors much of the best stone. Extracting is much less expensive there, as are the workers, and their skill in stonecraft is superior. Moreover, export restrictions and cutthroat competition among small family-owned producers in the West Bank ensure that product prices are undervalued, to the benefit of Israeli buyers. The net result is that the industry, along with its pollution and other environmentally harmful impacts, has been very effectively outsourced across the Green Line.

Before 1967, the extraction of stone in the West Bank was a local craft-based enterprise. But from the onset of the Occupation, Israel's "invitation to industrialize" brought about a sea change. In *White Oil*, Judy Price's documentary film about quarrying, a security guard at the Rafat quarry near Ramallah neatly described the outcomes:

> Traditionally, quarries existed in Beit Nabala and Deir Tareef. After the 1967 war, Israeli authorities gathered the owners of the quarries, they met with the head of the Civil Administration, and they offered the owners competitive loans to expand their quarries to use the stone to build the state of Israel. Our village refused, and they chose to shut down the quarries. But the owners in Beit Nabala accepted the offer and they prospered. Now Beit Nabala is well-built, it's a city but our town remains as it was. It's a dump, and has really declined. There is nothing there, just orchards on the outskirts, and the downtown is derelict.[8]

Similar offers were made in other parts of the West Bank, and industrial activity picked up even more when Israeli authorities permitted exports to Jordan and the Gulf states in 1973. As new Palestinian quarries and factories opened, production inside the Green Line declined. Today, there is only one major stone producer, Grebelsky & Son, operating in Israel itself, and it is the oldest Jewish-owned company in the business. Founded in 1923 by Aharon Grebelsky, a flour merchant from the Ukraine, the firm started out quarrying from the mountains of Jerusalem, with a predominantly Arab workforce. After the 1967 war, the company won a commission to supply and lay stone for the new Western Wall plaza (on the site where the 700-year-old Moroccan, or Mughrabi, Quarter was razed and cleared overnight by Israeli forces), and then to fortify the walls of the Church of the Holy Sepulcher. Other high-visibility orders followed, raising the firm's profile above that of its competitors. The post-Occupation policy of "integrating" the Palestinian and Israeli economies more or less sealed the fate of the rest of the Israeli stone industry. With the West Bank opened for business, Palestinian producers, with ready access to the best stone, were a much cheaper option.

By the early 1980s, Grebelsky's Israeli rivals had all closed down, and the firm survived by sourcing stone from Bethlehem's Nassar company and by marketing the products for international export by using the "Jerusalem Stone" brand name. Arik, the founder's grandson (who now runs the company with his brother Hanan), told me that "we changed the name from Jerusalem Marble Company back to Grebelsky to distinguish ourselves from the competition." In many overseas markets, a family company with a Jewish name has an advantage over an Arab one, especially in North America where Grebelsky has thrived. Its success spawned several imitators in the export business, like Jerusalem Gardens, along with a host of US-based importers looking to service the booming suburban market for custom homes built in the "Mediterranean" style. One such firm, Kansas-based Jerusalem Stone, advertises its product in a typically misleading fashion as "cut from natural white stone imported from Hebron, Israel."[9]

Arik Grebelsky and I met in the company's new location in a dusty industrial park in Beit Shemesh. His father, Yechiel, who took over the company after Aharon's death in 1950, also showed up for the interview, and although his mind was wandering and generating erratic comments on occasion, he was treated with reverence by the son. At the mention of Kibbutz Ginosar, where I had worked as a volunteer in the late 1970s, he interrupted to reminisce about the Palmach, the Haganah's elite military organization, founded at that kibbutz by Yigal Allon in 1941. But the main point he seemed to want to communicate to me was that the company was "only Jews, no foreigners" and that the family had succeeded in building it into a Jewish-only workforce.

He was clearly not referring to the current workforce, which his son Arik described as a mixture of Jews, Eritreans, and Palestinians from Israel and the West Bank. But his interjections reminded me that the struggle over control of quarries in the pre-1948 decades was a particularly abrasive chapter in the Zionist "conquest of labor." No doubt, and especially because of its Jerusalem location, the first twenty-five years of the company's existence must have been quite turbulent. If

Yechiel and Arik Grebelsky, Beit Shemesh.

Photo by author

the Grebelsky family had achieved an all-Jewish workforce, or anything like it, in the period after 1948, it did not last for long. Indeed, a 1968 picture on the firm's website clearly shows a Palestinian mason in a kaffiyeh chiseling the firm's stones for the Western Wall plaza.

In the late 1980s, high-quality stone in a range of colors was discovered during excavations for a military airport in Mitzpe Ramon, in the Negev (*Naqab*) desert of southern Israel. Grebelsky established a quarry there, which employed Israeli Palestinians, as did the firm's other smaller quarry in the Galilee. Palestinian workers also traveled from the West Bank to work at the Beit Shemesh factory location. "They are the best workers," Arik reported, "their art of hand chiseling has not changed much in two thousand years, and they have worked for us since I was a boy." In addition, he declared, "these days, Israelis are spoiled, they don't want to do the hard work." Indeed, hand-chiseled surfaces were among the full range of finishes that the company could offer clients. But the most intriguing was called "Reclaimed," and the description in the company's marketing catalog spoke volumes about how politics was shaping taste among the industry's consumer base:

> Ancient 200–300 year old floors taken from the old city of Jerusalem are very rare and costly. There is increasing demand for this type of authentic floors (sic) due to its unique mysterious look and history. In order to be able to offer this type of look without relying on limited supply and extreme prices, Grebelsky has developed a unique finish, having a similar ancient appeal.

The Grebelskys' claim to have originated the "Jerusalem Stone" brand was a contested one. Nassar Nassar, the founder and owner of the largest and most successful Palestinian stone company, gave me a different account when I met him in his executive office in Bethlehem's industrial suburb of Doha. When he started his company in the mid-1980s, Nassar told me he spent four years, some of it in the United States, promoting the Jerusalem Stone concept and building trust in his firm's capacity to deliver it. "Then, in the 1990s," he recalled, "everyone started to use the brand, Turks, Jordanians, Israelis, but I tried to give some other Palestinian producers the opportunity to take advantage of the name." Grebelsky, according to Nassar, was one of those cashing in at the time, but, unlike the Palestinians, the Israeli firm "was able to exploit its Jewish identity and leverage the Jewish connection to Jerusalem to win overseas orders." Grebelsky had effectively appropriated his work, cornering as much of the international Jerusalem Stone market as it could. Needless to say, the two companies no longer had a trading relationship. "Now, I compete with them on quality and price," Nassar concluded, visibly vexed at having to tell this story about bad faith between businessmen.

Although he is the richest man in Bethlehem, with quarries and subsidiary companies in Oman, Brazil, and Jordan, Nassar was dressed in worn jeans and a sports shirt on the day of our interview, and he had a blue-collar air about him. At twelve years old, he had started working in his father's quarry in Yatta, near Hebron, and, to compensate for his lack

Photo by author

Nassar Nassar, Maestro d'Arte Della Pietra.

of education, he had judiciously employed top professionals to help open the export market where he now reigned supreme among fellow Palestinian producers; in 2013, he won the coveted Master of Stone Award at the premier International Stone Fair, staged annually in Verona. Stone company owners, I would soon find, liked to express their passion for stone, but Nassar was in a class of his own: "Some men flirt with women," he confided, "but sometimes, I feel that I am flirting with the stones."

Costs of Business

While environmental regulations and economic attrition all but killed off quarrying in Israel, some Jewish producers have found a way to directly operate across the Green Line. Taking advantage of massive land grabs during the 1970s, as many as ten Israeli-owned quarries and crushers opened up in Area C to directly supply Israeli demand for aggregate gravel. The Civil Administration licensed these facilities in clear violation of international humanitarian law that prohibits the expropriation of natural resources for the use or profit of the occupying power.[10] Some of the quarries were attached to settlements, while others, like the Nahal Raba quarry, run by the Israeli subsidiary of Heidelberg Cement and operating on land taken from al-Zawiya village, were deliberately facilitated by the rerouting of the Separation Wall.[11] Because they lie in Area C, they are not subject to any environmental regulation, while Israeli and Palestinian labor laws are barely, if ever, observed. In defiance of the Israeli High Court's 2007 ruling that Israeli labor laws should be observed by enterprises in West Bank settlements, employers routinely claim that they are bound by 1967-era Jordanian law, much weaker by far and all but impossible to enforce.

For the Palestinians employed in these Israeli quarries, this no-man's land of rights results in the most precarious form of at-will employment, without payslips or paper records of any kind, and offers little or no protection from the environmental hazards of extraction, processing, and asphalt production on site. In 2011, deteriorating conditions prompted the workforce at Salit Quarry, located in the Mishor Adumim industrial zone, to organize through the Israeli trade union Workers Advice Center (WAC-MAAN). Workers went on strike for several months to win what would have been the first collective bargaining agreement for Palestinians in the settlements. Rather than bargain, the quarry owners filed for bankruptcy, which required the courts to adjudicate the workers' legal case for compensation in accord with Israel's national insurance regulations. In a mixed decision on the creditors' agreement, the court ruled for compensation for the workers but did not require the new owners to reemploy them. Despite the loss of their jobs, the workers were able to win a landmark case that proved collective action could yield material results along with recognition of their rights.[12]

Two years earlier, the Israeli Supreme Court handed down another mixed decision, this time in response to a suit from the Israeli NGO Yesh Din challenging the legality of the settlement quarries. In a 1992 opinion, the same court had determined that the transfer of natural resources from the West Bank was unlawful: "a territory held through belligerent seizure is not a field open for economic or other exploitation."[13] The Yesh Din petition cited that earlier opinion as part of its appeal to the 1907 Hague Convention on Land Warfare. In this instance, however, the court, which has deferred any opinion on the legality of the West Bank settlements themselves, rejected the Yesh Din suit, citing "adjustment to the prolonged duration of the occupation." Arguing that Palestinians were beneficiaries of the employment provided by the quarries, the court backed the Civil Administration's procedure of collecting taxes from facility owners as a way of benefiting all Palestinians residents in Area C. However, the judges also discouraged the approval of any new quarries.[14]

In a scathing 2016 report on settlement businesses, Human Rights Watch drew attention to the double standard by which the Civil Administration granted concessions to these Israeli mining concerns (which supply more than a quarter of Israel's sand and gravel needs) while denying permits to Palestinian quarry owners in the same areas. Since the Paris Protocol was adopted in 1995, and in violation of the spirit of the Oslo Accords, no new quarry permits had been issued to Palestinians, and most of the preexisting ones in Area C had been denied renewal.[15] In the wake of international attention to the lawsuit and the Human Rights Watch report, the Civil Administration issued five new three-year permits: Nassar told me that he possessed one of them. In 2013, the World Bank estimated that the quarry restrictions cost the Palestinian economy upwards of $250 million annually, while the total loss from Area C restrictions amounted to $3.4 billion.[16] Many of the other Israeli-owned business enterprises located in settlements and Area C land illegally draw upon the West Bank's natural resources, but none of them so blatantly transfer the contents of the land itself, leaving behind open pits to scar the landscape.

Aside from their lawlessness, these strip-mining operations are able to supply the Israeli aggregates industry much more efficiently than Palestinian producers. Half of the West Bank's twenty-five integrated crushers (which process stone *in situ* at the quarry) are Israeli-owned, but, with ready access to explosives to break up the stone face, they can produce much more cheaply, at a scale and consistency that allow them to fill large orders for quality concrete. Since the al-Aqsa intifada, almost all Palestinian operators have been denied the use of explosives. Fallback technology like diggers and jackhammers makes extraction three times more expensive; Israeli-owned quarries can excavate 5,000 tons of stone in one hour using explosives, whereas Palestinian operators might take two to three days to produce one ton using a jackhammer.[17] Logistical obstacles to moving and distributing Palestinian product also amplify the transaction costs, rendering them less competitive in the main Israeli markets. As a result, according to one estimate, "the Israeli-run operators ($105m) generate approximately five times the value of Palestinian-run integrated crushers ($21m)." By comparison, almost all of the West Bank's fifty recycling crushers, which process stone waste from the top cover of quarries elsewhere, are Palestinian-owned and operated. But because their product is inferior to that of the integrated crushers, they generate much less revenue ($38 million) and cannot compete well for tenders from large contractors in the construction industry.[18] Consequently, the Palestinian quarries operate well under capacity, and at a considerable market disadvantage, as intended by the Israeli restrictions.

The Palestinian side of the industry is also severely constrained by the Israeli rationing of energy and water and denial of access to Area C, where most of the known stone deposits are located in estimated deposits of 20,000 dunums (2,000 hectares) of minable land. The border controls hamper the movement of Palestinian goods through enforcement of what is called the "back-to-back system." Maher Hshayesh, director of the Union of Stone and Marble (USM), the trade association that represents the owners, explained how the system works: "The driver will have to wait several hours at the checkpoints, which are only open during the day, unload everything, and then reload to an Israeli truck on the other side of the border." Although "Hebron is only one hour from the port of Ashdod," he pointed out, "a truckload of goods from here will take a long time to get there." The Tunnels checkpoint near Bethlehem is the only one of the West Bank's five commercial crossings through which large stone blocks can pass to Jerusalem, and only a limited number of trucks (125) are allowed to pass daily. "The transportation costs are doubled as a result of back-to-back," he estimated, "and goods are damaged in the process." For those firms with access to export markets, he added, "there will be many clearance delays at the port," on account of the complex rules of the PA–Israel customs union. Hshayesh, who acknowledged that the sector is almost "saturated" and "blocked from future growth" by the Area C constraints, visibly chafed at mention of all the obstacles, pointing out, with no small amount of irony, that "these are the actions of our main trading partner." Little headway had been made on loosening the restrictions, he reported, despite negotiations with the EU, the Quartet, and the US Consulate. "The Israeli goal is not to shut us down but to restrict and contain our business in every way possible."

With limited options, even in a construction boom, his USM members were directly selling product, albeit discreetly, to the settlements. This was a violation of PA policy, as was the acceptance of employment in settlements (officially punishable by a prison sentence of up to five years), but the PA had no plan B and the cost of absorbing all the workers back into the Palestinian economy was prohibitive. "From a national point of view, we don't encourage any contact with the settlements," Hshayesh explained, "but we cannot enforce the prohibition. If you cannot offer an alternative, you cannot punish." Nor was there much help for the industry from the PA, which had not responded to owners' requests for tax breaks and subsidies, along with formal industrial zones offering infrastructural services.

For him, the only upside was the growing volume of exports by the forty or so local producers with the resources to promote their brand at the big international trade fairs in Verona and Dubai. Wherever they are allowed access, he said, "their products are increasingly able to compete at the quality end of the market." Indeed, between the years 2007 and 2011, exports grew by almost 13 percent, targeting as many as twenty-five countries around the world, and by 2017, accounted for 17 percent of Palestinian external trade (and 25 percent overall).[19] The volume would be much greater if it included the large portion of cross-border stone product which Israeli distributors brand (unlawfully) as Made in Israel and sell overseas at a considerable markup.[20]

The USM, which represents more than half of the sector's firms (and 70 percent of output volume), is not without its industry critics. In my interviews with small factory owners, several reported efforts on the part of members to pressure the union to use its power to set price floors. In a very tight market, producers are routinely under-cut by their neighbors, and the rivalry between family businesses (the same names come up repeatedly in the USM's membership directory—Taqatqa, Deirya, Thawabta, Nassar, Halaika) is ampli-fied by the competition between village clusters. Under these circumstances, it is easy to understand why there was so much inter-est in price regulation and a corresponding frustration about the USM's inertia. USM's acting director, Wisam Al-Taraweh, insisted that the union supported the idea but could not get enough buy-in from members. According to one Bethlehem-based factory owner, "there were lots of meetings, but the advocates could not get total agreement among the members. Their idea was to stop factories from selling low to Israel buyers, but the small companies in Beit Fajjar were always breaking the agreement and were not punished. Over there," he added, gesturing southwards, "they operate like cowboys."

Beit Fajjar, nine kilometers to the south of Bethlehem, is one of the oldest and most important centers of stone production in the West Bank; Jama'in, near Nablus; Qabatiya, near Jenin; and Sioukh, Sa'ir, and Bani Na'im, close to Hebron, share the honors. Genera-tions of villagers have scratched out a living from the quarries and factories, dust collecting in their lungs, the angle of their backs bent from chronic occupational ailments. Trucks with jumbo blocks of raw white stone strapped to their bodies rumble through the narrow road network of the village, and stacks of blocks, slabs, and shards are lined up in fields and yards. Yawning quarry pits are gouged out of the hills on every side, and the dimmed sunlit air has a powdery taste. The town hosts 150 factories and as many as forty quarries, employing more than 80 percent of its 11,000 residents. Almost all of the factories are in Area B, but most of the quarries are operating without permits in Area C, and many only on Fridays and Saturdays, around the clock, when Israeli soldiers are off-duty. Some of the best stone is tantalizingly close yet politically difficult to extract. Nor can the full extent of the deposits be known, because Israeli authorities have blocked efforts to mount a comprehensive geological survey.

Like most firms in the business, the town's companies are family owned and typically employ only a handful of workers, some working the machines, others chiseling or dressing the slab surfaces in a variety of styles. "I was working as a decorator in the United Arab Emirates, and I saw a market need for a particular product," reported Ahmed, one of the first owners I interviewed, "so I bought some land here and started digging." He coyly added that he "didn't know whether the land was in B or C," though this distinction was highly consequential and unlikely to be a matter of interpretation. In any event, he only ever had a PA license to operate, but he knew of other quarry owners who had been mining in Area C for decades and were recently denied their license renewals. Many firms had no license whatsoever and operated in the cowboy mode, wholly outside of the regulatory and taxation orbit and always on the verge of being fined and shut down. Later in the day, Omar, one of his neighbors, described to me how his machinery and tools had been confiscated by the Israeli soldiers in his Area C facility. In fact, this happened quite regularly. Just to retrieve his assets, he said: "I had to pay fines, storage fees, transport costs, and even the salaries of the soldiers for bringing them back." The threat of seizure had become more common but the policy seemed to be one of random harassment. "Sometimes they come twice in a month," Ahmed said, "and then not again until three months later."

Badil, a worker at another quarry, described the labor and cost involved in these illicit Friday and Saturday operations. "We have to bring all the machinery in and out through illegal routes, and also employ lookouts to keep watch for soldiers who have beaten and arrested my co-workers." Once on site, he said, his crew worked eighteen or nineteen hour shifts to maximize their temporary access. Israeli officials had found a way to take advantage of their predicament. Badil recounted that "some of the quarry owners had been

pressured by the authorities to offer discount prices on their products in return for unhindered access to Area C, while other firms
were harassed for refusing." Needless to say, this shady arrangement
divided the community. "The collaborators," as he called them,
"are shunned within Beit Fajjar—everyone knows who they are."
At times, Israeli reprisals took on the more overt form of collective
punishment following incidents of resistance or unrest. When two
Beit Fajjar youth stabbed a soldier near the settlement of Ariel, in
March 2016, the authorities raided and shut down three dozen Beit
Fajjar quarries, confiscating much of the equipment.[21] The Gush
Etzion traffic junction that fed the approach road to the town also
became a conflict zone, heavily policed by armed settlers and sol-
diers who periodically placed the village on lockdown during the
"knife intifada" of 2015–16 when I was first visiting the locality.

I asked Ahmed where he sold his products. "Some of it locally, but
mostly I sell to an Israeli distributor," he responded, "though everyone around here knows owners who sell directly to the settlements or
even to the Israeli crushers. These owners don't get much respect—
it's a small community—but we all have to survive." The stone
trade was part of his family history. Before machines arrived in the
1960s, he recalled, "my grandfather's generation used hammers and
saws, and they always talked about how hard it used to be." He grew
up listening to their taunts. "They told us that we were not strong
enough today to use a stone saw," and added respectfully, "but they
were really good at working with stone." Ahmed did not inherit
a factory from his father, as was the case with many of the town's
small owners. Instead, he had earned his start-up capital by working
in the Gulf. But his company was similar in scale to most of the
others and just as under-resourced.

Mohammed, an owner–manager in another sector of the village,
was one of the fortunate sons. His father had been an engineer in the
United States and had returned to start up a factory after the Oslo
Accords in the mid-1990s. The firm, which only did cutting and finishing, was beginning to register some success in export markets like
Dubai and Qatar—"they only want polished stone," he remarked,
"just like the Pharaohs." But there was a lot of construction going

on in Ramallah and in Israel, so there was plenty of demand for *taltis* and *tubʒeh*—locally the most favored of the traditional, hand-chiseled finishes. He had also developed a specialty line for Israeli buyers who were prepared to pay more for a product that looked like old stone. "If you mix in some oil and dust to the finish, then it will look weathered," he explained, "and Israeli home owners want it to look as if they have been here for a long time." Was that a growing trend? I asked him. "The Israelis have to use what we call 'Jerusalem Stone,'" he explained, "but now they also want the stone to look natural and textured, the same way it is here and in Arab countries like Jordan." In Israel, this market taste was geographically uneven. Where the stark modernity of Tel Aviv and the coastal cities was still at odds with traditional regional styles, the goal of the religious-settler movement in the east was to be at one with the stony aura of the biblical homelands.

Aside from a complaint, in passing, about the shortage of workers willing to sign up for the minimum wage—a 65 shekel ($16) daily pay rate—Mohammed was upbeat about his firm's current business prospects. The longterm future of the industry was another matter, however. "There are only twenty more years of Jerusalem Stone left in the areas where we can quarry," he lamented. "Much of the best stone is mined out, and we have to go deeper and deeper—up to a hundred meters in some cases—to get at it." Palestine's overseas competitors had some clear advantages in this regard. "Turkey has limestone just like ours," he pointed out, "and it is much closer to the surface."

At that point, his father, Mahmoud, who had entered the room, joined the conversation and immediately countered his son's pessimism. "There is lots of stone left in the mountains, in Area C," he insisted, "and at some point the Israelis will have to permit access to it." However, he was worried about the foreign competition from other low-wage countries, like Jordan, Egypt, and Turkey, and most recently from Iran and India, and he warned about a new entrant, with inventive techniques. "The Chinese come here and buy flawed blocks on the cheap," he related. "They have developed a machine at home that pulverizes the raw stone and mixes it with their own stone powder to produce Jerusalem Gold slabs." Sure enough, on Alibaba.com, China's leading online marketplace, I found such products for purchase from Xiamen, the country's primary stone center. Mahmoud marveled at the ingenuity of the Chinese, as did several other owners whom I interviewed, but he also placed some faith in Hebron's production workshops, where stone-cutting and finishing technologies were manufactured more cheaply than in Italy and Turkey, the industry leaders. "In Hebron, they are good at knockoffs too," his son Mohammed joked, "so maybe they can make a version of the Chinese machine."

Careful Competition

In 2005, the Palestinian Federation of Industries commissioned a survey to assess the stone industry's potential for growth and development. The report touched on several of the chief obstacles facing producers: constraints placed on energy supply and mobility by the Israeli authorities; the lopsided playing field of the customs union set up under the Paris Protocol; the poor state of the PA's industrial policymaking; the lack of sound scientific and geological surveys; uneven access to leading technologies; ineffective worker safety regulations and job training; inexperience in marketing to overseas buyers; and the lack of cooperation among owners to boost efficiency and reduce net damage from overcompetition.[22] Elaborating on the last of these, the report drew attention to the familial ownership structure as one of the sector's prime weaknesses. Its authors cited the custom of passing on the business to a son in order to retain family control over decision-making as a major obstacle to the professionalization of the industry. Among other things, this meant that the operating capital of firms typically came from savings and not from commercial loans that would allow for more investment in upgraded technology.

This viewpoint may have been in sync with standard corporate practices, even in medium-sized firms, but it is largely ignored by the owners of the smaller West Bank family firms who struggle to keep their businesses afloat. A quarry without a license in Area

C, for example, that can only operate two days a week and is regularly raided by Israeli soldiers could only be a sideline and not a professional operation with growth potential. Moreover, as one of those quarry owners in Beit Fajjar pointed out to me, "ultimately, the family members are there to support, not compete with, one another, and since we have all been living in the same community for hundreds of years, the competition between families is very careful." Even without the constraints of the Occupation, the Beit Fajjar model of "careful competition" is at odds with the more cutthroat one embraced by entrepreneurial capitalism. In addition, the family ownership model is often governed by noncommercial considerations. Suhail Sultan, a Birzeit University expert on the industry, explained to me that "some owners will sell for less than the production costs just to protect the family name, its honor, and its reputation." However, these costs are by no means easy to estimate, at least not with any fiscal precision. "They don't count the labor of family members," he pointed out, "they don't pay taxes, or the full cost of electricity or water, and so their invoices, if they have any at all, are not very accurate."

Samir Hazboun, the chief author of the federation's report, seemed to think that things had not changed much in the decade since it was issued, especially in the area of underprofessionalization. "Owners should not be directors, managers, or accountants," he insisted, "that is a reflection of the impact of culture upon the economy." He continued: "If I am the owner, should I have complete control? And just because I have four sons, do they have to work in the factory? Why? Because I trust them more or want to keep wealth in the family? That is feudalism. I should be hiring professionals to do these jobs." A free market economist, Hazboun had worked in academe and the private sector, and, in conversation, switched effortlessly from discussing the pragmatic details of industry logistics to theoretical analysis of political economy. "American capitalism moved from managerialism to entrepreneurialism," he pronounced, "but we Palestinians are still stuck in the comprador stage. We have not yet achieved a capitalist economy."

Hazboun hailed from one of Bethlehem's oldest families. Serving as the president of the Bethlehem Chamber of Commerce, he was well-connected to national elites and partial to the suggestion that a truly fair Israeli–Palestinian customs union would make for an ideal kind of joint venture: "Israel would be the capital-intensive partner, and Palestine the labor-intensive one." Hazboun was invoking the Ricardian principle of national comparative advantage by which small countries ought to trade on the basis of their domestic assets and not try to substitute local products for those that were more cost-effective to import. The primary Palestinian asset was low-cost labor, and the PA had ensured it would remain that way by setting a minimum monthly wage at 1,450 shekels ($415), or less than a third of the Israeli rate.

But how should the PA seek to regulate Palestinians' other great asset? Adopting the confident air of the notable class, Hazboun disclosed that "initially we considered nationalizing the stone industry," following the example of resource-rich nations like Libya, "but we decided to tax it instead, so that owners would submit a share of their revenues." No doubt, pressure from owners and investors helped to determine the PA's decision to exempt stone and sand from its 1999 law declaring all natural resources to be publicly owned.[23] Even though the industry is wholly privatized, regulation of the industry is also hands-off, with scant enforcement of safety or health provisions. As a result, many quarry and factory owners operate without licenses and despoil the environment without any fear of sanction.

Even the proposal mentioned by Hazboun to tax the industry had yet to be adopted into law. Neither the PA nor the municipalities hosting the industrial facilities were able to collect much revenue, while, in most cases, these governments were footing the costs of building and maintaining infrastructure used by the industry, not to mention the more onerous burden of mitigating the harmful environmental and public health impacts. Even if enforceable tax laws were to be passed, Hazboun conceded that "many of the assets lie in Area C, so it will be a challenge to collect the taxes."

In the meantime, factories that could no longer obtain stone quarried from a local source were importing it from overseas or from other parts of the West Bank. Owners were bringing in raw marble from Brazil and Oman, and even limestone from Jenin that fell within the Jerusalem range of colors, to be cut and finished in Beit Fajjar. Nor did the authorities in Ramallah see much tax revenue from these imports. As Hazboun pointed out, an overseas shipment could "sit in the bonded area of an Israeli port for twenty-eight days if a Palestinian name and destination was on its cargo bill," whereas "if an Israeli name is on the container, then the contents will be here in three days, but the taxes will be paid to Israel and not to the PA." A similar advantage accrued when Palestinian stones were exported with an Israeli origin certificate. "An Israeli exporter in Tel Aviv will sell Beit Fajjar stone in his name at a large profit and thereby take advantage of the services of Palestinians, and it's the same in agriculture with strawberries," he pointed out. "It's just easier for the Palestinian to use his Israeli counterpart for the exports, and for Israel, of course, this is the best kind of Occupation—one that lays golden eggs."

Bethlehem's Doha industrial district is choc-a-bloc with small family-owned stone factories struggling to adjust to a volatile market. Internationally, the industry has undergone a boom over the last two decades, as the use of natural stone in interior decor, especially on kitchen countertops, has become more common. This upturn, and the corresponding shift in taste, has been driven by the development of diamond wire saw technologies that significantly reduced the time, and the price, of stone cutting. Factories without this advanced machinery are at a disadvantage. Regional trend swings also make it difficult to find, and hold on to, a market niche. Niveen Odeh, a manager at the Al Jabary Company in Bethlehem's Doha zone, explained how this had affected her firm's trade with Jordanian buyers: "Before, they only wanted *taltis* [a traditional hand-dressed treatment], but now they want brushed stone," which reinforces the vein structure of the stone and gives it a rustic appearance. "Brushed is not so labor-intensive and so it is cheaper," she pointed out, "but to get a decent price we need special machines to produce that finish, and then we have to bring technicians from Italy to fix the machines when they break down." "In the Gulf countries," she continued, "they only want a smooth classic finish, they want to pretend that their stone comes from Europe (like Carrara from Italy or Crema from Spain), because they want to be in that league and not have anything to do with the Middle East, and certainly not Palestine." On the upside, she observed that the "Israelis still want the traditional look of *taltis* because they want their buildings to look local, they don't want the look of the 'new.'"

Odeh was one of the few women, aside from secretarial staff, whom I met in the industry, and it was easy to see why she was so prized. In the absence of the company boss, she was running the ship single-handedly. In the course of our interview, she fielded phone calls and seamlessly answered queries from clerical employees while all the time attending closely to our conversation. "Initially," she recalled, "it was quite difficult to work as a woman at this level in a male industry where there are so few of us," but "I am strong and capable, and so I have thrived." She said that when clients meet her, they think she is a professional, "someone like an engineer, while everyone here treats me just like one of the owner's family."

Like the other Bethlehem producers, she expressed frustration not only with the pint-sized Beit Fajjar factories—"they undercut our prices all the time, so that we can only really survive on our big orders"—but also with the USM for holding back on setting price floors. Mohammed Al-Jundi, the general manager of a firm next door, shared the sentiment. Indeed, he lamented, "the prices had been driven so low by Beit Fajjar we cannot get a decent profit out of the Israeli trade anymore." The only one of the Jundi sons to have developed a passion for stone, he could only see a future, for midsized companies at least, in more and more automation. Hand-dressed *taltis* stone, he predicted, "would still be popular in Palestine and Israel, but only the small firms and workshops will be able to compete." Economic pressure on all but the largest companies had become "intense," in his view, and, like other owners, he was nostalgic for an earlier period (the 1990s usually) when transaction costs were lower and earnings easier to come by.

Yet for all the grumbling about falling rates of profit, many owners appeared to be doing well. At the end of several of my interviews, factory owners insisted that I come to visit their own homes. Usually this meant driving up to a freshly built villa that enjoyed capacious views from a hilltop shared with similar mansions belonging to other family members in the business. In some respects, these were model homes, showcasing the firm's range of stone products, but they also doubled as trophies of personal wealth. The visits culminated in a typically gracious reception period, with successive rounds of coffee, teas, juices, and snacks. For sure, the ever more restrictive Occupation had put a dent in their revenue, but many of these industry families were still extracting a good living from the metastasizing of Jerusalem and the settlement blocs.

Rank and File

Like employers in every industry under the sun, the factory owners I interviewed complained about the shortage of "good employees." Sometimes, they blamed the steadily increasing volume of Israeli work permits, which could generate wages at two or three times the West Bank pay rates. Yet there still was a large pool of available workers who had been denied a permit, either for "security reasons" or because they did not fit the required profile. At other times, owners bemoaned the lack of work ethic among employees reluctant to operate machines for long hours or undertake the backbreaking work of hand chiseling. In truth, the only shortage was of "ideal" workers, loyal and willing to labor hard for low wages and under industrial conditions that were unhealthy and hazardous. After all, the quarries and stone factories offered reasonably steady jobs in a local labor market with high unemployment and at wage levels higher than in any other West Bank industry. A 1999 study by the Palestine Economic Policy Research Institute estimated that average yearly employee compensation was $7,937 (compared to $2,659 in the industrial sector in general).[24] The federation's report in 2005 offered a lower estimate, at $6,000, but my own informal interviews suggested that the salaries were even lower. I also found there was a discrepancy between what owners told me their employees were paid and what the workers themselves reported. Typically, an owner would estimate his workers' daily rate at between 100 and 130 shekels, depending on skills, while the numbers offered by workers were often 10 to 20 percent lower.

Jamal was one of the first factory workers I met and interviewed in Beit Fajjar. He had been in the workforce since the mid-1970s and was able to recall the arduous labor of manually pulling stones out of the ground in an era before quarrying was more fully mechanized. He left for a while to work in a settlement, where the daily pay ranged from 300 to 350 shekels. After he lost his permit access, he returned to the factories, where he currently earned 100 shekels a day, working at a hand-operated machine that finished the slabs. "After forty years of acquiring skills, it's really not much money," he conceded, "I would not be here, believe me, if I did not have to support my daughters' education." His sons worked in a quarry, overseeing block-cutting machinery, but they "had no skills," at least by his definition. By contrast, he recalled, "my grandfather was a real craftsman, and helped to build the Jacir Palace Hotel in Bethlehem, which was highly technical work, and is still a place of great beauty." Commissioned in 1910 as a family home by the mayor

Jacir Palace Hotel, Bethlehem.

of Bethlehem, and subsequently used as a school and a military detention center, the five-star hotel, lately fallen on hard times, is one of the most remarkable monuments to local stone craft in the central West Bank. Reflecting on the hotel's elegance and the decline of craft within his family history, he found one bright spot: "now at least we have a union."

Though the Bethlehem owners I interviewed denied any knowledge of unions in the industry, the stone workers in Beit Fajjar certainly had one, and many of them belonged to it, paying 50 shekels a year for membership dues. The union was formed in 1996 after an owner beat a striker during a walkout at one firm, and sixty-five workers in neighboring factories struck in support. "The construction union officials in Bethlehem came to talk to us and to raise awareness about our rights," recalled Hamed Taqatqa, the current union president. "We knew very little about the law in these days—child labor was quite common—and the owners used Israeli army and PA soldiers to harass the organizers." Nassar Nassar, USM director at the time, advocated for raising wages to stave off the formation of the union, but the local was successfully established and became part of the Palestinian General Federation of Trade Unions' (PGFTU) national construction union, with 750 members initially, and doubling in size since then. "Since 1996, there have been four strikes for higher wages," according to Taqatqa, "and the union has tried to get agreements on standard pay rates: 100–130 for regular workers, and up to 200 for the more specialized chiselers, who do piece work on demand at up to 3 shekels a meter." The piece workers could take home more cash for their chiseling handicraft, but, unlike the regulars, they had no protection or benefits under the PA's labor laws; typically, they worked on a casual basis for several firms at a time, and so they left no record on the books.

From the stone workers' perspective, the PA's 2012 implementation of a minimum monthly wage, set at 1,450 shekels ($15), changed the landscape of the industry for the worse. "Before that, we could get 100 shekels a day," recalled Hamed, "but then the owners tried to push the rate down to the new legal minimum level, and now the new hires only get 65 shekels." He concluded that "these labor laws really protect the owners more than the workers." In particular, he supported the widely held view that the minimum wage was too low for stone workers, though it might be appropriate for garment workers. Was that because the latter were predominantly female? "No," he replied, "it's because our jobs are more dangerous and also much harder." Some might take issue with that proposition— the repetitious labor of garment sewing and assembly is a grueling challenge—but there is no denying that stone extraction and processing is a hazard to life and limb. Workplace accidents are a regular occupational hazard, if not a certainty, and many of the fly-by-night firms have limited insurance at best. Samir Hazboun went so far as to depict Beit Fajjar as "environmentally destroyed." Though that description could match any of the industry towns, ravaged by strip mining and contamination of air and water, he was referring to the fact that the factories (located in Areas A and B) were not enclosed spaces, and so airborne pollution generated chronic ailments for villagers, even when they did not work inside the facilities.

Hazboun was critical of how the authorities adjudicated medical costs relating to injuries. "Some accident victims had filed for awards that were greater than the company's capitalization value," he objected, and so he welcomed the PA's ongoing efforts (finalized in 2016) to "institute a national insurance scheme." But the real problem lay with the conditions that gave rise to the accidents in the first place. "The Labor Ministry is supposed to enforce safety regulations in the factories," said Hamed, the union president, "but we rarely see inspectors, and owners don't provide protective clothing, they prefer to run the risk of having the injuries and then paying the hospital costs." The union itself offered workshops on safety, and, in 2009, it won workers compensation insurance at some factories but had limited resources to protect members' health when owners failed to pay up. "Many of us suffer asthma from the dust," he reported, "and, over time, some workers develop chronic disk injuries in their backs from chiseling." In all my factory visits, I hardly ever saw workers wear face masks, helmets, goggles, or reinforced footwear, and some of them looked too young to be in the workplace. The quarry work of cutting, extracting, and hauling huge stone blocks was more arduous and dangerous (and marginally better paid as a result), and although some employees I interviewed reported that they wore steel-reinforced boots, at one quarry that I visited the operators of heavy machinery were wearing sneakers and baseball caps.

Photo by author

Stone-cutting quarry machinery and operator.

Back in Bethlehem, I quizzed Rasslan Abu Rihan, the director of the local Ministry of Labor office, about the lack of protective gear. "We have only two inspectors for the whole region here," he conceded, "but at least they do arrive in factories unannounced." The main problem with safety, according to him, was the workers' mentality: "It's because of the culture within the industry. We can provide the clothing but the workers won't wear it, they put their faith in religion, and say to themselves, 'God will decide my fate.'" It was not the first time I had heard about God's judgment; factory owners were also quite fond of this explanation. The same afternoon, I visited Mahmoud Abu Odeh, the legal director for the regional union in his Bethlehem office, who had quite a different perspective. "When we bring problems to them, the ministry officials always complain that they don't have enough inspectors," he said, "but just look at all the police and soldiers that the PA employs. Surely they can hire a few more labor inspectors instead." On the issue of protective clothing he was firm: "It's in the law, but the owners won't provide it, or require workers to wear it." Nor, according to him, did all owners abide by the bargaining agreements. "Some do, but others don't, and the Ministry won't make them, and if we try to go into a factory to find out the wages and the conditions, they will shut us out." Odeh had nothing good to say about the low minimum wage rate, pointing out that it was well below the official poverty line, set in 2011 at 2,293 shekels ($637) for a family of two adults and three children. Even so, in 2016, about 17.4 percent of wage employees in the West Bank's private sector were not even earning the minimum wage (and 69.2 percent in Gaza, where there was no legal minimum), while 25.8 percent of Palestinians overall were living in poverty.[25]

Over the next week, I interviewed many Beit Fajjar workers in their homes, after their day shift. An interview session would begin with two or three, and then others—either family members or neighbors—would join us. In the course of the evening, the conversation would typically segue into a discussion about the politics of the Occupation. The groups invariably included a college-educated worker, since almost every factory had a graduate or two in its workforce. Rashid, one of the union's founders, who had grown disillusioned by its impotence, was a participant in one of the more lively sessions. "I know the labor laws and am not satisfied with what the union does, these days it is mostly associated with handouts of flour and other food staples." He acknowledged that, in a single-industry town like Beit Fajjar, the "owners are always going to be very powerful" but insisted that "they are still allowed to get away with too much." According to him, those violations included failing to pay wages on time or to abide by agreements about pay rates, forcing workers to waive end-of-service benefits, and bribing the factory inspectors to issue clean bills of health. "The protective clothing gets handed out," he reported, "on the one day of the year when the inspector visits." Rashid had worked in several different factories and claimed that employees routinely asked for face masks, only to be denied. As for grievances, he advised that "you can get further if you go to the Bethlehem union office than to the Beit Fajjar union officials, who are too friendly with the owners, but, in the end, lodging a claim will cost you a lot of legal fees."

Other workers in the room deferred to his informed opinion on such matters, and, since he came from a refugee family, they expected him to be more militant. But everyone had something to say about the workplace hazards. "It is just not healthy to work or even live here, everything is covered with the dust" remarked one of them, "and I have heard of studies showing higher levels of cancer in Beit Fajjar." Another claimed that he also knew of such studies, but expressed the view that "there is no proof about the causal connection between the disease and the conditions." Besides, "cancer is only for old people, and they have not been able to connect it to places these people have worked." A medical intern at Bethlehem's Beit Jala hospital told me that, in his estimate, 80 percent or more of their patients were either from Beit Fajjar or the two other stone-producing towns in the area, a ratio far out of proportion to the area's population distribution. In his experience, blood cancers, kidney diseases, pneumonia, and other pulmonary ailments were prevalent among these patients, though the hospital itself kept no systematic records. "It is a sensitive topic at the hospital," he confided, while acknowledging that the occupational health hazards of working with stone had been thoroughly researched and were largely avoidable through appropriate protection.

While the workers I interviewed that night did not deny that they often found the protective gear too uncomfortable to wear, there was a consensus that the owners should be providing it and that it was their responsibility to insist that workers wear the gear. The oldest man in the room aimed at a higher target, blaming the PA for "not valuing the lives of ordinary Palestinians—they only want to stay in power and make profits for their friends." After that the talk turned to politics, and, as elsewhere, contempt for the PA ran almost as strong as the anti-Zionist sentiment. Notwithstanding the anger directed at Israeli policies, no one was prepared to express remorse about producing for the occupier. "I am not paid enough to accept this burden of guilt," Rashid insisted. "That is for the owners to live with. I am proud of my work and of the Palestinian stone products, but have no feelings beyond that."

While they had no interest in sharing the presumed shame of their bosses, they were acutely aware of the profitability to owners of different markets, because it directly affected their own employability. Kamal, whom I interviewed the following evening, explained the industry's tripartite structure: "the top-level companies produce for Israelis and for overseas export, the mid-level ones for Israelis and the Palestinian market, and the bottom-level are the most labor-intensive and underautomated, selling only to Palestinians." Stone extraction and fabrication is increasingly capital-intensive, dependent on advanced machinery, and he knew that Palestinians who could not muster the investment were competing solely on the cost of his labor. He himself was a hand carver—"I am the Michelangelo of Beit Fajjar," he declared—and so he aimed for employment in the middle-level firms. Regular work was never assured, and the pay was better at the top level, but he knew his niche. "Word gets around town when openings are available and who is paying better," he reported. "If an owner is not paying on time or treating employees badly, everyone hears about it. But we also know which companies are losing money, because we have to be aware of such things." In this regard, the union's formal structure was no match for the informal network of hearsay and information sharing.

Of course, the owners have their own version of pooled data, some of it useful for competing against one another, or another village, but also for knowing how and when to act in their common interest. In Beit Fajjar, there is no middle layer of information. In that regard I found it to be a precorporate industrial landscape, where the owners' villas command the high ground, a world apart from the workers' self-built houses beneath, but where the fortunes and livelihoods of all are intimately connected. And since the underfunded municipality is unable to collect taxes or fees from the owners it cannot offer much of an alternative in the way of public amenities and resources. As Hamed, the union president, put it, "this is a town of rich and poor, there is no middle class."

Efficiency or Rights?

The Palestinian Federation of Industries' 2005 report on the stone and marble industry included a long list of recommendations, many of them aimed at integrating the needs of the hundreds of family businesses in order to boost the overall health of the sector. Management, even in the smaller, maverick outfits, should be more professionalized, existing stone resources should be surveyed and assessed to reduce duplication and waste, and every institution with a stake in the industry—government ministries, the owners association (USM), vocational associations, universities, banks, and investor groups—should cooperate more in realizing these goals. The report advised USM to set up a multipurpose research and service center for the entire sector (to showcase products, train employees, and conduct surveys for the general benefit of members) as well as a single Palestinian marketing company to promote the region's brand overseas.

Scattered among the recommendations was some language about stronger implementation of labor laws and environmental regulations. But the concerns expressed were directed less at worker protection than at industrial efficiency. For example, the report commended the productivity of stone sector employees relative to the domestic workforce; "average annual sales per employee" was estimated at "approximately $27,000, which is five times more than that of the average productivity per employee across all industries in Palestine." But the same performance was far below internationally competitive levels; according to the report, the "productivity of the Palestinian worker is still only 10 percent of that of an Italian worker," due to factors like underequipped machinery, poor safety standards, and lack of worker incentives and on-the-job training. In other words, the authors were seeing workers' quality of work life through the lens of manpower capacity and not from the standpoint of their welfare.

Most of the report's recommendations had not borne fruit, though by 2017, the USM had settled on the name for a regional trade brand—"Palestinian Stone–Jerusalem"—which members were encouraged to use. So, too, the proposal for a research and service center was realized when the Palestine Polytechnic University in Hebron launched the Palestinian Stone and Marble Center in 2009. In partnership with the USM and Ministry of National Economy, and funded in part by government agencies in Italy (the stone industry's leading global producer) and the United Nations Industrial Development Organization, the center had set up a vocational program to train students in specialized skills and careers relevant to the industry. It soon boasted a research arm and offered consulting services and a laboratory to test the quality of stone samples. The center's initial survey of the industry showed that there were 605 factories, 252 quarries, 50 crushers, and 280 workshops operating in the West Bank, and that they were producing as many as 100 different stone types and colors.

Jawad Alhaj, the center's director at the time of my visit, was an ex-employee of Nassar, the industry's leading firm, and so he was well-versed in all commercial and technical aspects of production. Though training and placing students was the center's main purpose, he emphasized that one of its primary research goals was to make the industry more environmentally efficient. The industrial process already includes utilization of factory by-product, ground down by crushers into aggregate for concrete, cement, and asphalt, but there is still a good deal of waste in the throughput, especially in the disposal of stone slurry. Globally, the industry generates as much as one ton of waste for every 2.5 tons of stone product. Some of the West Bank's most beautiful highlands and agricultural resources are marred by open pits and vast mounds of waste material, while many of its municipal wastewater lines are routinely clogged by slurry.[26]

Very few of the spent quarries have been rehabilitated for public use—as parks, swimming pools, wildlife preserves, open-air theaters, malls, and residence complexes—an industry practice more common in Europe and North America.[27] Indeed, Alhaj saw "a potential boom in employment opportunities for graduates who could work in recycling, restoration, and waste management." But, in his opinion, the PA would first have to more clearly communicate that environmental protection was a priority. Currently, the only real penalties for excess pollution are being issued not by the PA but by the Israeli authorities, in the form of tax revenue deductions as a penalty for contaminated wastewater that finds its way through rivers and streams inside the Green Line.[28]

Alhaj's faculty colleague, Nabil Al-Joulani, who had helped to draft industrial regulations for the Ministry of Environment, told me he was saddened by the poor implementation of safety standards in the industry's workplaces. "The factory owners should be holding mandatory workshops," he asserted, "and they should be providing masks, at least three per day." Unlike ministry officials and factory managers with whom I spoke previously, he placed no blame on the "mentality" of the workers; "they are very needy people, not well-informed, and they have to take work where they can find it." At the center, Joulani's research was focused on the recycling of stone slurry into new products, especially bricks for use in construction. The West Bank's stone factories generate more than a million tons of slurry waste annually, and it is typically disposed of in open, underpopulated areas, degrading the air and contaminating flora, fauna, and soil, along with surface and ground water.[29] Heavy metals in the slurry are not soluble in water, and the smaller firms, with fewer resources for disposal, simply flush the waste into sewage networks. "Recycling this sludge," he told me, "is the biggest environmental challenge for the industry, and if we succeed we can make our own concrete."

Joulani lamented that he did not have a high-tech research lab at his disposal. "I used my own sugar grinder in the kitchen," he recalled, "to grind down the sludge filter cake into fine powder for compression into bricks." He wanted to prove that this stony dust could be used as an industrial substitute for the sand ingredient in concrete by applying the result to ready-mix product, but, for the time being, he was focused on making the bricks. Joulani insisted that the compressive strength of his handmade bricks was comparable to that of a typical concrete block, and that they were more resistant to acid attacks and less water-absorbent. In the center's first commercial offshoot, his bricks were being fabricated in a production line of a Hebron firm. But even if Joulani's bricks did not catch on, there is a growing commercial market for the use of slurry waste in ready-mix concrete. Because of the restrictions on building outside of Area A and B, the trend in vertical building is likely to continue, and so, in those locations, ready-mix is more practical than concrete that is mixed and cast on site. There are already more than sixty ready-mix facilities in the West Bank and they could surely save money and resources by using the stone dust.

But they would still not be self-sufficient in the use of local materials because concrete production depends on cement, and Palestinians have none of their own. In recent years, the dependence on Israeli cement imports, almost 90 percent of which came from the Nesher monopoly, has become an urgent concern. In 2007, after Hamas assumed power in Gaza (which hosts many sand-quarrying operations), Israeli authorities banned the import of cement, gravel, and other building materials on the basis that they could be used for belligerent purposes. The ban, which grievously hampered reconstruction efforts after the widespread devastation of the 2012 attack on Gaza, was only lifted in 2016. But the lesson was clear enough. Palestinians use more than 2.2 million tons of cement annually (1.7 million in the West Bank alone), they need it for housing and for the rentier wealth that housing generates, and so they can ill-afford to have this strategic resource be withheld by the occupying power.

Cement in the Wilderness

I n 2014, Israel's Antitrust Commission took steps to break up Nesher's official monopoly, requiring the company to sell off its Har Tuv plant that produced 30 percent of the country's cement. The conglomerate was no longer in a position to take full advantage of the Palestinian market exclusively handed to the company by the 1994 Paris Protocol; until recently, more than 20 percent of Nesher's annual production had been sold to the PA's marketing company for distribution in the Occupied Territories. To make up for the shortfall in supply, the PA decided that Palestinians would finally have their own cement plant, and that it should be a national-level priority to build one. Influenced by Theodor Herzl, Zionist settlers had pressed hard on the nation-building need for a cement plant of their own, realized in the establishment of Nesher in 1923. A similar, though long-deferred, moment seemed to have finally arrived for the Palestinians. Or had it? Economists in the orbit of the PA were not so easily persuaded. Responding to the economic prospects for the proposed Palestine Cement Factory (PCF), Samir Hazboun explained that "the cost of processing the clinker and absorbing the high energy and logistics bills might be too high a price to pay" simply to have Made in Palestine stamped on the cement bags. "From a Ricardian perspective," he added, "it might be cheaper just to import cement from Turkey, Jordan, and Israel. We damage ourselves economically if we only do things for nationalist reasons." Business owners in the construction industry also voiced skepticism about whether the PCF would deliver prices low enough to undercut the imports.[30]

In this case, however, the PA's nationalist sentiment seemed to be running high—the provision of cement "without interruption" had to be guaranteed—and so the Palestine Investment Fund (PIF) subsidiary, Sanad Construction Resources, which already handled the Nesher cement imports, was green-lighted to launch the top-level PCF project. At the launch ceremony in October 2016, in Bethlehem's Jacir Palace Hotel, with PA president Mahmoud Abbas at his side, PIF chair Mohammad Mustafa made an ambitious declaration: "This mega national project, alongside the accumulated achievements that the PIF has realized, are vital steps towards freeing the Palestinian economy from the Israeli economic hegemony; and once realized, it would be a key contributor to the establishment of Palestinian statehood, and thus the advancement of the two states solution."

Sanad's first effort to locate a feasible site, east of Tulkarm, had run aground the previous year. Residents near the proposed location strongly objected to the health hazards posed by the facility. A new site was found in a more remote location in the al-Bariya desert wilderness southeast of Bethlehem, and the PIF secured an area of 3.3 square kilometers to host the plant. Since the site would be more than the required four kilometers from the nearest residential home, and, since the prevailing wind blew away from those residents, the PA's Environment Quality Authority had approved the plan. But support from the local residents—members of al-Rashaida, a Bedouin community with a deep attachment to their desert lands—was a much tougher proposition. Aside from tending to their livestock (large herds of camels, sheep, and goats), the Bedouin catered to eco-tourists, helping them camp out in the pristine lands of the 172 square kilometer al-Kanub Nature Reserve, which borders their village of 'Arab al-Rashaida. Any visitor can see how intrusive a huge industrial plant would be amidst the stunningly beautiful Rashaida territory, which stretches over fifteen kilometers of the desert's eroded plateaux and wadis all the way to a curtain of cliffs overlooking the Dead Sea.

The Rashaida are dispersed all across the Middle East, from Jordan to Sudan, but the West Bank groupings have been displaced by Israeli authorities on several occasions, most notably after a large, long-standing encampment was evicted during the *Nakba* from Ein Gedi Springs, on the shores of the Dead Sea. In recent years, Israeli authorities served several different Bedouin groups in the region (from the Jahalin, Kaabna, and Rashaida tribes) with eviction notices as they tried to move forward with settlement plans for the highly contested E1 area, east of Jerusalem. In the south, many more are threatened with eviction as part of a decades-long effort to

Photo by author

Village of 'Arab al-Rashaida, al-Bariya desert.

ethnically cleanse the Negev (*Naqab*) desert. Though many of them have long given up their nomadic lifestyles in favor of settlement, the traditionally nonurbanized Bedouin still use large expanses of Area C land for herding purposes. Israeli policies of forcible transfer are aimed at squeezing their numbers into compact townships with limited space to graze their livestock.

'Arab al-Rashaida is one such township, and it borders the proposed PCF site. When its residents learned of the plans, their ever-present fears about relocation by the Israelis were sharpened by resentment about being chosen by the PA to host an industrial facility that directly threatens their livelihoods through its pollution of the grazing lands. Community members blocked surveyors from approaching the proposed PCF site, and the town council mobilized opposition to the project. By the time I visited 'Arab al-Rashaida in January 2017, both sides had dug in. The PA's governor of Bethlehem had recently fired and replaced the dissident chairman of the council, but his allies subsequently resigned and formed an alternative People's Community Committee. Careful not to present their opposition to the project as unpatriotic, Ahmed Rashaida, a committee representative, affirmed: "We are not against promoting Palestinian investments." On the contrary, he pointed out, the national interest would be adversely affected by the PCF plan because the Bedouin played a vital role in supplying regional food markets. "According to the statistics of the Ministry of Agriculture," Ahmed explained, "the 'Arab al-Rashaida area includes one third of livestock in Palestine. A cement factory would threaten their existence as it will be built on a natural reserve, comprising water wells that we use in grazing livestock."[31]

PA officials initially dismissed the community's claims and reaffirmed that the plant would be sited beyond the regulation distance from the village. Technically, this would make it compliant, but the nearest place of Rashaida residence was actually much closer—an encampment of tents and shacks built out of walls of a valley and inhabited by several extended families. These families have houses in the township but prefer to live more in the open, where there is ample room for grazing. Their original encampment had been

Photo by author

Talab al-Rashaida, in his family tent.

demolished by Israeli forces as punishment for smuggling guns across the Dead Sea from Jordan during the al-Aqsa intifada, but the families had moved back because they found that township life was stifling. Talab, one of the elders in the camp, said that there was another reason: "we really feared that Israeli forces would seize the land, even though we have been here for centuries and have Ottoman and British land titles." Under the Oslo agreement, he explained, "the Rashaida land was divided into three parts: an Israeli Nature Reserve in Ein Gedi, a large military zone, and we were left with a much smaller portion for our sheep and goats to graze." Talab insisted that his family would not budge—"not even if we were offered a lot of money"—pointing out that "it would be much easier to move the factory site than my people."

Wouldn't they be able to bargain for good jobs in the plant? "That's not Bedouin work," he responded. "Maybe workers will come from Bethlehem or even from Nablus, but I doubt that anyone here would sign up." Moreover, once the polluting plant was there, he reckoned that other dirty industrial facilities would surely follow. Indeed, the road that led to their village already hosted a new landfill at al-Minya as part of the World Bank-sponsored Southern West Bank Solid

Waste Management Project. Serving thirty-three municipalities, and replacing thirty of the region's random dump sites, the landfill was beginning to generate its share of heavy traffic. In the years to come, many more trucks would be trundling out of the proposed cement factory. The small rural road would quickly become a busy thoroughfare, pumping out diesel fumes and blighting this fragile desert landscape. Over the years, Israel authorities designated the Negev's "concentration towns" (created for displaced Bedouins after the *Nakba*) as locations for hazardous waste or noxious industry.[32] The PA seemed to be on the verge of replicating a similar pattern of environmental injustice against a poor, minority population.

Israeli approval for the PCF had also drawn suspicion. "Maybe it does have something to do with logistics," Talab conceded, "but the fact is that the PA's investors are also putting a lot of money into this, and of course there must be some secret agreement with the Israelis—why else would they allow a cement factory in Palestine?" In their minds, there was little reason to trust either of the two national authorities. Rima Abboud, a Bethlehem-based activist with ties to the Rashaida community, was more skeptical by far. She suggested that the plant was simply part of Nesher's strategy to circumvent the antitrust decision by relocating production across the Green Line. "Not for the first time," she mused, "a company had found that the Occupation was a convenient way to avoid Israeli law by outsourcing to the West Bank. Naturally, the PA leadership was also profiting from the arrangement."

The Rashaida, whom I visited with some Bethlehem University students, were more focused on showing us how their lands, and their own landed rights, would be affected by the planned facility. After lunch in the encampment's big tent, we packed ourselves into a beat-up van and headed east, over dry desert stream beds and craggy rock trails, to the steep escarpment above the Dead Sea, which marks the limits of the Rashaida claims. Directly below, by the water side, was their ancestral domain, now forbidden to them. As we took in the breathtaking view, no commentary about this lost paradise was needed, either from Talab or any of our party.

Why was this face-off in the desert so noteworthy? It would be

Photo by author

Looking down on former Rashaida lands by the Dead Sea.

too banal to conclude that the Rashaida, as members of the most vulnerable population in the Occupied Territories, were standing up for values that could not be bought or traded. After all, they were basically defending their livelihoods and their lands against perceived and real threats. As refugees in the past, and quite possibly in the future too, they had earned the moral right to show some grit. Nor was the apparent conflict between their own pastoral "land ethic" and one reliant on industrial growth anything like a straightforward clash. However marginal their pastoral lifestyle, the livestock they tend are essential to urban food markets. Bedouin herding, traditionally associated with the *Negev/Naqab*, has high symbolic value for Palestinians, like the tending of olive trees or stonemasonry, and, in common with these others, it is an important supplier of livelihoods.

The economic decisions that Palestinians have to make under the boot of the Occupation regularly pit industrial interests against agricultural ones, and there is often little room to factor in environmental outcomes: for example, officials often have to weigh the potential production revenue between olive trees and stone quarries in deciding whether to grant licenses to extract in Area B.[33] Here, in a part of Area C, a similar cost accounting was being played out with the herders of the al-Bariya desert. Whatever the outcome (and, at the time of writing, I heard rumors that the authorities were considering another site near Jericho), the cement in question is nothing if not a highly political product. Because it is a material needed for constructing new Palestinian facts on the ground, and for housing an exploding population with one of the highest birth rates in the world, control over its production gives it a national significance far beyond its market value.

The Israeli decision to green-light the plant on Area C land, at a time when stone quarrying was prohibited in such areas, had been met with cynicism, for obvious reasons. But what about the likely environmental harms from the planned facility? Palestinian stone producers, operating in survival mode and in a position of dependency on Israeli buyers, are already lagging far behind the international curve of achieving a measure of sustainability within the industry. Domestic regulation is light, and so West Bank extractors have few incentives to meet their obligations to worker safety and to environmental security. The result is a ravaged landscape and a sickened workforce, all in the cause of utilizing Palestinians' most precious natural resource for the building of the Zionist "national home."

Bedouins faced with eviction can often arouse strong public sympathy. Yet the Rashaida herders I talked to complained of a blackout in the Palestinian media. Ironically, they had found an unlikely source of support from Jewish settlements in the locality. The leadership of the Gush Etzion Regional Council had met with 'Arab al-Rashaida council members and made common cause over concerns about environmental damage to the regional ecosystem, or "the Judaean Desert," as the Israeli press typically described it.[34] The Gush Etzion bloc, which contains twenty-two settlements and more than 70,000 colonists, straddles the Bethlehem–Hebron road and has been in a state of near continuous expansion since its Kfar Etzion core was established as 1967 as the first Jewish settlement on the West Bank. Israeli plans are under way to expropriate areas to the north and northeast. That land grab will make the bloc contiguous with the Green Line and allow its territory to expand to the outskirts of Bethlehem itself. Under these circumstances, it is difficult not to see the settlers' concern for the environment as something other than disinterested. In the imagined geography of Greater Jerusalem, the city boundaries extend to embrace their houses, and so they already see the Rashaida land to the east as their future recreational backyard.

There are other plans for these desert lands, however. As part of the Palestinian effort to protect its cultural heritage from Israeli seizure and settlement, the PA nominated al-Bariya wilderness in 2012 as a UNESCO World Heritage Site. The case was supported by several justifications: extensive archeological evidence of pre-historic habitation; worldwide identification with Jesus, who joined the eremitic tradition in the desert, generating a cluster of import-ant monasteries in the region; the legacy of the Herodion fortress, outside Bethlehem; the region's unique geological formation and bio-geographic location as a world-renowned site of breeding and migration for birds; and, more generally, its historical significance as a place of refuge from civilization.[35]

As with other Palestinian nominations, the UNESCO protection of al-Bariya would hamper Zionist goals, in this case not just to annex the entire Gush Etzion bloc but also to establish a cross-desert road to the Dead Sea. Considerable Israeli funding is already being used to develop tourism in the area, especially around the Herodion and related archeological sites. Planners curate these investments exclusively to highlight the area's links to ancient Jewish history and to consolidate the Israeli claim to sovereignty over it. By contrast with the Zionist representation of the territory as a proprietary part of the once and future Land of Israel, the UNESCO nomination pointedly made reference to an *inclusive* heritage, ranging across the entire history of habitation, from Paleolithic times through the Hellenistic, Roman, Byzantine, and Ottoman eras.[36]

5

Human Gold

I've been building homes every day over there for thirty years. In a way, it's really my country too, isn't it?

—West Bank worker at Israeli checkpoint

In the course of reporting for this book, I met many Palestinians who struggled to describe how they felt about working for "the occupier." Whether they were employed in Israel, or in the West Bank settlements, they knew all too well that they were being compelled to build a settler state on land seized from their own people. The emotional sting of that quandary was bad enough, but consider what goes through the mind of those who went further and helped build the Separation Wall itself. Most of them must have judged that putting food on their family's table outweighed everything else, even the shame that might sour the conversation around that table.

During a visit to a refugee camp that was dominated on one side by the separation barrier, I sat down with someone who had worked on a section of the Wall not far from his home. Samir and I met in a friend's house, and, as word got around, others dropped by to join in the discussion, including close relatives. It was not an ideal setting for him to tell his story, but the dialogue with others in the room more than made up for the lack of privacy. Samir's family were refugees from a village not far across the Green Line, and he recounted how he had saved enough money from working in Israel to buy some land near the camp, only to find out that it lay in the path of the Wall's planned route. "I had learned a lot about construction in Israel," he said, "so I started to build my own house, but then I had to watch it being destroyed by soldiers to make way for the Wall, and after that we had to live in tents." Jailed during the al-Aqsa intifada, he was subsequently denied an Israeli work permit. "I did not have much work, and because I also wanted revenge for the demolition, I took the job on the Wall through a friend in Jerusalem, so that I could take back what had been stolen from me." Samir was referring to building materials that he pilfered from the building site and either gave away or sold. "I was a good thief," he reported, "I took steel, wood, cables, and other things." He admitted to his share of remorse about taking the job, but not about the theft itself.

His friend Omar had done whatever he could to amp up Samir's guilt. "Every day the youth of the camp came and threw stones at us," recounted Samir, "and Omar was with them." By then, Omar had joined us in the room, and, although he was in a congenial mood, he wanted to make his friend relive the disgrace. "I think he betrayed us," he insisted, "and when I was throwing the stones, I really wanted to kill him." Had he forgiven his friend? "Not really. He was a traitor, but we are still friends." Samir recalled that many of his co-workers were Israeli Palestinians and that they wore baseball caps and sunglasses to conceal their identity. No doubt, the contractors found it convenient to have Arab workers on the frontline, perhaps as human shields to deflect, or absorb, any physical protests. By contrast, the managerial and security personnel, Russian Jews mostly, were issued bulletproof vests and helmets.

With his friend's rebuke still hanging in the air, Samir had a chance to redeem himself, and he took it. "If I had the choice again, I would not do it," he confessed. "I was driven by revenge, but that was a bad reason, because I helped put my people in a prison." That said, he clung to the notion that the entire infrastructure of the Occupation could one day be demolished, a fantasy shared by many of my interviewees: "I learned how to build that Wall, so I also know how to take it down, and I have earned the right to do so." One of the cousins in the room came to his defense. "He had no income, and we are poor people, so what choices do we have?" "Besides," he continued, "Samir gets a lot of respect in this camp for his skill as a peace-maker, resolving disputes between others, so it was a little easier for people to forgive him." The Separation Wall was another matter; "every day it is there as an act of violence," commented Omar, "and yet somehow we are seen as the violent ones?"

Far from an inert barrier that separates two populations (its route through the West Bank actually encircles several Palestinian towns), the Separation Wall is more like an active force field with many functions. The Israeli military uses it for population surveillance and as a base for raids and strike operations; it harbors checkpoints for containing traffic and controlling or harassing border crossers; and its implacable presence has all but erased the Green Line, increasingly regarded by the Israeli leadership as a political boundary of the past (and often scorned as an "Auschwitz border") with no enduring legitimacy.[1] Indeed, the projected 700-kilometer length is more than twice as long as the Green Line. The *seam zone* between the Green Line and the Separation Wall, which officially "protects" hundreds of thousands of settlers while stranding many Palestinian communities within it, was created as part of an ongoing land grab (9.4 percent of the West Bank's land mass) that started in 2002. Fertile farmland and vital water wells belonging to Palestinian villages on the east side of the Wall are no longer easily accessible and are at risk of being converted into "state land" by Israel under the 1858 Ottoman law of underutilization (*makhlul*) that authorized seizure of land if it had not been cultivated for three years. Israeli authorities expediently renewed this law after the *Nakba*, and, in October 1948, the Fallow Lands emergency regulations (preceding the more comprehensive 1950 Absentees Property Law) helped to legalize possession of "absentee" lands from which Palestinian owners had been expelled. Seventy years later, the "state of emergency" is still officially in effect.

The borderline between Israel and the Occupied Territories does not appear on any Israeli map. In common with other settler colonial enterprises, military authorities alter at will the exact geographical status of Israel's "frontier" zone. By contrast with the Separation

Wall's unsanctioned status, Israel does have a sovereign exclusion boundary—currently under construction on a 200-mile zone of its southern border with Egypt—to block the flow of asylum-seeking refugees and their traffickers, along with other non-nationals. But to all intents and purposes, the "real" border with Palestine is defined by the mesh of bypass roads, flying checkpoints (numbering in the hundreds), military stations, fresh settler outposts, and other forms of mobile infrastructure in Area C of the West Bank. This ever more invasive perimeter has an optional terrestrial shape on any given day. For settlers themselves, the only bounded limit to their armed roving is marked by the warning red signs at the edge of the Palestinian Authority (PA)–controlled cities of Area A—"Entrance for Israeli Citizens Is Forbidden, Dangerous to Your Lives, and Is Against the Israeli Law"—and, of course, this advisory does not apply to soldiers, who conduct raids at will.

While it is officially regarded as "movable" and "temporary," the Wall (built by more than fifty major construction firms and 700 different subcontractors as part of the most expensive public works project in Israel's history) has a hard-nosed presence that echoes the mid-century Brutalist cult of Hebrew concrete. Although the International Court of Justice ruled in 2004 that it was illegal, the Wall has become normalized, in line with the intended policy of "facts on the ground," and so it no longer generates outrage in the way that new settlements do. Its concrete parts are pieced together from precast panels (three meters wide and up to eight meters high), and the smooth surface—ostensibly to prevent climbers from gaining traction—is an inviting canvas on which to fashion slogans, graffiti, and some of the world's most poignant political murals. These include several signature works by British artist Banksy, whose Walled Off Hotel in Bethlehem offers guests the in-house amenity of stenciling their statement of choice over the closest section. Visitors (who can pay up to $1,000 a night for the presidential suite) can access the hotel's small Museum of the Occupation, which hosts artifacts and relics from street clashes with soldiers, and, if they take a walk around the block at the right time (usually after Friday prayers), they can witness the clashes themselves.

Despite its official *raison d'être* as a security measure, the Separation Wall does not really stop Palestinians from crossing it. Tens of thousands without a work permit whose labor is so critical to the Israeli construction industry go across on a regular basis, typically with the help of fixers on the other side. They go over by ladder or through holes in the concrete sections, or they sneak through the no-go firing zones, military roads, ditches, razor wire barricades, and electric fencing that make up the majority of its length. Border barriers all over the world facilitate the exploitation of cheap and vulnerable workers, and those that straddle unequal labor markets are always highly porous in practice: it is often said of the United States–Mexico border fence that the only thing it does not stop are humans.

Surrounded

Every new Israeli settlement insists on its own security zone, often extending to several hundred meters on all sides. These are the buffer belts, typically patrolled by armed personnel or volunteers, through which Palestinian workers with permits have to pass every day. Like the commuter flow across the Green Line, thousands without permits slip in, at some risk to their lives. For residents of villages surrounded by ever-expanding settlement blocs, employment inside these colonies is often their only option, especially if their access to work elsewhere in the West Bank or in Israel is obstructed by road closures and checkpoint delays. Men as young as eighteen years can obtain settlement work permits, whereas the permits to work inside the Green Line require holders to be at least twenty-two years old and married. (Anyone with a family member who has been arrested or injured by Israeli soldiers is blacklisted, the former for security reasons, the latter for being a "potential avenger.") There has never been a clampdown on settlement permits, and the announcement of new construction generates the expectation of more of these jobs, however odious.

In Husan, a village of almost 7,000 that abuts the Green Line several kilometers to the southwest of Bethlehem, I was told that almost every household sent at least one family member to work in the surrounding colonies. One of these settlements, the second largest in the West Bank, is Beitar Illit, a small city of 43,000 ultra-Orthodox Jews, built on Husan's land, steadily confiscated since 1985. The theft is ongoing, as is the demolition of their homes in Area C parcels where Husan residents are forced to move due to overcrowding in the village core. Since Beitar Illit's *haredi* residents shun employment, there is no shortage of work for outsiders. But workers from Husan cannot earn a decent wage there because these ultra-Orthodox populations are relatively poor (many West Bank settlers are economic refugees from Israel's housing market and they co-exist, sometimes uneasily, with national-religious zealots).

Better pay is on offer in the settlements just to the south where the Gush Etzion bloc lies. That is why residents like Amir, who grew up in Aida Camp and moved out to Husan when he married, prefers to work there. Unlike some of his neighbors who put in long days (sixteen hours door-to-door is not uncommon) crossing over to construction sites in Tel Aviv and Jerusalem, it was relatively simple for him to pass through the checkpoint that led to his settlement workplace. But getting there might cost him his life. I interviewed him during the "knife intifada," when armed settlers and soldiers were stationed around the traffic circle he had to cross en route. "If you get close to a settler they will shoot you," he reported, "and they decide when and why that will happen. I honestly do not know if I am coming home when I leave in the morning." Just the week before I interviewed him, soldiers killed three youths from the neighboring village of Sa'ir at the same Gush Etzion traffic circle and gunned down a fourth, allegedly a stabber fixed on revenge for their deaths, whom settlers allowed to bleed to death. "I force myself to go there," he added. "I am disgusted at myself, and I want no relationship with any settler, but my family needs to eat."

In a series of cluster interviews in Husan, where family, relatives, and neighbors joined the conversation over the course of several evenings, I learned how dependent the village had become on their settler neighbors who are intent on taking their land. (There are only 7,000 dunums left of the 12,000 that once belonged to Husan.)

According to Salim, a tiler in his late fifties who had been working inside the Green Line since 1978, "the work they offer us is supposed to be a benefit we get from the existence of their settlement, or maybe it is a compensation for our losses. At least this is the way it is presented, or else it is designed to be this way," he explained, adding that "you are supposed to have a permit to work there, but many don't, and that encourages the settlers to think they can pay you less, or try to cheat you, even of your back pay."

Nor was employment in the settlements less risky than working in Israel; of the reported instances of physical coercion against Palestinians, and exposure to toxic substances, the highest rates were among settlement workers.[2] According to the son of Salim's neighbor, a college graduate who had completed a two-year work stint in the Gush Etzion bloc, the threat of violence was omnipresent: "You cannot walk alone on the street, you always have to be in a car or near a security guard" because of settler distrust and hostility. "Children scream when they see you," he added, "because they are taught to be afraid, women never speak to you, and the contractor warns you not to make sudden movements." He had just been approved for his first Green Line permit, and was happy to see the back of "people who treated me like an animal—I felt like I was working in a prison." His brother, who had studied law in college, was unmarried and unemployed. "I cannot bring myself to work in a settlement," he declared, though without any bluster, "it's a personal principle, and besides, it would disgust me physically to do it."

Their father, an electrician who wired new Beitar Illit houses, said he had a good relationship with a former Jewish employer who used to come and visit him in Husan. He acknowledged that this kind of cordiality was rare. But in the village's retail core, goodwill appeared to be the currency of business as usual. Yellow Israeli license plates were a common sight in Husan, since Beitar Illit residents flocked to the village to take advantage of the "Arab prices" of everything from eggs to construction materials and auto repairs (25–50 percent lower than in the settlement or in Israel). As one *haredi* shopper tellingly commented to a reporter, "Don't make a mistake, I'm not a left-winger. I'm right-wing, even extreme, but cheap is cheap."[3]

Amiability in retail transactions was easier to stomach, but the settlement workplace was another matter. Badi, a builder who said he was lucky to bring home 110 shekels a day (more like a Palestinian wage than an Israeli one), reported that "settlers are openly disrespectful to us, one of them called me a donkey, which is quite racist. I really wanted to hit him and then just walk out, but I could not, I needed the money badly." Badi admitted that he talked about such feelings with other male friends—"it's therapeutic"—but he found it painful to describe to me how, on another occasion, a settler asked him to work on a house being constructed on land stolen from his own family. "My father and grandfather built houses, and that's what I really like doing, but this was too much. I could not do it." He had found his elastic limit, but there was a comeback. "I have a fantasy," he confessed, "of blowing up that house with dynamite. Every free man or woman in Palestine has the same fantasy."

The next day, I heard a more poignant story from Mohammed, a middle-aged worker from nearby Nahalin, who was helping to build a new house for his brother on his day off: "On one occasion, I was asked to renovate an old Palestinian house for an Israeli owner who wanted to preserve the antique exterior but modernize the inside." His strong repulsion for the job made it difficult to concentrate on the work, but then he overheard a conversation between the owner and his son: "He was telling the son that his grandfather had built the house originally, and I cried when I heard that." Like many others I interviewed, Mohammed made no distinction between towns inside Israel and colonies in the West Bank—"to me, they are all settlements." He also admitted that he and other work mates employed by settlers sometimes indulged in small acts of sabotage on the job: poorly mixed cement, adulterated paint, leaky drainage pipes.

More public displays of resistance were reserved for the villagers' responses to land seizures. Aware of the Israeli intention to create territorial contiguity between the Green Line and the Gush Etzion bloc, Husan residents mobilized in large numbers in 2014 to try to block a 1,000 acre land grab. The town saw weeks of protests, reprisals, and not a few prison sentences for those who participated. In some individual cases, the authorities offered compensation for land parcels, but because of the stigma attached to selling to settlers, several owners refused to take the money. Yet stories circulate in every village like Husan about those who had sold and pocketed the proceeds. As land prices have risen, the rewards are sizable, and the penalties—loss of respect from neighbors—are not so harsh. Others are cheated by overseas relatives who try to cash in by selling a fake, or incomplete, land title.

"Our village is almost cut off on three sides," the host of one of our cluster sessions pointed out. "They cut down our olive trees, take our dunums, and now we live here in a state of siege." I asked him whether the settlers would eventually take over the village. "Yes, maybe," he replied, but he didn't like the question, and others wondered why I would ask it. It was bad manners to even raise the prospect, and I apologized, moving on to the topic of the Occupation, which was guaranteed to spark a lively discussion. As in most conversations with workers about politics, I found that no one spoke up for the "two-state solution," and any talk of the "peace process" was roundly dismissed. "All we got from 'peace' so far is to watch our land being stolen," snorted the host. "But talking about one state is important for us because it means never giving up on our right to return to '48," he explained, using a preferred Palestinian term for Israel. His brother, who arrived late from working inside the Green Line, was not so sure about the single state—"a chicken and a turkey," he grinned, "cannot live in the same cage"—but he was no advocate of the status quo or of "any plan that involves the thieves of the Palestinian Authority."

Husan is one of many Palestinian villages where residents have little choice but to take employment from settlers who have stolen their land and bulldozed their orchards and homes. By one estimate, 11 percent of Palestinians employed on Israeli settlements are working on land formerly owned by them.[4] Historically, colonialism forced occupied populations into the most humiliating forms of compliance, but the psychology of this particular dilemma—we must build the houses of those who are demolishing ours—is especially perverse. Husan's state of siege is shared by many towns that lie within the imagined orbit of Greater Jerusalem, but the threat of being downsized, surrounded, or cut off hangs over any West Bank village located near settlers bent on increasing their holdings.

On my first visit to Nablus, in 2015, the film crew I was assisting went to cover one of the most grievous and long-running sieges, in the village of Kafr Qaddum, thirteen kilometers to the east of the city. Israeli forces had closed off the road from the village to Nablus since 2003, ostensibly to protect the ever-expanding nearby settlement of Kedumim. The roadblock had decimated the village economy by corralling the 3,500 residents and shunting all traffic in and out of town to a rocky, looping track over the mountains. Villagers' resistance to the siege had stepped up since 2011, and it usually took the form of nonviolent demonstrations every Friday after the midday prayer. Soldiers advanced into the town to subdue the protesters, routinely deploying rubber bullets (often steel-coated), sound bombs, tear gas, and skunkwater cannons. The record of casualties and arrests was long and gruesome.

Our film crew set up cameras in the centrally located home of the head of the Popular Committee. The house had a frontline vantage point on the clashes between stone-throwing youth and soldiers. Aware of our presence, advancing snipers selected his home as a potential target, and, eventually, an armored vehicle used its tank gun to spray us with skunkwater, a noxious mix of sewage and chemicals developed by Israelis as a crowd control weapon. The

Tires on fire after the Friday protest, Kafr Qaddum.

Photo by Nitasha Dhillon

soldiers shot out our car windows with rubber bullets, and, on their retreat back to the roadblock toward the end of the clashes, they lobbed a barrage of teargas at the jubilantly advancing villagers. On that day, as on other Fridays, tires were burned on the road to signal the end of the actions, and, if the wind was blowing in the right direction, the pungent smoke would carry over into the backyards of the settlement.

Though we stank to high heaven (the smell of skunkwater can linger on skin and clothing for several weeks), we bluffed our way into Kedumim afterward and found a calm hilltop haven of suburban tract houses, where many of the younger residents were mustered in prayer and religious study in a central hall. The tranquility was starkly at odds with the mayhem that had convulsed the Palestinian village below, and it conveyed nothing of the settlement's own history of extremism. Established by the Garin Elon Moreh group of Gush Emunim as a strategic cluster of mobile homes in 1975, its highly contested existence was officially recognized by the Begin administration two years later in a landmark decision that greenlighted the aggressive efforts of the settler movement. Self-titled as "the vanguard of Jewish resettlement in Samaria," its longest-serving mayor, Daniella Weiss, was also one of the movement's most prominent and zealous leaders, using her office and influence to expand Kedumim (and other West Bank colonies) far beyond the designated 1977 allotment of "state land." Kedumim's status as a pioneer settlement afforded it priority whenever the Israeli government decided to convert military zones into state land to be built on by settlers. Most recently, in 2015, another such conversion was announced, resulting in the confiscation of a further 165 dunums on the eastern side of Kedumim.[5]

Each new encroachment that cut off Kafr Qaddum from the outside world also closed down opportunities to earn a livelihood. Out-migration has been on the rise ever since the road was first blocked, and villagers who have had to take work in the settlement's orchards or industrial zone are not likely to be open about it. So, too, the town's reputation for resistance means that no resident, or any close relative, has been issued a permit to work in Israel. The young men from surrounding villages who are still able to secure permits consider themselves fortunate. Their Israeli wages are a lifeline, even if the money is offered in return for their own acquiescence in the face of the Occupation.

Inside the Green Line

The Green Line may have been erased from the Zionist geography of Eretz Israel, but Palestinians traveling from the West Bank still experience it as a very real and daunting border. Since 1967, human traffic across it has ebbed and flowed, in response to the needs of the Israeli labor market. In times of full employment, such as the 1960s and 1970s, or in the heat of a construction boom, authorities increase permit quotas to admit more surplus labor from the West Bank (and, at least until 2007, Gaza). When demand slackens, or when a recession kicks in, they cut the numbers back. But often the needs of Israeli employers are secondary to (or at odds with) the government's political manipulation of the right to work as a reward for Palestinian quiescence. Officials routinely use denial of access to employment as a form of collective punishment, even though Article 33 of the Geneva Convention (to which Israel is a signatory) explicitly outlaws this practice.

After 1967, in the first steps toward an integrated economy anchored by a joint Israeli–Palestinian labor market, Israel allocated a limited quota of 40,000 work permits to select industrial sectors. But labor shortages at a time of brisk economic growth prompted impatient Israeli employers to bring over workers without permits. Within a few years the quota arrangement was abandoned, and Israel set up labor exchanges on the West Bank to connect workers directly to employers inside the Green Line.[6] From the employers' perspective, these Palestinians were a godsend. Unlike Israeli Palestinians, they were unable to join the Histadrut, and so they were an unorganized, casual workforce of commuters, with no power to press grievances, let alone bargain over wages and conditions. As for the workers themselves, the lack of leverage and protections was far outweighed by the promised increase in income and standard of living.

From the early 1970s until the first intifada, there were relatively few barriers to movement between Israel and the West Bank or Gaza, and the official numbers of those employed in the Israeli labor market rose steadily, reaching an official peak of 115,600 in 1992, comprising more than 40 percent of the Palestinian workforce and earning an aggregate income that accounted for 42 percent of the GDP of the Occupied Territories.[7] At least a third more were crossing illegally and staying at or near construction sites for days or weeks at a time.[8] According to one estimate, during the 1970s and 1980s, only 50–70 percent of the West Bank and Gazan Palestinians working in Israel had permits.[9] In the course of the first decade of the open borders policy, Palestinian unemployment decreased, and the remittances raised household incomes. In the mid-1970s, however, the wage differential between the Occupied Territories and Israel began to narrow, coming close to parity. As wages in the former rose, employers stepped back from hiring, and domestic growth stalled.[10]

Leaving aside the impact of the remittances, Israel's highly restrictive tariffs, price and export controls, and commercial permissions effectively stifled all internal efforts to develop the productive economy of the West Bank and Gaza. A small number of industrial sectors—textile, footwear, chemicals, and stone and marble—were allowed to operate as offshore producers for the Israeli market. By contrast, Israel protected its own consumer goods by imposing Israeli prices on its exports to the Palestinian market. During periodic incursions, Israeli forces targeted and destroyed infrastructure specifically funded by foreign donors to support development. So, too, the assumption of Israeli control over utilities such as energy, water, and telecommunications meant that the supply of vital resources could be turned on and off at will whenever resistance to the Occupation flared up. Nor was the growth path projected by the Oslo Accords and the Paris Protocol allowed to proceed on track. The overall outcome was a policy of economic containment that economist Sara Roy, in reference to Gaza in particular, described as "de-development."[11]

During the first two decades of the Occupation, Israel's construction sector absorbed a generation of male Palestinian youth, typically at the pay grade of unskilled laborers.[12] But if the political goal was to use the reward of Israeli wages to quell resistance, the outcome was quite the opposite. Exposure to Israel's standards of living and to its well-serviced landscapes of modernity bred resentment among the border-crossers, and rural youth in particular used their access to higher wages to break free from the moderating authority of village elders. Employment in Israel watered the roots of nationalist consciousness and directly prepared the way for the first intifada. Palestinians' experience of swapping a customary agricultural livelihood (typically as a sharecropper, locked into peasant–landlord conflicts) for waged work helped shape their growing conviction that they might lay aside class differences and unite against a common enemy. The loosening of patriarchal authority extended beyond young males, impacting women traditionally confined to household labor. Rural women, who stepped up to take on the agricultural tasks, and female urbanites, who became politically active in the cross-class Women's Work Committees, played a key role in spreading the unity that led to the uprising of 1987.[13]

The border-crossers' capacity to withhold their labor was central to the first intifada, which was launched by a call for a general strike, to be backed up by commercial boycotts and tax refusals. In the absence of total cooperation, operatives of the Unified National Leadership of the Uprising enforced the strike by blocking workers from leaving their villages and encouraging Palestinian employers to create alternatives for the strikers. Israel's retribution for mass absenteeism from its workplaces eventually took the form of border closures and a sharp reduction of work permits. Palestinians' withdrawal of their labor had been a bold act of resistance with steep individual risks. The Israeli decision to exclude their labor was a cruel act of collective punishment, to show there was a price to be paid for opposing the Occupation. The reprisals extended to Israeli Palestinians who were also heavily employed in the construction industry (more than 25 percent of employed males) and who were hard hit by the subsequent decision to import a substitute workforce from overseas.[14]

In the immediate aftermath of the border closures, and in response to employer outcry about the curtailment of their cheap labor supply, officials launched the campaign to replace Palestinians, from both Israel and the Occupied Territories, with what are officially referred to as "foreign workers" (*ovdim zarim*). A largely unplanned, and ill-considered, recruitment drive brought significant numbers of Romanian, Bulgarian, Turkish, and Chinese men into the construction sector, Thai women into agriculture, and Filipinas into caregiving, while smaller pools were recruited from Bolivia, Colombia, Egypt, Ghana, Jordan, Nigeria, Poland, Russia, and Ukraine. Their numbers rose throughout the 1990s and peaked in the early 2000s at 300,000, or almost 12.5 percent of the Israeli workforce, among the highest rates of guest workers in the developed world.[15] Of that total, an estimated 60 percent had overstayed the duration of their permits or their tourist visas or had jumped ship from their sponsors under the binding system (*hesder ha'kvila*) that tied them to specific employers. So, too, the privatization of the recruitment business led to the growth of a highly lucrative black market, benefiting employers and personnel agents who lobbied hard for permits they did not need and subsequently sold off to bidders, often in other industrial sectors.[16]

In the short term, migrant recruitment eased employers off their addiction to cheap Palestinian labor, but it introduced no end of domestic strife over the presence of these "foreigners" who occupied an uncertain status as permanent temporary workers. Like Palestinian workers, the migrants were treated as integral to the labor market but were socially segregated and denied any rights within Israel's ethnocratic state. Jewish immigrants, simply by setting foot on Israeli soil, immediately enjoyed national rights under the Law of Return (1950), including permanent residence, citizenship, and full welfare entitlements and services, none of which were extended to migrant families, or their children, not even after more than a decade of contributing to the building of the Israeli state.[17] This discrepant treatment was a legal and human rights quagmire, and any humanitarian claims made on behalf of migrants only inflamed hostile right-wing officials, looking to trumpet a new "existential threat" to the country's Jewish national identity.[18] The belligerent backlash against these noncitizens mounted in volume, especially at a time of growing unemployment among Israelis, and culminated in mass deportations by a specially formed Migration Police force. From 2003 to 2005, its officers rounded up and sent home as many as 140,000 migrants.

Since 2006, a similar policy of exclusion and deportation has been directed toward asylum seekers from Africa's civil wars in Eritrea, Sudan, and Darfur. As a signatory to the UN Convention on Refugees, Israel was obliged to admit the refugees. Issuing them with temporary work visas (which did not ensure any social benefits) was a considerable boost to the country's tarnished international image. But the unwelcome prospect of their long-term residence meant that they would have to be treated as a temporary inconvenience. According to Noa Kaufman, the refugee specialist for Kav LaOved, Israel's leading labor NGO, government policy encouraged self-deportation, as in "we will make their lives so miserable that they will leave by themselves." In response to mounting right-wing pressure, the Netanyahu administration stepped up its hardline rhetoric and retreaded the old staple of security alarmism by labelling the refugees as "infiltrators" (*mistanenim*), the term originally used to describe Palestinians trying to return to their homes after the *Nakba*. With no evidence that the policy of self-deportation was working, the government sweetened the offer with rewards ($3,500 plus airfare) for leaving while vowing that refugees would face imprisonment if they chose to ignore the deal. Payments of $5,000 a head were made to receiving countries (like Uganda and Rwanda) for taking them, and civilians were also offered stipends ($8,700) to act as vigilantes in rounding up potential deportees. In a 2017 Supreme Court case, Kav LaOved, which provides legal services to all classes of underpaid workers in Israel and the Occupied Territories, successfully challenged a desperate Netanyahu policy mandating that 20 percent of the asylum seekers' salaries would be deducted and deposited in a fund only accessible to the refugees upon leaving Israel.

In the interim, the domestic demand for their temporary labor generated a cynical response from officials. "The government is so worried about the border-crossers' status becoming one of refugees entitled to asylum," explained Kaufman, "that they took away the work visas, so they are not officially allowed to work, but this regulation is not enforced at all, and so as many as 40,000 are casually employed in the 3Ds—dangerous, difficult, and dirty jobs." At the time, several thousand were being held under wretched conditions in the detention complex of the Holot camp, run by the neighboring Saharonim prison, in the temperature extremes of the Negev (*Naqab*) desert. Despite their detention, employers were all too willing to take advantage of this super-vulnerable workforce. Kaufman reported that the (mostly Eritrean) majority were competing for day labor with West Bank Palestinians and that some were even working in the settlements, living there in makeshift shelters.

The hiring of migrants brought more flexibility and competition to the labor market, enabling employers to depress wages, just as they had used West Bank Palestinians after 1967 to control, or drive down, Israeli Palestinian pay levels. But despite their availability, employers in Israel's construction industry had several reasons to continue to prefer the West Bank workers, many of whom had a stable, long-term commitment to their employers and commuter workplaces. The latter were more skilled, had a working knowledge of Hebrew, returned home every night, and spent their wages on Israeli goods. So, too, their deference was more or less guaranteed for fear of losing their permits. As one of my Palestinian interviewees put it, such workers are like "human gold." By contrast, the migrants sent their earnings home, they required accommodation and services, they often jumped ship and went "underground," and their long-term habitation in Israeli cities posed a political problem for Jewish ethnocrats.

There are other, less obvious, reasons that Israelis recruit workers from a population regarded by many as the "enemy." The policy of jobs-for-peace has strong political advocates on the left and the right. It is also considered good for public relations to show that Palestinians are benefiting in some way from a dynamic Israeli economy and that Israel is meeting some of its minimal obligations, as an occupying force, to look after their livelihoods. Since the early years of the Zionist presence in the region, building houses has been seen as a preserve of Arab labor, and this fixed perception has endured, in spite of the pre-1948 drive for Hebrew Labor and the more recent experiment with an overseas substitute. Moreover, at least since the 1960s, Israeli Jews have shown little interest in employment in the labor-intensive sectors of construction and agriculture. The initial tolerance for manual work of ex-Soviet Jews (many of them well educated) eroded quickly in a society where such employment was stigmatized as "Arab work" and where generous state aid was available to help new immigrants (*olim*) find their footing and attain the social mobility promised to them. Even unskilled immigrants expected higher status work in Israel as a dividend of their Jewish identity. National guilt at being unable to recruit Jews for construction periodically prompted the government to launch training programs to persuade them to "go back to the scaffolds" and take up a vocation redolent of the pioneering Labor Zionist past.[19]

The most recent government initiative, in 2014, promised employers subsidies to offer an attractive wage to skilled Israeli workers, at 9,000 shekels per month ($2,602), or more than double the 4,300 shekel minimum wage at that time.[20] The agreement, forged between the Finance Ministry, the Association of National Builders, and the construction workers' union, was also aimed at recruiting ultra-Orthodox Jews, who have a relatively low workforce participation rate (44.5 percent). Such efforts harked back to the early twentieth-century policy of using overseas Zionist funds to subsidize the "European wage" demanded by Jewish pioneers, but they were a far cry from the Hebrew Labor campaigns of Mandatory Palestine; their goal was not to conquer the labor market but to secure a small, symbolic foothold in a sector dominated by Palestinians and migrant workers. The nationalist impulse behind them was to show that Jews, especially *haredim*, were capable of physically building the Israeli state instead of living off it.

The following year, in June 2015, the Builders Association and Histadrut's Federation of Builders and Woodworkers signed a general collective agreement that gave construction workers the highest minimum pay of any industrial sector, with scheduled increases over three years. By the time I interviewed the union president, Yitzhak Moyal, two years later, basic pay had been hiked to 5,600 shekels (or 600 shekels above the general minimum wage), and for foremen the minimum had risen to 7,500 shekels. Moyal pointed out to me that "these pay grades applied to all workers, regardless of ethnicity or national origin." He also described the legal services the union now provides through a new arbitration unit for Palestinians mired in conflicts over pay with employers, and he reported that he had pushed the government to issue more permits for West Bank workers: "two of our employees of the year," he reported to me with pride, "were Palestinians." Yet Moyal's preamble to the 2015 master contract suggested that the agreement was sealed as part of the drive specifically to attract Israeli Jews with the promise of training them for the better paying foreman positions least likely to be occupied by Palestinians: "These moves," he wrote, "constitute a dramatic improvement in pay and a broadening of professional training, arising from our wish to recruit new Israeli workers to this industry and to create a new generation of work foremen."

In any case, these targeted conscription drives generally produced few results. None of my Palestinian interviewees reported working alongside Jews on the same crew, though they did encounter some employed as foremen and others in the highest skilled trades on the same construction sites. Israeli Palestinians, on the other hand, made up a sizable portion—up to one-fifth—of the construction industry workforce. As official Histadrut members, their rights were better protected than those of migrant workers or West Bank Palestinians, though overall they were still paid less than Jews.[21] In 2014, the average Israeli Palestinian male earned only 60 percent of his Jewish counterpart's wages, and two years later the gap had widened to 53 percent.[22]

From the long-term perspective of Zionist settlement, the advantage to Israel of employing Palestinians from the Occupied Territories is clear. Rural workers from landed families have been converted into wage laborers; as a result, they have gradually lost their vested interest in the land, making it easier to expropriate. A family can earn much more by sending their sons out to a construction site in Tel Aviv or a factory in Ma'ale Adumim than by eking out a hardscrabble livelihood from their small holdings. Over time, the plots are either neglected, and risk being seized as "state land" in accordance with the refurbished Ottoman law (*makhlul*) of underutilization, or they are sold to settlers because they are more valuable as commodities than as a source of agricultural revenue. Either way, the will to hold on to the tracts has weakened. How many dunums of Palestinian land have passed into settler hands as a result? Between 1967 and 1993, during the period when the settlement movement made its first big gains, the Palestinian workforce in agrarian employment dropped from 40 percent to 20 percent.[23] In tandem with the decrease, Israeli import policies pushed Palestinian farmers toward cash or seasonal crops for export and away from subsistence agriculture.[24] In this way, each new advance in settlement building was facilitated by Israeli strategies that encouraged transfer of workers off the land, whether to urban centers or to the Palestinian diaspora.

Trial by Checkpoint

For rural Palestinians, at least, grueling commutes to work are nothing new. During the Mandate, and especially during World War II, when the British Army commandeered large labor pools through its Middle Eastern Supply Center, employment on British military bases and public work sites often required extensive travel and periods away from home. In the 1960s and 1970s, many households sent members to Jordan, Kuwait, Saudi Arabia, and the United Arab Emirates to build these fledgling nations. In other words, crossing borders or checkpoints to get to workplaces was a common experience, and, until the 1990s, entering Israel was much less arduous than it is today. But the abandonment of the open border policy in the early 1990s transformed the transit into an exhausting, demeaning, and often dangerous daily journey. Passing through a portal checkpoint into Israel is an ordeal at the best of times.[25] Waiting in line for hours eats away the precious nonworking portion of the waking day. Aside from the physical abuse—more than 80 percent of border-crossers reportedly experience harassment, and many have died en route—the humiliation of being treated so badly exacts a more grievous toll on the spirit.[26] If Palestinians working inside the Green Line were once akin to commuters, albeit as migrants in their own land, the increasing control over their movements today invites comparisons to apartheid-era South Africa. Indeed, the fragmentation of the West Bank into (more than twenty) shrunken, noncontiguous enclaves is regularly labeled as "Bantustanization," in reference to the apartheid system's creation of separate micro-states, or homelands. The bounded territories of the South African Bantustans functioned as labor reservoirs, from which residents required a travel pass or permit to leave, often traveling long distances to work. Today, there are as many as 100 permits required by Palestinians for a wide range of economic activities and types of travel, comprising a regime comparable to, but even more restrictive than, South Africa's apartheid pass laws.[27]

As the archipelago of settlement blocs expand, a gridded network of bypass roads, military zones, nature preserves, "state lands," earth mounds, concrete blocks, road gates, and flying checkpoints crisscross the West Bank, sequestering the now amputated and economically dysfunctional cantons from one another. As a result, the terminal checkpoints at the Separation Wall that are the entry portals to Israel now operate like ghetto gates, closing at the informal curfew hour when workers are required to return to their designated West Bank territory. Gaza, routinely described as an open-air prison, was blockaded after Hamas took control in 2007 and put under quarantine since then. In keeping with the aims behind the creation of the original Bantustans in South Africa, these enclaves are not economically viable on their own, and it is all but futile to imagine how they could function in noncontiguous combination to support a free-standing state.

Nor are the border barriers designed to fully exclude those without permits. Israeli employers, eager to circumvent domestic labor and taxation regulations, stand to benefit from access to unregistered workers whose unauthorized crossing is unofficially tolerated. If they are apprehended, workers without permits are briefly detained and issued fines of several thousand shekels; after four arrests, they are handed jail sentences of several months. Given the limited alternatives on the West Bank, these punitive costs are not enough to deter them, and the extensive illegal traffic belies the official rhetoric about the security function of the Separation Wall. One worker I interviewed from the Bethlehem district, a tiler who spent a week at a time in Israel, explained the calculus behind the risk of being caught without papers. "I am from a family where no one has a permit, so I have no choice," he said, "but with my wages I can afford the fines." And the detention? "Many Palestinians are used to jail, that is no shame for us." Of course, employers take full advantage of workers like him, paying them less, stealing their wages, and enjoying their exemption from tax or insurance payroll obligations. Many sleep on site or in the rough, and so there are minimal employer overheads. Their availability helps to hold down wage levels and placate employers who want maximum flexibility over their workforce.

In recent years, the permit system has given rise to an additional layer of exploitation. Roughly 70 percent of my checkpoint interviewees reported that they had to pay for permits, at a cost that could consume up to one-half of their wages. This commission, which is often (spuriously) explained to them as a way for employers to cover payroll deductions for social benefits, is charged by either the labor contractor or the employer. Though it is not legal, the practice is now widespread. "Only six years ago, this was not common at all," Castro Daoud, an Israeli Palestinian labor lawyer, informed me. "It is a felony to charge commission for a permit," he continued, "but it is one of the ways that employers have perfected the techniques they use to cheat workers." Employers are also able to pay off the books for workers whose permits are issued for another company and sold on the black market. Another relatively recent development, according to Daoud, is "the practice of hiring Palestinian workers through Palestinian subcontractors, which only began after workers started suing the Israeli employers for labor violations."

The chain of contracting, which can involve Palestinians on both sides of the Green Line, is designed to shield the employer from any legal accountability. All recruitment and logistical arrangements are taken care of by the (sub)contractor, whose name sometimes appears on the permit itself and typically functions in an employer capacity. Workers have limited contact, if any, with the actual employer. Dependence on these unregulated middlemen introduces a further level of vulnerability, including, for women, the threat of sexual assault.[28] Of course, the permit brokers and the (sub)contractors, or labor recruiters, each take a cut. "There is a mutual interest between them all, and therefore no chance of solidarity among Palestinians," Daoud commented, "and then the worker always ends up paying the price." An even greater price is paid by the victims of swindlers who sell permits online, preying on the desperation of workers in times of high unemployment. (More than 350,000 are jobless on the West Bank, and the unemployment rate in Gaza is a staggering 60 percent.)[29]

Under a 1997 agreement with the Histadrut, Daoud explained, workers who have the resources to hire a lawyer "can sue for reparations in the Israeli labor courts, and occasionally will win damages and restitution, but felony charges can only be brought through the criminal courts and, even if successful, will not result in compensation." One percent of their pay is deducted for a representation fee to the Histadrut, and so the Israeli federation is obliged to provide some services, even legal aid. But until recently, the workers' best resort was to contact under-resourced Israeli labor organizations like Kav LaOved. For many years, the Histadrut held the position that organizing Palestinians would only serve to normalize the Occupation, but, in 2008, the union entered into a controversial arrangement with the Palestinian General Federation of Trade Unions (PGFTU) to offer protection for Palestinian workers inside the Green Line. The Histadrut also agreed to reimburse the PGFTU for the accrued sum, since 1995, of the long-disputed 1 percent representation fee.

Agreements to transfer to the PA the much more substantial Israeli payroll deductions for social insurance (unemployment benefits, child allowances, social security, disability allowances, old age pensions, and nursing care) proved more elusive. These deductions, equivalent to those taken out of Israeli workers' wages, amounted to almost 20 percent of net pay; they had been withheld for decades and allegedly deposited in a Treasury trust fund. Officially, the lion's share of those monies was supposed to be allocated to the Civil Administration to be used for infrastructure improvements in the Occupied Territories, but there was never any accountability in this arrangement, nor any evidence that authorities had complied over the years. So, too, the subterfuges used to avoid employer contributions, such as registering employees as day laborers or underreporting wages and hours, ended up drastically reducing the sums and benefits to be claimed. Article 38 of the Paris Protocol (April 1994) stipulated that the deductions were to be transferred to the Palestinian social security authority once it was established. But even then, Section 34(1) of the separate Gaza Strip–Jericho Area Agreement Law (signed five days later) precluded any claims on the payments withheld from 1968 to 1994.[30]

In Ramallah, the long-delayed effort to establish the social security authority was finally initiated in 2013, though the process was far from transparent and all but devoid of any civil society input. By the time the PA leadership produced an initial draft in 2015, a coalition of trade unions, women's organizations, and youth associations had sprung into action to protest the top-down operation and also the ratio of distributions proposed in the draft. A series of labor strikes brought tens of thousands of workers out on Ramallah's streets, attesting to the strength of public sentiment on the topic. Pressure from these groups resulted in changes, and legislation was finally signed in September 2016, followed by negotiations with Israel about the accumulated sum of post-1994 money to be handed over to the PA. Some initial media reports put that sum at 31 billion shekels (or $8.2 billion).[31]

A full eighteen months after these reports, Mohammed Aruri, a longtime labor official who served as one of the labor representatives appointed to the social security authority's fifteen-person executive board, assured me that the Israelis had yet to name a figure. "Some estimates on our side are as high as $20 billion, but we don't have the receipts to prove it. The Israelis mentioned 2 or 3 billion shekels as an initial payment, and they are supposed to hand over all the records of payments, but we are still waiting on a final number." Aruri, who, as former head of PGFTU's Legal Affairs

Department had successfully negotiated hundreds of workers' settlements through Israeli lawyers, had learned to be stoic in the face of Israeli stonewalling. With a deadpan expression on his face, he predicted that payments would be delivered in a matter of months. But he preferred to talk about the benefits the PA would eventually be able to generate: "We will invest the money well, to create jobs for the unemployed and ensure that workers are able to retire at the designated age (sixty for men, fifty-five for women) and be comfortable." When I quizzed him much later in the year, he reported, with regret, that the commission had yet to receive any payments.

Aruri, who commuted to Ramallah from Arura village (near Rawabi) to work for the FIDA Party (Palestinian Democratic Union), had been active in the coalition to amend the PA's initial plan and said that he had not seen anything like it in Palestinian civil society. At the height of the coalition's activities, I met informally in Ramallah with a group of trade unionists and labor advisors who were centrally involved. They were affiliated or aligned with the Federation of Independent & Democratic Trade Unions & Workers' Committees (GFITUP), which broke away from the PGFTU in 2007 because of the federation's lack of democratic process (no elections had been held since 1981) and in protest against its close ties with Fatah. "The PGFTU does not represent the working class," explained Abu Mahmoud, a cadre from one of the federation's unions, "they even approved of the PA's first social security draft." According to those present, there were several points of contention with the draft document; among them, the unfair proportion of employer and employee contributions, meager maternity and disability benefits, and the lack of provision for labor courts.

But the most animated conversation in the room was about the transfer to Ramallah of the payroll deductions and whether the money could be fairly distributed. How much of the final sum would the PA and its cronies try to siphon off? Who would oversee those responsible for disbursements? Would the widows of deceased workers see anything? "Workers want the money transferred directly," explained Azzam Abedin, a longtime public health advocate, "because they don't trust the government or anyone appointed by it." With particular emphasis, he added, "this is not a simple financial transaction, it is central to decades of injustice."

Why had the Israeli retention of social insurance payments caused so much bitterness? The withholding of these payments over the course of fifty years sent a blunt message—Palestinian workers could expect nothing from a state they had spent most of their daily lives building, stone by stone. Not only was their labor taken for granted, but the means to protect their welfare and the well-being of their families had been converted into a scheme to fill the Israeli government's treasury. So the return of the payments was not just the settlement of a long overdue monetary debt; it was also seen as reparation for their lack of recognition as human beings and thus as a small milestone in the larger campaign to seek compensation for losses sustained during the long *Nakba*. In spite of the Oslo agreements, labor advocates like Aruri had continued to pursue the return of the pre-1994 payments. With the assistance of Kav LaOved, four workers filed claims as a test case before the Israeli Supreme Court. When it seemed likely the court would side with the government, Aruri and others decided to "withdraw the suits before the judgment became a matter of law in order to keep the door open for other workers to demand their right from the period before 1994."

New Unions, Old Challenges

Earlier in the year, I met with Mahmoud Ziadeh, who, as general secretary of the GFITUP (formally recognized by the PA in 2011), was also active in the coalition to reform the social security draft law. "This secret process was a violation of Palestinian Basic Law," he thundered, "and the draft proposal, as it stood, was heavily biased toward private sector employers." Like the unionists I had met earlier, Ziadeh directed his concerns at the cross-border transfer but was more pointed in his criticism. In his view, the 2008 PGFTU accord with the Histadrut was a particularly corrosive factor in the negotiations. The Histadrut's history as a pillar of Zionist expansion—"it actively supports and builds the settlements"—should disqualify its consideration, he believed, as a potential partner for Palestinian workers. "Cooperation is only possible," he insisted, "with Israeli workers and unions who are opposed to colonialism and who support an independent Palestine." Besides, even if the Israeli authorities handed over all of the social insurance payments, the Histadrut–PGFTU agreement still allowed the 1 percent representation fee to be split between the two big unions. "Our union considers that to be a theft, because Histadrut is doing nothing for our workers."

Imprisoned for several years during the Israeli crackdown on the labor movement for its role in the first intifada, Ziadeh was a legendary organizer whose career cut across the fractured, historical landscape of the Palestinian trade union movement. Over the decades, efforts have been made to unite the major federations and breakaway factions, but concord remains elusive between the three main federations—the PGFTU, GFITUP, and the General Union of Palestinian Workers—not to mention the unions organized through Hamas. Though the right to organize and to collectively bargain are guaranteed under Palestinian Basic Law, no unified trade union law has been drafted, and the exercise of these basic union rights is barred in the case of public sector employees, whose unions are considered illegal. Legal protection is minimal in the private sector, where, in the first quarter of 2014, a mere 0.2 percent of workers were covered by collective bargaining agreements.[32]

In March 2016, another federation, the New Federation of Trade Unions (New Unions), was recognized by the PA and made its official debut with twenty-six regional branches in a variety of industries. The most immediate origins of New Unions lay in efforts to organize Palestinian workers that resulted in strikes at two chemical factories located in the Nitzanei Shalom (Buds of Peace) industrial zone in Area C just to the east of the Separation Wall near Tulkarm. Israeli factory owners in high-polluting industries (waste recycling, nylon manufacture, fertilizer, pesticide, and chemical production) had moved their facilities there to evade domestic environmental regulations, and the zone was notorious for its hazardous working conditions and noxious impacts on the surrounding communities. Tulkarm, close to the Tel Aviv metro area, developed a reputation as the go-to location for the dumping of Israeli toxic waste: according to

Mohammed al-Hmaidi, the director of the Palestine Environmental Authority, "it costs about $65 to hire a driver—usually a Palestinian—to dump a five-ton truck of waste chemicals [in the West Bank] ... to dispose of the same volume at Ramat Hovay in the Negev desert, Israel's only approved dump site for toxic chemicals, costs more than $11,000."[33] Probably as a result, Tulkarm and its environs have the highest cancer rate in the West Bank.

The strike organizers in the chemical factories were aiming to test the Israeli High Court's landmark 2007 ruling (in a suit brought by Kav LaOved) that Israeli labor law applied to workers in the settlements. Under a 1982 order, the military governor had extended the Israeli minimum wage to settlements in the Occupied Territories, but the rule was never implemented or monitored. Instead, employers looking to relocate in the West Bank were led to believe that the 1967 Jordanian labor laws, which were much weaker, would be applied (while Egyptian law would cover the Erez industrial zone in Gaza). The 2007 decision was double-edged because it provided a potential legal pathway for annexation of the settlement blocs, but tens of thousands of Palestinian employees covered by the ruling still regarded it as a significant win. In the aftermath of the decision, Palestinians employed in the twenty or more affected industrial zones and parks launched a barrage of legal complaints.

Occupying twice the acreage of the residential settlements, these parks comprised almost a thousand industrial facilities and many large farms, employing more than 30,000 workers and generating billions of dollars in Israeli exports.[34] Boycott, Divestment, and Sanctions (BDS) movement activists selected some of the facilities, like the SodaStream factory in Mishor Adumim and the Royalife plant in the Barkan Industrial Zone near Ariel, as boycott targets because of international brand recognition, but their campaigns also helped draw attention to the abuse of basic rights in all the settlement zones, where subminimum wages are issued to workers without any benefits or pay slips to document employment.

Since the Tulkarm chemical factories were not producing high-profile brand exports, the 2010 strikes were not well-publicized, but the union's campaign for higher wages, benefits, and workplace protections registered some success. During the strikes, workers asked the PGFTU for support. Speaking to me in his Tulkarm home, where he was recovering from surgery, Mohammed Blaidi, New Unions' general secretary, described the outcome: "The workers called a large meeting at the union office, and decided among themselves that they needed an alternative to the PGFTU. During the strike there had been no help from the federation, so they said, 'Why should we wait for them? We should go and create something new by ourselves.'" After the new federation's launch, it rapidly branched out to cover textiles, services, and other sectors not included in the General Union of Palestinian Workers, another Palestinian rival of the PGFTU. Blaidi insisted that "it was the workers' needs that had made it essential to create something new, despite the lack of any funding at the outset."

Palestinian unions cannot operate legally in a settlement, and so efforts to organize within the Nitzanei Shalom zone continued with the assistance of the Israeli labor union Workers Advice Center (WAC-MAAN). But these activities were stymied by a 2015 decision from Israel's National Labor Court, which ruled that the old 1967 Jordanian laws still applied to the zone because it had been established to "promote economic cooperation between Israelis and Palestinians, and the employment of Palestinians"—in other words, territorially, it was located in a "no-man's-land."[35] Many court decisions about the status of Palestinian land were surreal, but this one was particularly absurd since worker legal protections in Jordan itself had been considerably strengthened since 1967, and Palestinian law, which applied just outside the zone walls, was also superior. In effect, there were no courts in existence that could rule under the old Jordanian law.[36]

Blocked from further organizing, Blaidi and his New Unions colleagues were operating a workers center, providing legal advice and other kinds of support. They were also doing something else that was quite uncommon—showing up at the Green Line checkpoints to promote the cause of labor rights. "Every month we conduct four or five unscheduled visits," he told me, "so the workers are starting to see us on the ground. We are beginning to take on their cases and the word is spreading that someone who can be trusted is there to help them." On an early (and, for him, formative) visit, Blaidi recounted that a worker waiting in line in one of the caged pens told him "to go home, and stop coming out to look at us as if we were animals in a zoo." At first, Blaidi took this remark as an expression of the worker's self-loathing, but subsequently saw it as a comment on how trade unions were regarded by those whom they had neglected.[37]

Either way, my visit to Tulkarm's al-Tayba (Shaar Efraim) checkpoint after leaving Blaidi's house helped to clarify where the reference to the zoo came from. As I made my way through the market stalls of produce and clothing that greeted workers on their return, a fight broke out among several men who had just exited the turnstiles, their tempers badly frayed by the extensive wait in lines and metal pens to cross back over to the West Bank. The tussle didn't last long, and it was the only violence I saw between Palestinians in the course of my visits to the West Bank. Cooped up in the long series of fenced-in pathways and channels, the men had obviously rubbed one another the wrong way. That would not be hard to do. Al-Tayba was notorious for overcrowded, dehumanizing conditions that had caused many worker injuries and not a few deaths. The checkpoint was poorly managed by a private contractor, and a recent worker protest at the conditions had forced this company to add an extra terminal and turnstile to deal with the high volume of traffic.

Crossing the al-Tayba border checkpoint is particularly taxing—it involves passing through several hundred meters of turnstiles, metal detectors, X-ray machines, and inspection stations for IDs, permits, and fingerprints. A few of the workers I interviewed described the infamous circular "oven" room, which has no roof (ostensibly to limit the damage from bomb detonations), and where selected workers, including women, are taken to be stripped down and examined. Delays of several hours are common, as is the herding and crushing of users, some of whom are regularly forced to climb up the side of the pens to avoid suffocation. Among my interviewees at several checkpoint locations, those at al-Tayba were the only ones who focused so exclusively on the atrocious conditions

Workers coming out of Al-Tayba checkpoint past market stalls.

at the checkpoint complex itself. "I feel that everything in this place is like an instrument of torture," commented a worker exiting the last turnstile; he was a middle-aged resident of Tulkarm who used to be a high school teacher. "It has absolutely nothing to do with security," reported a carpenter who was about to take a taxi back to Jenin, "the whole process is designed to humiliate us in every way." He pointed out that "hundreds of thousands of us are allowed to pass freely during Ramadan and Eid al-Fitr, so how are we not a security threat then?" Another frequently voiced complaint concerned the delays from fingerprint inspections. Several workers alleged that the contractor was paid extra for reprocessing the prints, a common occurrence on account of work-related abrasions on fingers.

Among Israel's fifteen terminal checkpoints, al-Tayba sees the heaviest volume of crossers, most of them from Nablus and Jenin. By Blaidi's estimate, more than 15,000 cross daily. Overall, he reckoned that more than 60,000 West Bank Palestinians had work permits, 25,000 had commercial permits, and 15,000 crossed the Green Line without any documents. He also reported that 30,000 Palestinians had permits to work in settlements and more than 15,000 worked there without legal permission. In its labor force survey for the first quarter of 2017, the Palestinian Bureau of Statistics estimated that 139,600 were working, with or without permits, in Israel and in Israeli settlements (and a further 10,000 without permits in the latter): almost 60 percent of these were in construction.[38] According to the Israeli state comptroller, more than 50,000 were working without permits every day inside the Green Line.[39]

Overall, these slightly varying figures suggested that the numbers of Palestinians building the state of Israel were above the previous peaks of 115,000 in 1992 and 135,000 in 2000, and well above, if unregistered settlement workers were included.[40] At the end of 2016, the Israeli cabinet discussed plans to increase the number of standard permits for work in Israel to 78,000, though right-wing politicians, like Naftali Bennett, had been urging a higher allocation of 100,000 for some time.[41] Aside from the usual reason of "keeping the peace," Israeli authorities are under pressure from the housing shortage and have committed to expanding the pool of affordable homes. Employers in the construction industry, thirsty for cheap laborers, are always lobbying for more permits for the West Bank.

In contrast with the horrors of al-Tayba, the Eyal checkpoint at Qalqilya, eighteen miles to the south, has the reputation of being the best managed. At the time of my visits, it was handling about 7,000 crossers per day, though the PGFTU official who staffed a small union office there told me, in early 2016, that more permits were being issued and that the numbers were likely to rise to 10,000. He also casually confirmed that the brisk market in permits was probably reaping more profit than the wage economy itself. The going rate for permits had risen to between 2,000 and 2,500 shekels a month, at a time when the Israeli minimum wage was set at 4,650 shekels. Until recently, the general contractor or employer would control, or split, the permit commission, and the subcontractors and the recruiters further down the chain would have no claim on the profit; now that the returns were higher, everyone was trying to cash in.

Abdu, a plasterer from a village east of Nablus, who rose at 3 a.m. and did not return home until 9 p.m., explained how the permit market affected him: "Before, when I went across without a permit,

I earned 350 shekels a day, but now even though I earn more and work longer I have to pay for the permit, so in the end I take home the same pay." On the other hand, he added, "these days, the smugglers [usually Israeli Palestinians] who help you over the Separation Wall or through gaps in the fence want more and more, too." Many of those waiting in line had other calculations in their heads. I met, in short order, a cement worker who used to be a fashion designer, a tiler who had been trained as an electrical engineer, and an economist who said he was laying foundations for houses in Herzliya. Each of them had amassed a pile of student debt from earning degrees that can cost up to $40,000 in Palestine's private university system. Domestic unemployment in their professional fields had driven them to join the less skilled in the checkpoint lines. Rashid, from Jenin refugee camp, had no degrees, but his sons and daughters were trying to enter the educated class: "I have three children in college, and that's why I am here. If you cross over, you can earn enough to avoid taking out the college loans. Everyone who has to work in the West Bank is up to their neck in debt."

Rashid had just turned fifty-five, and so he no longer needed a work permit, but his age cohort was not allowed in until 7 a.m. (Regular permit holders entered at 4 a.m. and those with commercial permits from 6 a.m.) "From here I go to the traffic circle on the other side," he reported, "and if there is any work left, I can be lucky and get taken on for the day, but often I have to come back empty-handed." His home was in Qalqilya, which, like Gaza, is often compared to an open-air prison because it is almost entirely surrounded by the Wall and settlements. Women, bound for agricultural work, were part of the throng passing through, and a small number of the men had skilled jobs, in welding, carpentry, or ironwork, but 90 percent of those in the lines were employed in "wet" work—tiling, plastering, casting, framing, bricklaying, and paving—required to construct the skeleton of a building. These are the sectors typically reserved for Palestinians from the West Bank.

From Bed to Work, from Work to Bed

On all of my field trips to the West Bank I visited checkpoints regularly, and conducted more than 200 interviews with workers either waiting in line or exiting the turnstiles at the end of the work day. Indeed, I had originally imagined this book would be about the checkpoints themselves. Most of my interviews were done at the Bethlehem 300 checkpoint, in the city where I was usually based. I started out by showing up at 4 a.m., but over time I decided to make my visits later in the day if only because the workers had more time to chat on their return from work. In addition, since the soldiers were able to monitor my presence through surveillance cameras, workers sometimes got through the checkpoint more quickly when I was there, which made me uncomfortable. Whether they were coming or going to work, I felt uneasy about holding them up, but those who agreed to an interview were typically patient and polite, even when fielding questions that were sometimes quite intimate.

Though circumstances varied, I usually asked the same questions about the nature of their work; their employers, contractors, and pay; permit obligations; workplace safety; residence and family; and about their aspirations for the future. At times, when they had the time and inclination, the conversation got broader and deeper and invariably trended toward politics and the Occupation. By far the majority of those queuing or exiting were men, employed on construction sites. Occasionally, women who worked in food preparation, cleaning, or agriculture showed up, though I never once saw them being allowed to use the separate line officially designated for women, the disabled, and the sick. The women who agreed to talk with me were often the most articulate and militant of all those I interviewed about the political situation.

In the course of conducting the interviews, I occasionally thought about tabulating the results in some way, but over time I realized that I could not do it.[42] The checkpoints, even when they are functioning as "orderly" points of cross-border transit, are places of extreme duress, where people are processed in the most degrading and often capricious ways. The administrative mentality of the occupier is well represented in this classificatory ordeal of being herded, sorted, and judged by soldiers who are often youthful, nervous, and trigger-happy. Any thoughts I had about arranging data simply reminded me of the deliberative calculus that underpinned all this hardship; the criteria, for example, of selecting those who will be accepted for entry—if you are twenty-two and married, for example, you might qualify as part of the quota for construction, but you need to be twenty-eight to pick strawberries, and thirty-five years old to work in a field, and you can only enter at your designated regional checkpoint, and so on and so forth.[43]

The official security rationale for the endless layers of screening and vetting struck me as specious, given how many workers cross illegally and how few have ever been involved in acts of violence against Israelis. Most workers I interviewed experienced the checkpoint regime as nothing other than a ritual of debasement and punishment, especially since the speed of passage is almost entirely dependent on the whim of the soldiers on duty. It is easy to understand how some commentators interpret the daily endurance of the checkpoint as a form of *sumud*, a steadfast resilience in the face of the Zionist policy of "population transfer" that lies behind the security rhetoric. For sure, one of the lessons from the history of ethnic cleansing (including the wartime Jewish experience in Europe and North Africa) was that the target population must first be dehumanized in the eyes of the aggressor before the process of transfer or elimination is undertaken.

An initial step is to reduce people to serving merely as a source of labor, and for most border-crossers there is no time left in their day for anything else, so they could just as well be in a labor camp (though even that would be more costly to maintain). Under the regime of "from bed to work, from work to bed" (*min al-farsha la-l-warsha wa min al-warsha la-l-farsha*), many have only a few minutes, or an hour, to spend with their families, and when they enjoy a day off, it is likely to be on a Saturday (Jewish Shabbat) and not the Muslim (Friday) or the Christian (Sunday) day of prayer. In other words, their baseline access to humanity is treated as an avoided transaction cost by a society that does not need to waste any time, resources, or thought over their welfare. Instead, they are accounted for in numerical permit quotas, determined by the calculus of risk and profit to Israeli Jews. The risks faced by workers themselves do not enter into the equation.[44] I conducted many of my worker interviews during the "knife intifada" of 2015–16, and almost everyone whom I asked said they felt unsafe in Israel. This was a period when it was not uncommon for a knife to be thrown near the body of a Palestinian in order to justify a shooting or killing after the fact.

During the course of my visits, Israel increased its monthly minimum wage, in a series of hikes, from 4,200 shekels ($1,160) in early 2015 to 5,000 shekels ($1,380) at the beginning of 2017. The wages reported to me by workers doing unskilled "wet" work in construction were in the range of 4,000 to 5,000, but the fee charged for a permit (from 1,200 to 2,500), if it was borne by employees, was a huge toll. Veterans reminisced about the era of open borders, before permits and also before fees were taken in exchange for them. But more recent recruits typically had no idea it was illegal to charge for a permit. Employers very rarely covered transit costs, which could stretch to four or more taxi fares. (Israeli public buses are often avoided since they expose Arab workers to random violence.) Nor was the time expended to travel between work and home—more than eight hours a day for some—ever compensated, and those who had to change employers regularly said they experienced wage theft on a routine basis. Despite all of these add-ons and levies, the take-home pay inside the Green Line was still superior to a West Bank wage, even for educated professionals who were standing in line for the construction work every day. As for the unregistered workers I interviewed, none of them earned more than the Israeli minimum wage, and they earned no social insurance, but at least they were not shelling out for a permit.

With the exception of more highly skilled tradesmen, most of these workers experienced the minimum wage not as a floor but as a ceiling, and many were lucky to secure work for the full twenty-six days sanctioned by their monthly permits in order to earn that wage. Yet when I asked what they thought they should be paid, the numbers given were rarely more than 20 percent above their current wage. Was this an expression of low self-worth or a reflection of the meager expectations most had about the feasible improvement of their circumstances? No doubt these options were connected. In any event, I had hoped to learn more about their general frame of mind by wrapping up the interviews with two open-ended questions: What is your personal dream? And what is your dream for Palestine?

The second question proved the easier to answer. Very few workers expressed any faith in the future of the two-state solution or had anything good to say about the PA. "I once had dreams and the PA destroyed them," was one memorable reply, reflecting the post-Oslo experience of corrupt and ineffective Ramallah governance. Another estimated that "we only have a 10 percent democracy under the PA," while his mate, bitter about the role played by PA police in suppressing dissent, pitched in: "we are living under two occupations, Israel's and the PA's." Those who looked forward to "peace" and a "free Palestine" were rarely specific about what form that would take, though these were by far the most common responses. A few, when pressed, gave out some detail—"a lasting Fatah–Hamas reconciliation" or "the demolition of the Wall and the checkpoints"—and a few even gave a precise, political definition; they wanted an "Islamic state, from the river to the sea," and they were always willing to linger in order to explain their beliefs.

The first question, about their personal aspirations, invariably produced an awkward silence. When pressed, many ventured that they no longer had any dreams or hopes or that their plight under the Occupation had wiped out any prospects for betterment: "my only hope is that I can feed my family every day" was a common-place response. This low-key melancholy often segued into nihilism. One worker expressed a wish to be dead, explaining that "there is no future for people like me, because I feel that no one really cares about our fate," while another morbidly joked: "if the Israelis did not give us this work, we would have to eat each other." Yet there were also a goodly number who emphasized the importance of "pre-serving their dignity," and even more expressed their desire "to lead a normal life, as they do in other countries." Given the constraints they were living under, this wish for normality was almost utopian. Younger workers were more likely to give precise answers: to build my own house, to start my own business, to travel overseas, to watch Barcelona FC play at the Nou Camp, and, in one case (an unregistered youth), "to marry my contractor's daughter."

Not surprisingly, I often heard the wish "to never see this checkpoint again." Yet, however detested, the checkpoints were more than just places of duress and discipline; they were intensely social locations, where vital information was traded, transactions of all kinds were made, and an assortment of ancillary livelihoods were earned, by drivers of taxis and vans, retailers of food, clothing, tools, and household supplies, and other providers of useful services to those standing in line. Although they were dreaded, the checkpoints were also places of warm camaraderie, and the bonding could turn into solidarity in the face of particularly oppressive conditions.[45] In its own way, the common experience of degradation at checkpoints helped Palestinians learn, or understand, what they all shared in common, overriding the differences between them.[46]

Pathways to Authoritarianism

As a matter of course, I always asked my interviewees if migrant workers were employed alongside them, as general laborers, inside the Green Line. Eritrean and Sudanese (refugees) were mentioned most often, followed by Romanians, Chinese, Moldovans, Poles, Turks, Russians, and Ukrainians. A majority estimated that the migrant workers were paid more (and labored less); in particular, the compensation of the Chinese workers evoked a wide range of opinions. The discrepancy intrigued me, because the recruitment of Chinese to the construction industry was a topic of high-level concern in Israel.

When Chinese laborers were first brought over, they were all carrying heavy debts, from recruitment fees paid out to a series of brokers, including Chinese government officials who customarily took a hefty $6,000 commission. In some cases, according to Kav LaOved staff, the individual debt burden was as high as $30,000.

With an average monthly salary of 5,300 shekels ($1,500), a worker would be hard-pressed to pay down that volume of recruitment debt within the span of a typical three-year contract. In reality, the duration of the contract often turned out to be shorter than promised by private recruitment agencies, resulting in the termination of work permits long before expected.[47] According to one construction worker who used to own a textile business in China, coming to Israel "was not worth it for me because four years on I have only managed to save US$12,000 ... I would have made more than that in China in those years."[48] In addition, some of the documents turned out to be fake, issued by fly-by-night operators. In both circumstances, these Chinese were forced to go underground as a result and were especially vulnerable to wage theft and abuse by their employers. By contrast, migrant workers from countries with which Israel had bilateral treaties enjoyed nominal rights and protections: Bulgaria, Moldova, and Romania in construction; Thailand and Sri Lanka in agriculture; and Nepal for home care workers.

Initially, Israelis preferred Chinese workers because the tidy profits from the recruitment commissions flowed to headhunters and manpower agencies before a single shovel had been picked up. More returns were generated from the trading of surplus permits, through a system akin to trafficking. In response to widespread criticism of the profiteering and labor violations, including from US agencies especially concerned about human trafficking, the government floated a plan in 2015 to bypass the private recruiters and directly import an additional 20,000 workers from China. Trade unionists and labor advocates stiffly opposed the proposal, arguing that, in the absence of a bilateral treaty between Israel and China, the combination of recruitment debt and nonexistent protections would still expose the workers to super-exploitation. The industry's overall needs, they insisted, were better served by West Bank workers or by Israeli Palestinians whose access to the labor market had been hardest hit by the influx of migrants.[49] Subsequent efforts to forge a bilateral treaty with China, which would have outlawed the commissions, ran aground when Beijing repeatedly refused to allow workers to be employed in West Bank settlements. In April

2017, the two countries finally reached an agreement to bring an additional 6,000 construction workers. Specific work locations (none of them outside the Green Line) were named in order to avoid any explicit agreement on Israel's part to recognizing a boycott of the settlements.[50]

In the last few decades of globalization, as the transborder traffic of migrants has escalated, workers have no alternative but to pay high recruitment fees to travel to host countries. In the Persian Gulf, where I had previously done worker research and where South Asians had long replaced Arabs as the preferred labor supply, recruitment debt is key to the system of exploitation—no one would work that hard unless they had a debt to pay off.[51] In Israel, the debt burden is more uneven among migrant groups, and the differences are used to play workers off against one another. Kav LaOved's Einat Podjarny assured me that the indentured status of "the Chinese feeds into the industry mythology that they are the best workers, whereas the reality is that they probably work harder *because* of the debt." In addition, she explained, "the stereotype of the hard worker is used to reinforce contractors' demands for more Chinese permits." A similar principle applies to the semi-bonded status of migrants. As in the *kafala* sponsorship system of the Gulf states, Israel's migrant workers used to be tied (ostensibly because of security concerns) to employers who would routinely keep their passports and take advantage of their dependency. This system was relaxed after Israel was criticized in a human rights assessment from the US State Department, and it received even harsher condemnation in a 2002 report entitled *Migrant Workers in Israel—A Contemporary Form of Slavery*, jointly issued by the International Federation for Human Rights and the Euro-Mediterranean Human Rights Network. Even so, the binding system was partially reestablished in 2011 through a regulation that workers could have no more than three employers and only with Ministry of Interior approval.

Several of my Palestinian interviewees told me they believed that the commissions paid to Chinese officials emboldened workers to appeal to the Chinese Embassy to intercede on their behalf when they were badly treated or robbed of their wages. I could find no evidence of this. Indeed it took a widely publicized series of protests against unpaid wages in 2009—when Chinese workers climbed up cranes and threatened to jump—to get the attention of officials from their embassy.[52] The belief expressed by my interviewees may have had more to do with the absence of protections available to Palestinian workers who found themselves in a similar plight. Nor could I find evidence for the claim, which I also heard, that Palestinians were allocated more dangerous jobs than the migrants with whom they worked and competed. Nevertheless, the available evidence does show that Israel's construction sector is a deadly workplace, with one of the highest rates of accidents in the developed world—more than twice the European average and more than five times the British average—and that non-Israeli workers are twice as likely to lose their lives as Israeli ones.[53] Within a year of the Sino–Israeli agreement on migrant labor supply, the high rates of injury, and some deaths on site, prompted the Chinese authorities to veto as many as thirty-six locations approved as part of the treaty.[54] In the case of Palestinians, those injuries added to high disability rates on the West Bank already boosted by the Israeli military policy of shoot-to-maim.[55]

Some of the blame can also be attributed to the decomposition of Israel's construction industry. Neoliberal economic policies adopted in the 1990s led to the breakup and privatization of state-level companies, like the Histadrut-owned Solel Boneh, which had employed unionized workforces, well-trained in health and safety standards. These firms had largely been replaced by a network of contractors, controlling irregular labor pools, whether from the West Bank or from overseas. As in the Gulf countries, the increasing reliance on cheap casual labor means that construction methods and technologies have not kept up with upgraded standards and innovations elsewhere. This lack of investment in mechanization has led to stagnant productivity levels and a decline in workplace safety. Racism is undoubtedly also a factor; the lives of workers who are regarded as aliens, and as lesser beings, are not valued highly.

Another Future?

Unlike the Gulf states, Israel does not have to recruit expatriate professionals for its development needs. But its comprehensive reliance on a transborder working class with no civil rights or pathway to citizenship precludes its full membership in the northern club of nations to which it so aspires (in line with its carefully curated self-image as a small Western democracy besieged by Arab or Muslim terrorism). Instead, Israel is rapidly consigning itself to the same illiberal league as the Gulf monarchies with whom it has reached a diplomatic understanding, and it has set itself on a similar growth track to an even more authoritarian future.

If another future is possible, then perhaps its seedlings can be found in the work of labor advocates and organizers, enjoying a renaissance in Israel as well as the West Bank. As in other industrialized countries, the new working class is much more difficult to organize and responds better to bodies that are independent of the established national labor federations with their close ties to centralized power. This is certainly true of the new Palestinian unions, operating at a distance from the PGFTU/Fatah fold. So too, the new generation of Israeli labor and human rights groups have learned to work together effectively outside of the orbit of the once mighty Histadrut (representing 85 percent of the total national workforce in the 1970s, and less than 30 percent today), which traditionally did little to protect Palestinian and migrant workers.

In 2015, one such cooperative effort, the Coalition against Accidents in the Workplace, was formed by Kav LaOved's Worker's Hotline, Physicians for Human Rights, WAC-MAAN, and the Association for Civil Rights in Israel. Exposing the lack of routine inspections and the high rate of injury—in the course of 2016, two construction workers suffered serious injury every day, and there was one death every week—the coalition lobbied and shamed government agencies that were failing to enforce basic standards and regulations. Some legislation was passed in response, but arguably the most positive outcome lay in establishing a habit of flexible cooperation between such groups. The bigger challenge was to work with unions or other civil society groups across the Green Line: after the 1980s alliances with the Israeli "peace camp" produced meager results, Palestinian public opinion shifted, and so cooperation with any Israelis, even those opposed to the Occupation, is more and more fraught.

Traditional organizing is not beyond the reach of this new wave. Koach LaOvdim (Power to the Workers) was founded in 2007 as a more democratic union alternative to the Histadrut and immediately took aim at the 2.5 million unorganized workers in Israel. Harnessing the social energy of the mass 2011 street protests against social inequality, it won several significant contracts for groups considered "marginal": part-time professors, cleaners, nannies, and security guards. In response, the Histadrut roused itself and re-entered the field of organizing it had neglected for so long. Like Koach, the federation began to record victories in sectors like hi-tech, finance, and telecommunications that had been considered unorganizable.

When I met him in a café in northern Tel Aviv, Yaniv Bar-Ilan, a key Koach organizer, drew attention to his new union's lack of any party affiliation: "we are a non-partisan, social democratic organization which does not take political positions." He also admitted that "the topic of the Occupation is sensitive within our branches, and especially among rank and file who do not have a larger view of human rights." "Besides," he added, invoking the union's democratic principles, "it would be arrogant of us to impose a political view on new members." Bar-Ilan reported that a contract was in negotiation with Israeli Palestinian bus drivers in East Jerusalem but conceded that the union's neutral stance on the Occupation limited its ability to engage West Bank settlement workers where only Israeli trade unions could operate.

By contrast, Koach's smaller rival, WAC-MAAN, founded in the late 1990s to help workers hard hit by neoliberal deregulation and privatization, was in full-throated opposition to the Occupation. "WAC-MAAN is not so much a union per se," explained Assaf Adiv, the director, "as it is an organizational force for social change, and so taking a position on racism or on the Occupation is a democratic principle in itself." Building on its early success in placing

Israeli Palestinians in the construction industry, the center won the legal right to organize in 2009, and it set about organizing a variety of workforces: Palestinian women in agriculture, Jewish art school teachers, Jews and Palestinians in trucking and in bilingual schools. To date, WAC-MAAN is the only union organizing Palestinians in West Bank settlement zones. "We went there because it was an obligation, not an opportunity," explained Adiv. "In places where Palestinian unions are not allowed, we can support the workers, take on the bosses, and instigate a strike." While WAC-MAAN's campaign to organize the Salit Quarry workforce (described in the previous chapter) was ultimately unsuccessful, the union did subsequently prevail at another facility nearby—Zarfati Garage, a large auto repair firm in the Mishor Adumim zone.

The Zarfati owner had fired long-standing employee Hatem Abu Ziadeh for trying to organize his co-workers, and the legal campaign to have him reinstated turned into a cause. "One worker alone is weak," Abu Ziadeh explained, "because the owner is the one that makes the decisions, who's in control. The worker is afraid, but when the workers join hand-in-hand as one person together, there won't be a possibility for the owner to play one against the other. If he's trying to fire a worker who's from the union he will have to think very carefully, because he knows he will get a response from all of us."[56] At the encouragement of the PGFTU, who could offer no direct help, the workers turned to WAC-MAAN, and after three years of strikes and legal suits, they signed a collective bargaining agreement in February 2017, the first to be won by Palestinians in a West Bank settlement. The agreement (which reinstated Abu Ziadeh) not only granted the workers benefits but also compensation for lost payments, vacation and sick days, and established a professional wage scale based on seniority. Within months, workers at a nearby carpentry shop, Hayei Adam, voted to join the union. In response, employers within the industrial zone began to raise pay to the legal minimum, issue wage slips, and even pay into pension funds—all unheard of before the Zarfati contract.[57]

The Zarfati victory, and other recent wins by WAC-MAAN, Koach LaOvdim, and even the newly active Histadrut, echo the

Courtesy of WAC-MAAN

Workers voting for the Zarfati Garage contract, Mishor Adumim Industrial Zone.

aspirations of many non-Zionist Jewish settlers during the early decades of the twentieth century. In the brief window of time before the Hebrew Labor policy was adopted and zealously promoted by the Histadrut, Arab and Jewish socialists and communists dreamed of a commonwealth achieved through joint labor organizing and insisted that Arab and Jewish workers had mutual interests they could fight for together. The key to co-existence, they believed, lay in side-by-side struggles for workplace rights and shared industrial governance. But the Labor Zionists who got the upper hand opted for separation, exclusion, and territorial conquest, thereby laying the foundations for Israel's apartheid-style state, built largely with Palestinian hands, then and now.

The new organizing efforts among multiethnic groups of workers (and WAC-MAAN's across the Green Line) are being undertaken in a spirit similar to those a century before, though the economic and political landscape has been transformed in the interim. But WAC-MAAN's Adiv had little time for nostalgia: "Today, we are more developed in our thinking about unions and civil society," he pointed out, "we are more attentive to gender and racism—and, though we operate on the current reality, we are also preparing for a future that is not far away." For him, that future included "full political rights in a unitary common state," where the union principle of "one man equals one vote, regardless of origin, or nationality," would serve as a model.

The rightward march of Israeli society stands in the way, as does the economic drive toward private monopolistic power. Since the 1980s, the government has dismantled the strong welfare state built by and for Labor Zionists (though not for West Bank settlers, who continue to enjoy lavish subsidies and services) in order to make way for Israel's "startup nation" of entrepreneurs, with its promise of blockbuster rewards for the winners and small pickings for the rest. Like the well-connected capitalists around the PA who control the economic life of West Bank Palestinians, Israel's assets and wealth have fallen into the hands of a small number of powerful families, and its Gini index—which measures inequality and wealth distribution—is second only to the United States among developed nations. A massive volume of overseas aid props up government programs in both countries. The foreign donors who supply the PA with the wherewithal to pay the salaries of more than 180,000 public employees is well matched by the funding from world Jewry and the US government that pays the bills for Israel's militarized security sector, finances its settlement-building, and bankrolls Jewish immigrant absorption. Indeed, according to one 2012 estimate, the level of per capita aid from foreign donors and governments to Israel is higher than to Palestinians in the Occupied Territories.[58]

On the face of it, a single, secular-democratic state in historic Palestine is no more in the offing in 2018 than it was a century before. The destiny of the Middle East is still largely shaped by the say-so of foreign powers, though none is in a position any longer to make sweeping paternalistic promises, or, just as imperiously, turn around and break them. The most infamous instance of broken promises was the assurances of independence for the region's Arabs in return for their revolt against the Ottoman Empire. That offer (extended in the 1915–16 McMahon–Hussein correspondence) was undermined almost immediately by the Sykes–Picot Agreement, which "awarded" the Ottoman territories in southwestern Asia to Britain and France. The 1917 Balfour Declaration's pledge of a

Jewish "national home" (not exactly a state) in the predominantly Arab lands west of the Jordan was a further breach of faith. Moreover, as Rashid Khalidi pointed out, Balfour's rider—"nothing shall be done which may prejudice the civil and religious rights of existing non-Jewish communities in Palestine"—did not even name the indigenous population, let alone reference their "political rights."[59] Unlike other Arab peoples in the region who were granted some measure of self-government under the postwar British and French Mandates (in Iraq, Lebanon, Syria, and Transjordan), the Palestine Mandate authorities made no such concessions, and there would be no recognition of any rights for Palestinians until the 1974 UN resolutions that launched the idea of the two-state solution.

Though the region today is no longer under the direct sway of colonial overlords, any prospect of a single, multiethnic state in the lands between the Jordan River and the Mediterranean Sea conflicts with the geopolitical interests of a more varied array of foreign powers—Washington, Riyadh, Tehran, Moscow, and Brussels. Over the course of fifty years, the maximal goals of Zionist land annexation have been pursued with the tacit complicity of each of these powers in turn, even as they offered token recognition of Palestinian rights.

As for Arab neighbors in the region, their erstwhile sponsorship of the Palestinian cause has weakened considerably. Decimated by a series of foreign invasions, internal crises, regionwide sectarian antagonism between Saudi Arabia and Iran, and bilateral agreements with Israel, Palestine's natural allies are no longer able, or inclined, to throw their diplomatic weight (let alone their armies) behind support for a just solution. The result has been a shift away from government-level diplomacy toward global solidarity initiatives as part of what Richard Falk calls a "legitimacy war," whereby Palestinian civil society appeals to international law, morality, and human rights through campaigns like BDS, hunger strikes, and anti-apartheid discourse, and through the Boycott from Within from Israel's own dissident citizenry.[60]

By 2010, 42 percent of West Bank territory had already fallen under the jurisdiction of Jewish settlement councils,[61] and by the tail end of the second Obama administration, when John Kerry's State Department aides took fresh (and more accurate) maps of the Occupied Territories to the White House for presidential perusal, it was concluded that the combination of settlement zones and Palestine no-go areas covered almost 60 percent of the West Bank. "It looked like a brain tumor," remarked one official.[62] The settler population today is approaching 750,000, and, with no end in sight to the land grab, the "land for peace" formula is no longer remotely viable as a negotiating tool. While political elites still pay lip service to the vision of an autonomous Palestinian state, most other advocates have pivoted away from partition toward the thorny proposition of securing equal rights for all residents of a future unified state. They argue that a program of civic, and not ethnic, nationalism is needed to deliver a full-blown democracy in the lands of historic Palestine. If that scenario ever advances, then the record of labor contributions outlined in these pages ought to be part of the reckoning.

Given the experience to date, any bargaining over these labor contributions on a purely monetary basis is guaranteed to be a hard, and likely demoralizing, option. For a small taste, consider the long struggle, described earlier in this chapter, to get Israeli authorities to hand over the accumulated sum from decades of social insurance payments. Since Israel has consistently failed to abide by the Oslo agreements, why not add to the final tally all of the pre-1994 payments, blocked from consideration by the Oslo-related Gaza Strip–Jericho Area Agreement? After all, taking these sums off the table was tantamount to massive wage theft, and assessments of them could presumably be drawn up from payroll records.[63]

It would be more difficult to quantify other kinds of arrears from the decades of unfree labor. For example, there are no records pertaining to the denial of minimum wages and social benefits to settlement workers, nor any estimates for the loss of income from border closures, checkpoint blockages, and arbitrary revocations of work permits. One could reasonably add to the list compensations for the denial of the right to work, obstruction of access to collective bargaining and legal avenues for redress, and income deprivation from the policies of collective punishment and economic underdevelopment in the Occupied Territories. Finally, how to account for the common employer practice of underreporting wages and hours in order to avoid making social security payments?[64] These and other liabilities are all part of the inventory of debts run up in the course of the long *Nakba*. But a full settling of these obligations might have to go beyond monetary redress, and it should be inclusive of rights recognition.

Israeli officials, deeply fearful of opening the Pandora's box of the *Nakba*, have been loath to include any restitution claims in the roster of issues to be negotiated in final status talks. But a properly decolonial outcome cannot ignore the pattern of plunder that began in 1948 and has not yet run its course. Advocates for a fair-minded resolution of the national conflict have produced rough sketches for how to measure and discharge these debts. "Transitional justice" is one model for moving the parties beyond wrangling over restitution and return; its toolbox includes truth-telling, reconciliation, and other forms of symbolic recognition as part of reparations.[65] Omar Barghouti, prime architect of the BDS campaign, has gone further, outlining a blueprint for "ethical decolonization" in a single, secular state, where the settlers are accepted by the indigenous population as legitimate residents on the condition that they give up all colonial privileges.[66]

For obvious reasons, the remedies regarding confiscated land and property have taken precedence in the proposals for a *Nakba* settlement, but to my knowledge no one has considered the moral claims arising from the history of unfair labor utilization described in these pages. I have only touched on this line of argument in the course of this book. It is a complex topic, and it merits further elaboration by those with the proper reasoning and expertise. But the root principle of just deserts is a simple one. Or, as one of my cross-border interviewees put it, "I've been building homes every day over there for thirty years. In a way, it's really my country too, isn't it?"

Notes

Preface

1. Benny Morris, *The Birth of the Palestinian Refugee Problem Revisited, 1947–1949*, Cambridge: Cambridge University Press, 2004, 248–52; Walid Khalidi, ed., *All That Remains: The Palestinian Villages Occupied and Depopulated by Israel in 1948*, Washington, DC: Institute for Palestine Studies, 1992, 514–47.
2. Transcribed testimony of Yerachmiel Kahanovich in Kibbutz Degania Alef on July 23, 2012, exhibited in Eyal Sivan, *Towards a Common Archive—Video Testimonies of Zionist Fighters in 1948*, trans. Ami Asher, Arts & Humanities Research Council, thehypertexts.com.
3. Quoted in Walid Khalidi, "Plan Dalet: Master Plan for the Conquest of Palestine," *Journal of Palestine Studies* 18: 1, 1988, 4–33, is-studies.org.
4. Yigal Allon, *The Book of the Palmach*, vol. 2, Tel Aviv: Hakibbutz Hameuchad, 1965, 286. Quoted in Morris, *The Birth of the Palestinian Refugee Problem Revisited*, 250. Ilan Pappé references some of the cleansing language, and the subsequent renaming efforts to conceal it, in *The Ethnic Cleansing of Palestine*, Oxford: Oneworld Publications, 2006, 94, 158.
5. The Allon Plan called for Israeli annexation of the Jordan Valley, East Jerusalem, and the Gush Etzion settlement bloc and for returning the more heavily populated areas of the West Bank to Jordanian rule. The Oslo Accords more or less designated these latter areas as Area A, nominally under control of the Palestinian Authority.
6. In *My Enemy, My Self* (Garden City: Doubleday, 1989), his book about masquerading as a Palestinian from Balata refugee camp, Israeli Jewish journalist Yoram Binur recounts his fruitless application efforts to work as a volunteer in an Israeli kibbutz. He was finally

accepted at one in the Golan Heights, but only after his *Haaretz* editor interceded, and he almost inevitably fell under suspicion after a robbery occurred at the kibbutz.

7. Lara El-Jazairi, Fionna Smyth, and Marwa El-Ansary, *On the Brink: Israeli Settlements and Their Impact on Palestinians in the Jordan Valley*, Oxfam Briefing Paper 160, Oxfam International, July 2012, oxfam-wereldwinkels.be. Al Haq, *Water for One People Only: Discriminatory Access and "Water-Apartheid" in the OPT*, Ramallah, 2013, alhaq.org.

8. Amira Hass, "PA Farmers Hung Out to Dry While Israelis Flourish in Jordan Valley," *Haaretz*, December 2, 2012. For a longer analysis of blocked Palestinian access, see the Amnesty International report, *Troubled Waters: Palestinians Denied Fair Access to Water*, October 2009, amnestyusa.org, and Al Haq, *Water for One People Only*.

9. Tali Heruti-Sover, "Low Pay, No Leave: Jordan Valley Farmers Exploiting Palestinian Labor," *Haaretz*, May 14, 2014.

10. Bill Van Esveld, *Ripe for Abuse: Palestinian Child Labor in Israeli Agricultural Settlements in the West Bank*, Human Rights Watch, April 13, 2015, hrw.org.

Introduction

1. Quoted in Barbara McKean Parmenter, *Giving Voice to Stones: Place and Identity in Palestinian Literature*, Austin: Texas University Press, 1994, 1.

2. Cesar Chelala, "Palestinian Olive Trees: Destroying a Symbol of Life," *Counterpunch*, November 3, 2015.

3. The data is cited in Palestine Trade Center et al., *State of Palestine National Export Strategy: Stone and Marble: Sector Export Strategy 2014–2018*, Ramallah, 2014, 1, paltrade.org.

4. Physician and folklorist Tawfik Canaan documents the craft in *The Palestinian Arab House, Its Architecture and Folklore*, Jerusalem: Syrian Orphanage Press, 1933.

5. Although the percentage of the Palestinian workforce employed in Israel in 2017 was slightly lower than at its peak in 1988, the overall numbers were higher. According to the Palestinian Central Bureau of Statistics *Labor Force Survey*, January–March 2017, pcbs.gov.ps: "the number of employed individuals employed in Israel and Israeli settlements was 139,600 in the 1st quarter 2017 … Of these, 68,500 had a permit, 48,700 worked without any permit and 22,400 employed individuals have an Israeli identity card or foreign passport." An additional 24,000 worked in settlements, while almost 60 percent were

employed in construction. Bank of Israel data for the first quarter of 2018 showed unemployment rates in Israel at 3.7 percent, in a steady state of decline from the high levels after 2008. *Economic Indicators: Israeli Economic Data* (2017), boi.org.il.

6. National Economic Council, "Future Housing Needs in Israel, 2016–2040," 2016, cited in Bank of Israel, *Annual Report 2016*, Chapter 9, "Construction and the Housing Market," boi.org.il.

7. The estimate was based on 2011 employer reports and was published by the Interministerial Committee for the Regularization, Monitoring and Enforcement of Palestinian Employment in Israel (the "Eckstein Report"), cited in Shlomo Swirski and Noga Dagan-Buzaglo, *The Occupation: Who Pays the Price? The Impact of the Occupation on Israeli Society and Economy*, Tel Aviv: Adva Center, 2017, 48.

8. Records and registries of refugee losses have been compiled over the decades by a range of institutions—the United Nations Conciliation Commission for Palestine, UNRWA, and the Israeli State Archives—while others, such as Badil, International Development Research Centre, Chatham House, Palestine Refugee ResearchNet, and the Geneva Institute, have generated further research. Senechal and Hilal's estimate is laid out in "The Value of 1948 Palestinian Refugee Material Damages: An Estimate Based on International Standards," in Rex Brynen and Roula El-Rifai, eds., *Compensation to Palestinian Refugees and the Search for Palestinian–Israeli Peace*, London: Pluto Press, 2013, 132–58. For related analyses, see Michael Fischbach, *Records of Dispossession: Palestinian Refugee Property and the Arab–Israeli Conflict*, New York: Columbia University Press, 2003, and Megan Bradley, *Refugee Repatriation: Justice, Responsibility and Redress*, Cambridge: Cambridge University Press, 2013.

9. Andrzej Kapiszewski estimates that, by 2002, the Arab proportion of migrant workers in the Gulf had fallen to around 25–29 percent, from a peak of 72 percent in 1975. "Arab Labour Migration to the GCC States," in *Arab Migration in a Globalized World*, Geneva: International Organization for Migration, 2004, 115–34; Abdulhadi Khalaf, Omar Al-Shehabi, and Adam Hanieh, eds., *Transit States: Labour, Migration and Citizenship in the Gulf*, London: Pluto Press, 2015.

10. See Suad Amiry's account of traveling with a group of border crossers, in *Nothing to Lose but Your Life: An 18-Hour Journey with Murad*, New York: Bloomsbury, 2010.

11. In reference to Raja Shehadeh's description of the *samedin*, Edward Said writes: "Work first becomes a form of elementary resistance, a way of turning presence into small-scale obduracy. You accept

the narrowness of opportunity as a given, and you consider change, for the foreseeable future, as bringing worse, rather than better, conditions. Work then becomes a daily articulation of the formidably precise status quo into which you are bound; it brings you to a performance of your actual condition that, you find, sparks your consciousness of what you are all about, where you are to be found, how maddeningly complicated are the mechanisms that surround you. Raja Shehadeh says that sometimes at that very point you discover your freedom, which is neither capitulation nor 'blind, consuming hate,' but a sense that 'your mind is the one thing that you can prevent your oppressor from having the power to touch.'" *After the Last Sky: Palestinian Lives,* New York: Columbia University Press, 1999, 100.

12. Chaim Weizmann is often credited with coining, for Israel, the aspirational moniker of "the Switzerland of the Middle East."

13. Shlomo Sand, *The Invention of the Land of Israel: From Holy Land to Homeland,* London: Verso, 2014, 30.

14. Asa Maron and Michael Shalev, eds., *Neoliberalism as a State Project: Changing the Political Economy of Israel,* Oxford: Oxford University Press, 2017; Toufic Haddad, *Palestine Ltd.: Neoliberalism and Nationalism in the Occupied Territory,* London: I.B. Taurus, 2016; Idith Zertal and Akiva Eldar, *Lords of the Land: The War Over Israel's Settlements in the Occupied Territories, 1967–2007,* New York: Nation Books, 2007.

15. Statistics are from tradingeconomics.com.

16. The Israeli Supreme Court has ruled that there is no such thing as Israeli nationality, on the grounds that this would undermine the nation's Jewish character. See Ali Abunimah, *The Battle for Justice in Palestine,* Chicago: Haymarket, 2014, 26.

17. See the proposals collected in Joshua Simon, ed., *Solution 196–213 United States of Palestine–Israel,* Berlin: Sternberg Press, 2011.

18. B'Tselem, "By Hook and by Crook: Israeli Settlement Policy in the West Bank," July 2010, btselem.org.

19. See "The One State Declaration," issued by leading intellectuals after two meetings in 2007, published on *Electronic Intifada,* November 29, 2007, electronicintifada.net; and the essays collected in Antony Loewenstein and Ahmed Moor, eds., *After Zionism: One State for Israel and Palestine,* London: Saqi Books, 2012; Ali Abunimah, *One Country: A Bold Proposal to End the Israeli–Palestinian Impasse,* New York: Picador, 2007; Jamil Hilal, ed., *Where Now for Palestine? The Demise of the Two-State Solution,* London: Zed Books, 2007; Hani Faris, ed., *The Failure of the Two-State Solution: The Prospects of One*

State in the Israel–Palestine Conflict, London: I.B. Taurus, 2013; Mazin Qumsiyeh, *Sharing the Land of Canaan: Human Rights and the Israeli–Palestinian Struggle,* London: Pluto Press, 2004; Virginia Tilley, *The One-State Solution: A Breakthrough Plan for Peace in the Israeli–Palestinian Deadlock,* Manchester: Manchester University Press, 2005; Jeff Halper, "The One Democratic State Campaign," *Mondoweiss,* May 3, 2018, mondoweiss.net; and Ariella Azoulay and Adi Ophir, *The One-State Condition: Occupation and Democracy in Israel/Palestine,* Stanford: Stanford University, 2012. Salman Abu Sitta, founder and president of Palestine Land Society, is one of the most dedicated interpreters of, and advocates for, the feasibility of the right to return, estimating that 85 percent of the lands taken from the Palestinians in 1948 are still available for resettlement. See his essay, "The Implementation of the Right of Return," in Roane Carey, ed., *The New Intifada: Resisting Israel's Apartheid,* London: Verso, 2001, and *The Atlas of Palestine (1917–1966),* London: Palestine Land Society, 2010, plands.org; and *Mapping My Return: A Palestinian Memoir,* Cairo: American University in Cairo Press, 2016.

20. Gary Fields argues that Zionist land appropriation should be seen in the context of centuries of *enclosures* of the commons, primarily in Britain and North America. *Enclosure: Palestinian Landscapes in a Historical Mirror,* Berkeley: University of California Press, 2017.

21. Matthew Vickery argues that the conditions under which Palestinians work in the West Bank settlements merit the label of "forced labor," according to International Labour Organization definitions. *Employing the Enemy: The Story of Palestinian Labourers on Israeli Settlements,* London: Zed Books, 2017, 112–26.

1. Conquest and Manpower

1. Patrick Wolfe, "Settler Colonialism and the Elimination of the Native," *Journal of Genocide Research* 8: 4, 2006, 387–409. In discussions of Israeli settler colonialism, the most cited comparison is typically with the case of South Africa. See Ilan Pappé, *Israel and South Africa: The Many Faces of Apartheid,* London: Zed Books, 2015.

2. Theodor Herzl, *The Complete Diaries of Theodor Herzl, Vol. 1,* trans. Harry Zohn, New York: Herzl Press, 1960, 88 (entry for June 12, 1895).

3. Cited in Benny Morris, *Righteous Victims: A History of the Zionist Arab Conflict, 1881–2001,* New York: Knopf, 2001, 144.

4. Cited in Nur Masalha, *Expulsion of the Palestinians: The Concept of*

"Transfer" in Zionist Political Thought, 1882–1948, Beirut: Institute for Palestine Studies, 1992, 131–32.

5. The proletarianization of the Palestinian peasantry began in the 1930s, when rural families sent members to work in the fast-developing coastal enterprises, and picked up during the war, when the British Mandate employed an expanded workforce. See Rachelle Taqqu, "Peasants into Workmen: Internal Labor Migration and the Arab Village Community Under the Mandate," in Joel Migdal, ed., *Palestinian Society and Politics,* Princeton: Princeton University Press, 1980, 261–85.

6. Gershon Shafir argues that it was the early conflicts over labor competition between settlers and natives that shaped the career of Zionism on the ground in Palestine, transforming Jewish immigrants into Israelis and indigenous Arabs into Palestinians, both of them nationalist. *Land, Labor, and the Origins of the Israeli–Palestinian Conflict 1882–1914,* Cambridge: Cambridge University Press, 1989.

7. Their unauthorized squat on this land initiated a long-running dispute with Palestine Jewish Colonization Association over the legality of the new settlement. See Joshua Muravchik, *Heaven on Earth: The Rise and Fall of Socialism,* London: Encounter Books, 2003, 324. According to the invaluable inventory of Palestinian villages destroyed during the *Nakba,* the site was on traditional land belonging to the now lost village of Ghuwayr Abu Shusha. Walid Khalidi, ed., *All That Remains,* Washington, DC: Institute for Palestine Studies, 1992, 517.

8. According to Sharon Rotbard, "*Homa Umigdal* is the fundamental paradigm of all Jewish architecture in Israel, and it germinated the future characteristics of Israeli architecture and town planning; hasty translation of political agenda into an act of construction, occupation of territory through settlement and infrastructure, high priority given to the building's security functions and military capabilities … and informed use of modernity." Rotbard, "Wall and Tower (*Homa Umigdal*): The Mold of Israeli Architecture," in Rafi Segal and Eyal Weiznman, eds., *A Civilian Occupation: The Politics of Israeli Architecture,* Tel Aviv: Babel, 2003, 46.

9. After 1967, the Gush Emunim settler movement took further advantage of this rule, refurbished by Israeli lawmakers, in order to win government recognition for its improvised hilltop outposts.

10. The battle with the villagers and the longstanding conflict with Palestine Jewish Colonization Association is described by Anita Shapira in her biography, *Yigal Allon, Native Son,* Philadelphia: University of Pennsylvania Press, 2008, 51–78.

11. Muravchik, *Heaven on Earth*, 325.

12. A. D. Gordon, "Our Tasks Ahead" (1920), in Arthur Herzberg, ed., *The Zionist Idea: A Historical Analysis and Reader*, Garden City, NY: Doubleday and Herzl Press, 1959, 381–82.

13. A. D. Gordon, *Selected Essays by Aaron David Gordon*, trans. Frances Burnce, New York: League for Labor Palestine, 1938.

14. Avraham Granott, *The Land System in Palestine: History and Structure*, London: Eyre & Spottiswoode, 1952, 175.

15. Shafir, *Land, Labor, and the Origins of the Israeli–Palestinian Conflict*, 45–78.

16. Ibid., 96–105. When the Yemenite "solution" failed, interest was sparked in importing Bedouins from Baghdad who claimed to be Jews. Tom Segev, *One Palestine, Complete: Jews and Arabs Under the British Mandate*, New York: Metropolitan Books, 1999, 287.

17. See Moshe Semyonov and Noah Lewin-Epstein, *Hewers of Wood and Drawers of Water: Noncitizen Arabs in the Israeli Labor Market*, Ithaca, New York: ILR Press, 1987.

18. Shafir, *Land, Labor, and the Origins of the Israeli–Palestinian Conflict*, 56.

19. Steven A. Glazer, "Picketing for Hebrew Labor: A Window on Histadrut Tactics and Strategy," *Journal of Palestine Studies* 30: 4, 2001, 39–54; Hizky Shoham, "Buy Local or Buy Jewish? Separatist Consumption in Interwar Palestine," *International Journal of Middle East Studies* 45: 3, 2013, 469–89.

20. Michael Shalev analyzes the Histadrut's multiple functions in *Labour and the Political Economy in Israel*, Oxford: Oxford University Press, 1992, 23–80.

21. Elia Zureik, *Palestinians in Israel: A Study in Internal Colonialism*, New York: Routledge, 1979, 35.

22. Zeev Sternhell argues that the expressed socialist beliefs of Labor Zionist leaders, like David Ben-Gurion and Berl Katznelson, were mostly a rhetorical sideshow for their primary interest in promoting nationalism. *The Founding Myths of Israel*, Princeton: Princeton University Press, 1999, 134–78.

23. See Anita Shapira, *Futile Struggle: The Jewish Labor Controversy, 1929–1939*, Tel Aviv: Hakibbutz Hameuchad, 1977 (Hebrew).

24. Steven A. Glazer, "Language of Propaganda: The Histadrut, Hebrew Labor, and the Palestinian Worker," *Journal of Palestine Studies* 36: 2, 2007, 28.

25. Ibid., 25–38.

26. Ibid., 33.

27. David De Vries analyzes the long season of strike actions in the region in *Strike Action and Nation Building: Labor Unrest in Palestine/Israel, 1899–1951*, New York: Berghahn, 2015. By the 1930s, he argues that strike actions were more "politicized" than "nationalized" and that the Histadrut leadership had concluded that strikes were an "ineffective means" of persuading employers to prefer Jews over Arabs (53).

28. George Mansour, "The Arab Worker Under the Palestine Mandate (1937)," *Settler Colonial Studies* 2: 1, 2012, 200.

29. Bat-Sheva Margalit Stern, "'A Queen Without a Kingdom': Jewish Women Workers in the Labor Force in Mandatory Palestine," in *Economy and Society in Mandatory Palestine, 1918–1948*, Iyunim Bitkumat Israel, 2003, 107–53 (Hebrew).

30. Jacob Norris, *Land of Progress: Palestine in the Age of Colonial Development, 1905–1948*, Oxford: Oxford University Press, 2013, 173.

31. Lockman covers the controversy over joint organizing and the formation of PAWS in *Comrades and Enemies: Arab and Jewish Workers in Palestine, 1906–1948*, Berkeley: University of California Press, 1996, 80–85 and 145–47.

32. Baruch Kimmerling and Joel S. Migdal, *Palestinians: The Making of a People*, New York: Free Press, 1993, 51. Sawt el-Amel (The Laborer's Voice) summarizes the history of Arab organization under the Mandate in "Separate and Unequal: The History of Arab Labour in pre-1948 Palestine and Israel," December 2006, labournet.net.

33. De Vries, *Strike Action and Nation Building*, 51.

34. Ghassan Kanafani, *The 1936–1939 Revolt in Palestine*, New York: Committee for a Democratic Palestine, 1972, 12–20.

35. Zeev Studni, "The Nesher Workers' Strike," *Measef* 6, 1974, 166–75 (Hebrew).

36. See Lockman's account of the Nesher strikes in *Comrades and Enemies*, 85–88.

37. Ibid., 87.

38. Quoted in Deborah Bernstein, *Constructing Boundaries: Jewish and Arab Workers in Mandatory Palestine*, New York: SUNY Press, 2000, 136.

39. On the same website page, the company declares: "From the development and building of the Jewish home in Israel, through Israel's establishment as an independent state that supplies its own building materials, and up to the present, Nesher has supplied and still supplies most of the cement used in Israel today." Omitted is any mention of its near-monopoly on cement traded to the Occupied Territories,

which is distributed in green bags, whereas Israeli cement is in red bags; see nesher.co.il/en/history-nesher.

40. For example, this principle was more strictly observed, and for primarily religious reasons, at the Rishon LeZion wine cellar, where ritual wine products could only be touched by Jews.

41. Glenn Yago, "Whatever Happened to the Promised Land?: Capital Flows and the Israeli State," *Berkeley Journal of Sociology* 21, 1976–77, 117–146.

42. Zureik argues, in *Palestinians in Israel* (5, 33–66), that there were not two separate sectors but both "were interconnected in an asymmetrical relationship, mediated by the British presence."

43. Dorothy Willner, *Nation-Building and Community in Israel*, Princeton: Princeton University Press, 1969, 153, 321.

44. Quoted in David Hirst, *The Gun and the Olive Branch*, 2nd ed., New York: Nation Books, 2003, 185, citing *Haaretz*, November 15, 1969.

45. Lockman, *Comrades and Enemies*, 229–31.

46. Mansour, "The Arab Worker Under the Palestine Mandate (1937)," 202–3.

47. Ibid., 204.

48. Lockman, *Comrades and Enemies*, 245.

49. David Hacohen, *Time to Tell: An Israeli Life, 1898–1984*, trans. by Menachem Dagut, New York: Cornwall Books, 1985.

50. Rosemary Sayigh, *The Palestinians: From Peasants to Revolutionaries*, London: Zed Press, 1979, 60.

51. Yehouda Shenhav, *The Arab Jews: A Postcolonial Reading of Nationalism, Religion, and Ethnicity*, Stanford, CA: Stanford University Press, 2006, 37.

52. As reported by James MacDonald, the first US ambassador to Israel, in *My Mission in Israel, 1948–1951*, London: Gollancz, 1951, 160–1.

53. See Nur Masalha, *Expulsion of the Palestinians*, and *The Palestine Nakba: Decolonising History, Narrating the Subaltern, Reclaiming Memory*, London: Zed Books, 2012; 'Arif-al-'Arif, *Al-Nakba*, Beirut and Sidon: Al-Maktaba al-'Asriyya, 1956–1960. In his extensive registry of depopulated localities, *The Palestinian Nakba 1948*, London: Palestinian Return Centre, 2000, Salman Abu Sitta records the full geographical extent of the expulsions.

54. Adel Manna, *Nakba and Survival: The Story of the Palestinians Who Remained in Haifa and the Galilee, 1948–1956*, Jerusalem: Van Leer Institute and Hakibbutz Hameuchad, 2017 (Hebrew).

55. Nur Masalha, ed., *Catastrophe Remembered: Palestine, Israel, and the Internal Refugees*, London: Zed Books, 2005.

56. For details of the labor camps, see Ilan Pappé, *The Ethnic Cleansing of Palestine*, Oxford: Oneworld Publications, 2006, 202–3.

57. I undertook the trip along with Magid Shihade, native of the village and author of an incisive study of interethnic conflicts in the region, *Not Just a Soccer Game: Colonialism and Conflict Among Palestinians in Israel*, Syracuse: Syracuse University Press, 2011.

58. Shira Robinson uses this term in *Citizen Strangers: Palestinians and the Birth of Israel's Liberal Settler State*, Stanford, CA: Stanford University Press, 2013. For other comprehensive accounts of the situation of Israeli Palestinians, see Ben White, *Palestinians in Israel: Segregation, Discrimination and Democracy*, London: Pluto Press, 2011; Ilan Pappé, *The Forgotten Palestinians: A History of the Palestinians in Israel*, New Haven, CT, and London: Yale University Press, 2011; Nadim Rouhana, *Palestinian Citizens in an Ethnic Jewish State: Identities in Conflict*, New Haven, CT: Yale University Press, 1997; As'ad Ghanem, *The Palestinian-Arab Minority in Israel, 1948–2000*, New York: The State University of New York Press, 2001; Baruch Kimmerling and Joel S. Migdal, *The Palestinian People: A History*, Cambridge: Harvard University Press, 2003; David A. Wesley, *State Practices and Zionist Images: Shaping Economic Development in Arab Towns in Israel*, New York: Berghahn, 2006.

59. Shalev, *Labor and the Political Economy of Israel*, 46.

60. See Michael Shalev's analysis of the post-1948 exclusion and incorporation of Israeli Palestinians into the labor market, in "Jewish Organized Labor and the Palestinians: A Study of State/Society Relations in Israel," in Baruch Kimmerling, ed., *The Israeli State and Society: Boundaries and Frontiers*, Albany: State University of New York Press, 1989, 93–133.

61. Don Peretz, "Early State Policy Toward the Arab Population: 1948–1955," in Laurence Silberstein, ed., *New Perspectives on Israeli History: The Early Years of the State*, New York: New York University Press, 1991, 98; Yoram Ben-Porath, *The Arab Labor Force in Israel*, Jerusalem: Maurice Falk Institute for Economic Research, 1966, 62.

62. Sabri Jiryis, *The Arabs in Israel*, Beirut: Institute of Palestine Studies, 1969, 85–6.

63. Cited by Ian Lustick in *Arabs in the Jewish State: Israel's Control of a National Minority*, Austin: University of Texas Press, 1980, 17–18. Lustick also excerpts a 1957 journalist's report about Arab workers in Haifa: "Many are the children of peasant families that do not have enough land to feed every mouth. Others are the sons of landless refugees. With their weekly pay of 1£ 12–20 they must not only maintain

themselves but help support their parents and their younger brothers and sisters. In the summertime, the boys find themselves places to sleep in uncompleted houses under construction ... In the evening, the owner ... locks them up inside, releasing them in the morning when he comes to work."

64. Jiryis, *The Arabs in Israel*, 165.

65. See Ben-Porath's analysis of census data in *The Arab Labor Force in Israel*, 20–36 (Table 2-3. *Non-Jewish Employed Persons as a Per Cent of All Employed Persons, by Industry: 1961 and 1963*, 25; and Table 2-8. *Non-Jewish Employed Men by Occupation: 1954–1963*, 29).

66. Yael Allweil, "Israeli Housing and Nation Building: Establishment of the State-Citizen Contract, 1948–1953," in *Traditional Dwellings and Settlements Review* 23: 2, 2012, 55. Lustick cites the 200,000 number in *Arabs in the Jewish State*, 58.

67. The phrase, from an Immigration Department document, is cited by Tom Segev, *The First Israelis*, New York: Free Press, 1986, 171.

68. Allweil, "Israeli Housing and Nation Building," 59–61.

69. See Julie Peteet, *Landscape of Hope and Despair: Palestinian Refugee Camps*, Philadelphia: University of Pennsylvania Press, 2005.

70. G. Berg Kjersti, "From Chaos to Order and Back," in Sari Hanafi, Leila Hilal and Lex Takkenberg, eds., *UNRWA and Palestinian Refugees: From Relief and Works to Human Development*, London: Routledge, 2014, 109–28.

71. See Nasser Abourahme, "Assembling and Spilling-Over: Towards an 'Ethnography of Cement' in a Palestinian Refugee Camp," *International Journal of Urban and Regional Research* 39: 2, 2014, 200–17.

72. Sari Hanafi and Philipp Misselwitz, "Testing a New Paradigm: UNRWA's Camp Improvement Programme," *Refugee Survey Quarterly* 28: 2–3, 2009, 360–88.

73. Zvi Efrat refers to this centrally planned program of town and village building, administered and engineered from the top down, as "The Israeli Project," in a watershed 2004 exhibition of that title. See Zvi Efrat, *The Israeli Project: Building and Architecture 1948–1973*, Tel Aviv Museum of Art, 2005; and "The Plan: Drafting the Israeli National Space," in Segal and Weizman, eds., *A Civilian Occupation*, 59–76.

74. See Dorothy Willner's account of the *moshvei olim*, in *Nation-Building and Community in Israel*.

75. Robinson, *Citizen Strangers*, 49.

76. Ella Shohat initiated an influential line of inquiry about the structural subordination of Israel's "Oriental Jews" in Israel, in "Sephardim in

Israel: Zionism from the Standpoint of Its Jewish Victims," *Social Text*, no. 19/20, Autumn 1988, 1–35. Her related essays on this topic are collected in *On the Arab–Jew, Palestine, and Other Displacements*, London: Pluto Press, 2017.

77. See Sami Shalom Chetrit, *Intra-Jewish Conflict in Israel, White Jews, Black Jews,* London: Routledge, 2010; Oren Yiftachel, "The Consequences of Planning Control," in Jo Little, David Hedgcock, Ian Alexander, and Oren Yiftachel, eds., *The Power of Planning: Spaces of Control and Transformation*, Dordrecht: Kluwer, 2001, 117–34.

78. Arnon Golan, "Jewish Settlement of Former Arab Towns and Their Incorporation into the Urban Israeli System," in Alexander Bligh, ed., *The Israeli Palestinians: An Arab Minority in the Jewish State*, London: Taylor & Francis, 2003, 154.

79. Gideon Levy, "Exposing Israel's Original Sins," *Haaretz*, November 3, 2000. Also see Benny Morris, "The Transfer of Al Majdal's Remaining Arabs to Gaza, 1950," in *1948 and After: Israel and the Palestinians,* Oxford: Oxford University Press, 1994; and, more generally, Nur Masalha, *A Land Without a People: Israel, Transfer and the Palestinians 1949–96*, London: Faber & Faber, 2004, 9–10.

80. For more statistics, see Yechiel Harari, ed., *Arabs in Israel: Statistics and Facts*, 2nd and rev. ed., Givat Haviva, Center for Arab and Afro–Asian Studies, 1970, and Zureik, *Palestinians in Israel*, 122–29.

81. Haviv Rettig Gur, "Study Finds Huge Wage Gap Between Ashkenazim, Mizrahim," *Times of Israel*, January 29, 2014.

82. See Moshe Semyonov and Noah Lewin-Epstein, *Hewers of Wood and Drawers of Water.*

83. Even without the numbers of undocumented, Neve Gordon observes that this "phenomenon whereby almost 40 percent of the workforce is employed outside the local market has no parallel in the world." *Israel's Occupation*, Berkeley: University of California Press, 2008, 81.

84. The training programs were aimed at advanced skills and at moving recruits into site management after a few years on the job. See Nimrod Bousso, "Who Is Building Israel's Homes?" *Haaretz*, April 16, 2015.

2. From *Kurkar* to Concrete and Back

1. A typical example can be found in the photograph of a "Jewish building laborer" in Joachim Schlor, *Tel Aviv: From Dream to City,* London: Reaktion Books, 1999, 64, captioned by a quote from Oskar Neumann: "Here the classic people of cafes and of cafe writers has overcome that swamp fever of the *Galuth* and is instead dedicating

itself to achieving fitness of mind and body." Artist Dani Karavan, closely associated with White City mythologizing, conjured up a similar image of the philosopher-builder, who shares pride of place in the Labor Zionist pantheon with the educated kibbutznik farmer: "here on the distant white dunes, former students of medicine, law, and philosophy were mixing sand with gravel, water, and cement and pouring the mixture into wood and metal moulds to form brick and grey building blocks." "Tel-Aviv," in Nitza Smuk, ed., *Dwelling on the Dunes: Tel Aviv, Modern Movement and Bauhaus Ideals,* Paris: Editions de l'Eclat, 2004, 13.

2. According to Deborah Bernstein, these women were active in setting up cooperatives that competed for job contracts after they were shunned by the construction workers union. *Pioneers and Homemakers: Jewish Women in Pre-State Israel,* Albany: SUNY Press, 1992, 192–93. Tiling was the one trade where they made the most inroads, because they were competing with Arabs and Yemenite Jews and not Ashkenazis. Despite this breakthrough, in the mid-1920s, they were laid off in the subsequent economic slowdown (due to a decrease in immigrant capital), and it was another ten years before they were able to recover their niche. Deborah Bernstein, *The Struggle for Equality: Urban Women Workers in Prestate Israeli Society,* Westport, CT: Praeger, 1987, 48–51 and 124–25.

3. For documentation of the exhibition, see eretzmuseum.org.il/e/149.

4. JNF director Arthur Ruppin had grander aims: "The founding of a proper Jewish quarter is the best way for the Jews to take over Jaffa financially." Quoted in Annabel Jane Wharton, *Building the Cold War: Hilton International Hotels and Modern Architecture,* Chicago: University of Chicago Press, 2004, 109.

5. Hizky Shoham, "Tel Aviv's Foundation Myth," in Maoz Azaryahu and Ilan Troen, eds., *Tel Aviv: The First Century,* Bloomington: Indiana University Press, 2011, 38.

6. Mark LeVine, *Overthrowing Geography: Jaffa, Tel Aviv, and the Struggle for Palestine, 1880–1948,* Berkeley and Los Angeles: University of California Press, 2005, 71–2. LeVine also suggests that it is likely that Jaffan Arabs were hired to level and straighten the mythical sand dunes to grade the land (258, note 4) and that Arab guards were subsequently used to protect the settlement (290, note 71).

7. Yosef Eliyahu Chelouche, *Reminiscences of My Life, 1870–1930,* Tel Aviv: Babel, 1931, 2005, 126–7.

8. Ibid., 117.

9. Ibid., 427.

10. Or Aleksandrowicz offers an analysis of the competition over building materials in "*Kurkar*, Cement, Arabs, Jews: Building a Hebrew Town," *Theory and Criticism* 36, Spring 2010, 61–87 (Hebrew).

11. See Nathan Harpaz, *Zionist Architecture and Town Planning: The Building of Tel Aviv, 1919–1929*, West Lafayette, IN: Purdue University Press, 2013, 49–52.

12. Aleksandrowicz, "*Kurkar*, Cement, Arabs, Jews," 56–58.

13. Ofra Yeshua-Leit, "Hebrew and Arab, Zionist and Palestinian, Tel Aviv and Jaffa: The Case of *My Life*," *Haaretz*, August 15, 2005.

14 Harpaz, *Zionist Architecture and Town Planning*, 189.

15. Ibid., 203–4.

16. Mark Tessler, *A History of the Israeli–Palestinian Conflict*, Bloomington: Indiana University Press, 1994, 189.

17. The report, and the accompanying Passfield White Paper, recommended the limitation of Jewish immigration as a way of offsetting the pattern of exclusion. Worldwide Zionist backlash to Passfield resulted in a revresal by the British government, signaled by Ramsay MacDonald's infamous letter to Chaim Weizmann, president of the Zionist Organization, which reaffirmed the spirit of the Balfour Declaration. The climbdown set a pattern of forced withdrawals of criticism by foreign governments and lawmakers of Zionist policy-making that continues to this day.

18. John Hope Simpson, *Palestine: Report on Immigration, Land Settlement and Development*, October 1930, available at jewishvirtuallibrary.org/hope-simpson-report.

19. See Haim Yacobi, ed., *Constructing a Sense of Place: Architecture and The Zionist Discourse*, London: Routledge, 2004.

20. Quoted in LeVine, *Overthrowing Geography*, 161.

21. Ibid., 172.

22. Helen Meller, *Patrick Geddes: Social Evolutionist and City Planner*, Oxford: Oxford University Press, 1990, 195.

23. Quoted in Noah Hysler-Rubin, *Patrick Geddes and Town Planning: A Critical View*, London: Routledge, 2011, 98.

24. Some of the most eclectic buildings, ironically, were designed by Alexander Levy, who had earlier advocated for a more functional, pragmatic program for mass housing in Tel Aviv in *Building and Housing in the New Palestine* (1920). See Harpaz's chapters on Levy in *Zionist Architecture*, 33–113.

25. Yael Allweil, *Homeland: Zionism as Housing Regime, 1860–2011*, Abingdon: Routledge, 2017, 117–33.

26. Ibid., 126.

27. "This process [development by sweat equity] marks Tel Aviv as the only city in the world that was planned for through anarchist urbanism and executed by means of anarchist self-governance by disenfranchised urban workers under conditions of intense commodification of urban land and housing." Allweil develops this argument in "Geddes's 1925 Anarchist Housing-Based Plan for Tel Aviv and the 2011 Housing Protests," in Richard J. White, Simon Springer, and Marcelo Lopes de Souza, eds., *The Practice* of *Freedom*: *Anarchism, Geography, and the Spirit* of *Revolt*, London: Rowman & Littlefield International, 2016, 43–63.

28. Ironically, self-housing made a comeback in quite a different political context, in 1977, when the right-wing Likud Party came to power. The new administration tried to bring an end to the long season of statist building under the Histadrut's labor bureaucracy by launching a Build Your Own House program. This libertarian initiative gave license, in turn, to the first wave of definitively self-built settlements in the Occupied Territories.

29. Zvi Efrat's *The Israeli Project* (Leipzig, Germany: Spector Books, 2018) gives a fully documented account of the centrality of concrete to the post-1948 building of the state.

30. Raja Shehadeh writes eloquently about how the state of Israel's efforts to "make the desert bloom" has ruined the "biblical landscape" of the Central Highlands, in *Palestinian Walks: Notes on a Vanishing Landscape*, New York: Scribner, 2007.

31. LeVine, *Overthrowing Geography*, 96–97; Segev, *One Palestine, Complete: Jews and Arabs Under the British Mandate*, New York: Metropolitan Books, 1999, 389.

32. Amnon Rubinstein, "Jewish Labor, Arab Labor," *Haaretz*, April 27, 2003.

33. See touristisrael.com/the-white-city-tel-aviv/344.

34. Sharon Rotbard, *White City, Black City: Architecture and War in Tel Aviv and Jaffa*, Cambridge, MA: MIT Press, 2015, 16–24.

35. The French ambassador's residence on Toulouse Street, commissioned in the 1930s by Muhammed Abd al-Rahim, is one of the best surviving examples.

36. Before 1948, the indistinct border between the two cities was a vibrant contact zone for Jews and Arabs, hosting the kind of social commerce (cafes, nightlife, prostitution, narcotics, gay culture) that was shunned by Arab and Jewish conservatives. Deborah Bernstein, "South of Tel Aviv, North of Jaffa," in Maoz Azaryahu and Ilan Troen, eds., *Tel Aviv: The First Century*, 115–37.

37. The imminent gentrification prompted Rotbard to initiate an oral history of the neighborhood to capture the memories of its older residents. Sharon Rotbard and Muki Tsur, eds., *Neither in Jaffa, Nor in Tel Aviv: Stories, Testimonies and Documents from Shapira Neighborhood*, Tel Aviv: Babel, 2009 (Hebrew).

38. Sharon Rotbard, "Fauzi's Contract," in Zvi Efrat, curator, *Borderline Disorder*, 2002 Venice Architecture Biennale, 141.

39. In 2016, this village played host to the final session of the Truth Commission for the Events of 1948–1960 in the South, an investigation of the "Bedouin Nakba" by Zochrot, the Forensic Architecture project at Goldsmiths, University of London, and the inhabitants of al-Araqib. District court proceedings around a claim of one of the villagers is analyzed in Eyal Weizman and Fazal Sheikh, *The Conflict Shoreline: Colonization as Climate Change in the Negev Desert*, Berlin and Brooklyn: Steidl Verlag and Cabinet Books, 2015,

40. Rotbard, *White City, Black City*, 43.

41. The narrative about the wilderness/desert is not the only myth about Tel Aviv. For an analysis of how and why the city engendered so much mythmaking, see Maoz Azaryahu, *Tel Aviv: Mythography of a City*, Syracuse: Syracuse University Press, 2006.

42. Hizky Shoham dissects the controversy over Soskin's photograph in "Tel Aviv's Foundation Myth," 34–60. Rotbard cites the work of historian Ruth Kark (*Jaffa: A City in Evolution*, 1984) and Tamar Berger (*Dionysus in the Centre*, 1998) to support the claim that the lot was offered on the market after the failure of an agricultural venture. Kark is cited in Yael Allweil, *Homeland*, 2017, 111. Zochrot, an Israeli NGO committed to documenting the landscape of pre-1948 Palestinian settlement, has mapped remnants of that housing, especially the more solid "well houses" built and used by owners of orchards. These can be found all over Rotbard's Black City areas, as well as further to the north within the lines of flight along which Tel Aviv expanded. See Allison Deger, "Not an Empty Sand Dune: A Palestinian Mansion in Downtown Tel Aviv," *Mondoweiss*, April 15, 2013, mondoweiss.net.

43. See LeVine's description of the conflict along with the discrepancies between different descriptions of the parcel; its mixed usage, ownership, and tenure; and the presence of buildings on it, in *Overthrowing Geography*, 64–69.

44. Nahum Karlinsky, *California Dreaming: Ideology, Society, and Technology in the Citrus Industry of Palestine, 1890–1939*, Albany: SUNY Press, 2005. By some accounts, the first crate of Shamouti oranges

to be exported was sent by the British Vice Consul in Jaffa to Queen Victoria herself.

45. LeVine, *Overthrowing Geography*, 89.

46. Steven A. Glazer, "Picketing for Hebrew Labor: A Window on Histadrut Tactics and Strategy," *Journal of Palestine Studies* 30: 4, Summer 2001, 39–54.

47. In 2005, the Israeli Registrar of Trade Marks ruled that the brand should lose its protected status because South African growers had been permitted to cultivate and sell under the Jaffa name. The Jerusalem District Court overruled this decision in 2007. See Michael Factor, "Jerusalem District Court Overturns Ruling on Jaffa Trademark," *The IP Factor*, blog.ipfactor.co.il.

48. This market research finding is cited on a CMBI website, jaffa.co.il.

49. The Israeli Committee Against House Demolition (icahd.org), a human rights NGO, has focused its work on the almost daily demolitions inside the Occupied Territories, but thousands of Israeli Palestinians in the Galilee, the Triangle, and the Negev/Naqab face the same threat, because they are forced to build without permits.

50. The Jaffa port workers in particular were punished when the British authorities helped to realize the Zionist dream of a Tel Aviv port. (Ben-Gurion declared: "I want a Jewish sea.") Constructed in a matter of months, it would be staffed exclusively by Jewish labor. The new port immediately captured a large share of commercial activity on the coast, shifting the region's chief economic gateway to the north. Jaffa's defining identity as a port city was undercut and would never recover.

51. Salim Tamari, "Bourgeois Nostalgia and the Abandoned City," in Daniel Monterescu and Dan Rabinowitz, eds., *Mixed Towns, Trapped Communities: Historical Narratives, Spatial Dynamics, Gender Relations, and Cultural Encounters in Palestinian–Israeli Towns*, Aldershot: Ashgate, 2007, 45.

52. Nurit Alfasi and Roy Fabian analyze this first success, in "Preserving Urban Heritage: From Old Jaffa to Modern Tel Aviv," in Azaryahu and Troen, eds., *Tel Aviv: The First Century*, 326–47.

53. Simone Ricca, *Reinventing Jerusalem: Israel's Reconstruction of the Jewish Quarter After 1967*, London: I.B. Tauris, 2007, 87.

54. Ibid., 134–36.

55. Ben-Gurion, diary entry June 1948 and July 1936. The diaries are available online at bg-idea.bgu.ac.il/ideaweb/idea.asp.

56. Nassim Shaker, *The Arab Community in Jaffa at an Existential Crossroads*, Jaffa: Rabita–The League for the Arabs of Jaffa, 1996, 47 (Hebrew). Cited in Ravit Goldhaber, "The Jaffa Slope Project: An

Analysis of 'Jaffaesque' Narratives in the New Millennium," *Makan: Adalah's Journal for Land, Planning and Justice* 2, 2010, 53.

57. Daniel Monterescu gives an excellent frontline account of the evolution of this "mixed" environment in *Jaffa Shared and Shattered: Contrived Coexistence in Israel/Palestine*, Bloomington: Indiana University Press, 2015. He argues that a genuinely mixed city is not a divided one and that Jaffa is one of the places in Israel where the potential for ethnic co-existence is real.

58. A 1995 promise by the Israel Land Authority to provide 400 state-subsidized units of affordable housing in Jaffa resulted in only 22 being built. Sebastian Wallerstein and Emily Silverman (with Naama Meishar), *Housing Distress Within the Palestinian Community of Jaffa: The End of Protected Tenancy in Absentee Ownership Homes*, Technion University: Bimkom and Center for Urban and Regional Research, 2009, 3.

59. Daniel Monterescu, "The 'Housing Intifada' and Its Aftermath: Ethno-Gentrification and the Politics of Communal Existence in Jaffa," *Anthropology News* 49: 9, 2008, 21.

60. Adam LeBor, *City of Oranges: An Intimate History of Arabs and Jews in Jaffa*, London: Bloomsbury, 2006, 155. For more on Ismail Abu Shehadeh, see 206.

61. See Monterescu's analysis of the local conflict over Andromeda Hill in *Jaffa Shared and Shattered*, 177–207.

62. Keshet Rosenblum "Once a Hospice, Soon a Luxury Hotel: A Jaffa Story," *Haaretz*, July 8, 2014.

63. Barry Meier, "Popular Quartz Countertops Pose a Risk to Workers," *New York Times*, April 1, 2016.

3. Old and New Facts

1. In "The Albina Case," Raja Shehadeh recounts an Israeli judge's bizarre evisceration of one of his client's land claim on the grounds of "absenteeism." *Palestinian Walks: Notes on a Vanishing Landscape*, New York: Simon and Schuster, 2007, 41–97.

2. In Suad Amiry's account of her and her friends' visits to their old Jerusalem houses, she recalls that Golda Meir herself occupied one of the finest mansions, the Villa Harun al-Rashid, and, on the occasion of the UN secretary general's visit, "she made sure to sandblast the Arabic script to conceal the fact that she, the Prime Minister of Israel, was living in an Arab house." *Golda Slept Here*, Doha: Bloomsbury Qatar Foundation Publishing, 2014, 81.

3. For example, Jerusalem's Welfare Association produced a comprehensive mapping of the physical and social components of the old city, of which heritage restoration is but one component. Shadia Tuqan, ed., *Jerusalem Heritage and Life, the Old City Revitalization Plan,* Jerusalem: Welfare Association, 2003.

4. However, the Jordanian administration did take steps to clear away blocks of ancient houses surrounding religious monuments, like the Ibrahimi Mosque in Hebron and the Nativity Church in Bethlehem. Simone Ricca, *Reinventing Jerusalem: Israel's Reconstruction of the Jewish Quarter After 1967,* London: I.B. Tauris, 2007, 177–8.

5. Khaldun Bshara, ed., *Tashgheel: Riwaq's job Creation Through Conservation 2001–2011,* Ramallah: Riwaq–Centre for Architectural Conservation, 2011, 13.

6. Tawfik Canaan, *The Palestinian Arab House, Its Architecture and Folklore,* Jerusalem: Syrian Orphanage Press, 1933, 9.

7. "Palestine: Rehabilitation of Historic Centres and Job Creation Through Restoration," *Best Practices on Social Sustainability in Historic Districts,* Geneva: UN–HABITAT, 2008, 16.

8. Bshara, ed., *Tashgheel,* 46.

9. Khaldun Bshara and Suad Amiry, *Reclaiming Space: The 50 Village Project in Rural Palestine,* Ramallah: Riwaq Center for Architectural Conservation, 2016.

10. See Eyal Weizman's analysis of the defense-minded architecture of hilltop settlements, in *Hollow Land,* London: Verso, 2012, 111–36.

11. The ideas and practices behind the Beit Iksa restoration are covered in Bshara and Amiry, eds., *Reclaiming Space,* 33–69.

12. See, for example, this ICOMOS report, by Andrew Potts, on the UN Agenda 2030 and the Third UN Conference on Housing and Sustainable Urban Development: "Analysis of the Position of Cultural Heritage in the Final Draft of the Habitat 3 New Urban Agenda," October 10, 2016, usicomos.org.

13. Rosemary Sayigh, *The Palestinians: From Peasants to Revolutionaries,* London: Zed Press, 1979, 9.

14. Meir's comment was reported in the *Washington Post* in June 1969. A decade later, she published a *New York Times* op-ed article to clarify: "I have been charged with being rigidly insensitive to the question of the Palestinian Arabs. I am supposed to have said, 'There are no Palestinians.' My actual words were: 'There is no Palestinian people. There are Palestinian refugees.' The distinction is not semantic. My statement was based on a lifetime of debates with Arab nationalists who vehemently excluded a separatist Palestinian Arab

nationalism from their formulations." *New York Times*, January 4, 1976.

15. Riwaq has restored many of the fifteen remaining palaces, converting them into community centers. See Suad Amiry and Rana Anani, *Throne Village Architecture: Palestinian Rural Mansions in the 18th and 19th Centuries*, Ramallah: Riwaq–Center for Architectural Conservation, 2003.

16. Lisa Taraki, "Urban Modernity on the Periphery: A New Middle Class Reinvents the Palestinian City," *Social Text* 26: 2, 2008, 61–81.

17. Ali Abunimah, "Boycott Committee: Palestinian 'Rawabi' Tycoon Bashar Masri 'Must End All Normalization Activities with Israel,'" *Electronic Intifada*, September 10, 2012, electronicintifada.net.

18. Harriet Sherwood, "Story of Cities #49: The Long Road to Rawabi, Palestine's First Planned City," *The Guardian*, May 24, 2016.

19. Ali Abunimah, *The Battle for Justice in Palestine*, Chicago: Haymarket, 2014, 88–90.

20. Sherwood, "Story of Cities #49."

21. APCO/ARCON, "The New City of Rawabi–Road Construction," apcoarcon.com.

22. Ben Hattem, "Palestine's First Planned City Causes Tensions," *Middle East Eye*, August 29, 2014.

23. See Toufic Haddad, *Palestine Ltd: Neoliberalism and Nationalism in the Occupied Territory*, London: I.B. Tauris, 2016; Tariq Dana, "Palestine's Capitalists," *Jacobin*, February 20, 2012.

24. Mohammed Nasr, "Monopolies and the PNA," in Mushtaq Husain Khan, Inge Amundsen, and George Giacaman, eds., *State Formation in Palestine: Viability and Governance During a Social Transformation*, London: Routledge, 2004, 168–92.

25. Adam Hanieh describes the continuing importance of Gulf-based capital investment in the Occupied Territories and other Middle Eastern countries, in *Capitalism and Class in the Gulf Arab States*, New York: Palgrave Macmillan, 2011, 160–64.

26. Adam Hanieh, *Lineages of Revolt: Issues of Contemporary Capitalism in the Middle East*, Chicago: Haymarket Books, 2013, 99–122.

27. Khalil Nakhleh, *Globalized Palestine: The National Sell-Out of a Homeland*, Trenton, NJ: Red Sea Press, 2012, 37–130.

28. Quoted in N. Alva, "Palestinian Workers Campaign for Social Justice," *Middle East Research and Information Project* 281, Winter 2016, merip.org. The call for cross-class unity was initially taken up during the first intifada.

29. Palestinian Basic Law (amended 2003), palestinianbasiclaw.org/basic-law/2003-amended-basic-law (emphasis added).

30. The Paris Protocol limited the amount of cement that could be exported from Egypt and Jordan to 150,000 tons.

31. Amiry Haas, "Palestinians Invest Twice as Much in Israel as They Do in West Bank," *Haaretz*, November 22, 2011.

32. Tariq Dana, "The Palestinian Capitalists That Have Gone Too Far," *Al-Shabaka Policy Network*, January 14, 2014.

33. Khalid Amayreh, "Cement Scandal Highlights Corruption," *Al-Jazeera*, August 6, 2004.

34. Andrew Ross, *The Celebration Chronicles: Life, Liberty, and the Pursuit of Property Value in Disney's New Town*, New York: Ballantine Books, 1999.

35. Reported in Armin Rosen, "A Middle-Class Paradise in Palestine?" *The Atlantic*, February 11, 2013.

36. Tani Goldstein, "'Big Step' for New Palestinian City," *Ynet News*, January 26, 2012.

37. Arpan Roy, "Reimagining Resilience: Urbanization and Identity in Ramallah and Rawabi," *City* 20: 3, 2016, 386.

38. Abunimah, *The Battle for Justice in Palestine*, 92–96.

39. Christopher Harker, "Debt and Obligation in Contemporary Ramallah," *Jadaliyya*, October 19, 2014, jadaliyya.com.

40. This data is from the Palestine Monetary Authority, available at pma.ps.

41. Raja Khalidi and Sobhi Samour, "Neoliberalism as Liberation: The Statehood Program and the Remaking of the Palestinian National Movement," *Journal of Palestine Studies* 40: 2, 2011, 13.

42. From a 2006 speech by Fayyad, quoted in Haddad, *Palestine Ltd*, 212.

43. Ibid., 280.

44. UN General Assembly Resolution 31/15 of November 23, 1976, and UN General Assembly Resolution 34/52 of November 23, 1979.

45. See Alessandro Petti, "Refugee Heritage," *e-flux*, 2017, e-flux.com.

46. Human Rights Center, *No Safe Space: Health Consequences of Tear Gas Exposure Among Palestine Refugees*, University of California, Berkeley Law School, 2017, law.berkeley.edu/research/human-rights-center/programs/no-safe-space.

47. See Mazin Qumsiyeh, *Popular Resistance in Palestine: A History of Hope and Empowerment*, London: Pluto Press, 2011.

48. Bethlehem 2000 received strong backing, at every level, from the UN. See un.org/Depts/dpi/bethlehem2000/home.html.

49. The Israeli human rights organization B'Tselem issued detailed coverage of the first wave of Israeli army actions in 2001, in "Excessive Force: Human Rights Violations During IDF Incursions in Area A," 2001, btselem.org.

50. Hamdan Taha, "World Heritage in Palestine: From Inventory to Nomination," *This Week in Palestine*, March 2011, archive.thisweek inpalestine.com.

51. Nada Atrash, "World Heritage Site in Bethlehem and Its Potential Reflections on Tourism," in Rami Isaac, Michael Hall, and Freya Higgins-Desbiolles, eds., *The Politics and Power of Tourism in Palestine*, London: Routledge, 2015, 75–95.

52. Christiane Dabdoub Nasser and Markaz Hifz al-Turath al-Thaqafi, *Anatreh Quarter: An Urban and Architectural Study of a Bethlehem Quarter*, Bethlehem: Centre for Cultural Heritage Preservation, 2005.

53. Palestinian BDS National Committee, "From Standing Rock to Occupied Jerusalem: We Resist Desecration of Our Burial Sites and Colonizing Our Indigenous Lands," September 9, 2016, bdsmovement.net.

54. Nadia Abu El-Haj gives an incisive account of the emergence of "biblical archaeology" in *Facts on the Ground: Archaeological Practice and Territorial Self-Fashioning in Israeli Society*, Chicago: University of Chicago Press, 2001.

55. Ahmed Rjoob, "The Impact of Israeli Occupation on the Conservation of Cultural Heritage Sites in the Occupied Palestinian Territories: The Case of 'Salvage Excavations,'" *Conservation and Management of Archaeological Sites* 11: 3–4, 2009, 226. Evangelical Christian fundamentalists are also playing a significant role in these excavations. The Museum of the Bible funds illegal digs to gather material for its collections, distorting the historical record by applying exclusively Christian interpretations of the findings. Dylan Bergeson, "The Biblical Pseudo-Archaeologists Pillaging the West Bank," *The Atlantic*, February 28, 2013.

4. Extract, Export, and Extort

1. Yehoshua Ben-Arieh, *Jerusalem in the Nineteenth Century: The Emergence of the New City*, New York: St. Martin's Press, 1986, 400. Bethlehem's other traveling artisans were the olive wood and mother-of-pearl craftsmen, who achieved international fame in the nineteenth century. See Jacob Norris, "Exporting the Holy Land: Artisans and

Merchant Migrants in Ottoman-Era Bethlehem," *Mashriq & Mahjar* 1: 2, 2013, 14–40.

2. Tawfik Canaan, *The Palestinian Arab House, Its Architecture and Folklore,* Jerusalem: Syrian Orphanage Press, 1933, 25.

3. Avia Hashimshoni, Scweid Yosef, and Zion Hashimshoni, Municipality of Jerusalem, *Masterplan for the City of Jerusalem* 1968, 13 (quoted in Eyal Weizman, *Hollow Land*, London: Verso, 2012, 28).

4. Meron Benvenisti, *City of Stone: The Hidden History of Jerusalem,* Berkeley: University of California Press, 1996, 154. Yonatan Mendel, "New Jerusalem: On the Israeli Capital Metropolitan Disorder," *New Left Review* 81, June 2013, 35–56.

5. Issam Aruri, "Israel's Greater Jerusalem Bill: Settlers in, Palestinians Out," *Middle East Eye,* November 2, 2017.

6. Weizman, *Hollow Land*, 31–2.

7. Eran Tamir-Tawil, "To Start a City from Scratch: An Interview with Architect Thomas M. Leitersdorf," in Rafi Segal and Eyal Weizman, eds., *A Civilian Occupation*, 153.

8. Judy Price, "White Oil," *World of Matter,* 2013, worldofmatter.net.

9. See jerusalemstoneusa.com/white stone ceremony.html.

10. According to the watchdog group Who Profits?, the contested quarry facilities are Yatir, Meitarim, Beit Hagai/Lahav, Adora/Trans-Judea, Salit HaAdumim, Nahal Raba, Natuf Quarry, Beitar Illit, and Kochav Hashahar.

11. Human Rights Watch, *Occupation, Inc.: How Settlement Businesses Contribute to Israel's Violations of Palestinian Rights,* January 19, 2016, 45.

12. See Assaf Adiv's summary of the strike and its outcomes, "The Salit Workers' Struggle–Achievements and Limitations," *WAC-MAAN,* January 16, 2012, at eng.wac-maan.org.il.

13. Justice Aharon Barak's comments, in HCJ 393/82 *Jamait Askan v Commander of IDF Forces in Judea and Samaria,* were cited in the Yesh Din petition, *Yesh Din–Volunteers for Human Rights v. Commander of the IDF Forces in the West Bank et al.*, HCJ 2164/09, December 26, 2011, hamoked.org.

14. Zafrir Rinat, "High Court Says Israel Can Take Advantage of West Bank Resources," *Haaretz*, December 28, 2011.

15. Human Rights Watch, *Occupation, Inc.*, 42–52.

16. World Bank, *West Bank and Gaza—Area C and the Future of the Palestinian Economy,* Washington, DC: World Bank Group, 2013, 13–15, documents.worldbank.org.

17. Union of Stone and Marble, "The Aggregates Industry on the West Bank: A Consultation Paper," Bethlehem, December 2011, 12, usm-pal.ps.

18. Ibid., 6.

19. Palestine Trade Center, *State of Palestine National Export Strategy: Stones and Marble: Sector Export Strategy 2014–2018,* paltrade.org. Mohammed Al Ram'ah cites a 12.86 percent growth from 2012 to 2013, in "Marble From the Holy Land: The Pillar of the Palestinian Export Sector," *This Week in Palestine,* July 2014, thisweekin palestine.com.

20. Inexperience in sales and marketing was another obstacle for Palestinian producers looking to export. Industry groups like the USM advised their members to develop their own expertise, or to form consortia to pool resources, in these areas to take advantage of higher prices (50 to 100 percent) in the overseas market and not rely on Israeli "middle men." Union of Stone and Marble, *Stone & Marble in Palestine: Developing a Strategy for the Future,* Bethlehem, 2011, 24, usm-pal.ps.

21. B'Tselem, "Military Effectively Shutting Down Palestinian Quarries in Beit Fajjar to Aid De Facto Annexation of Area," April 21, 2016, btselem.org.

22. Palestinian Federation of Industries, *Palestinian Marble and Stone Industry,* Ramallah, May 2005.

23. "All existing natural sources within the Palestinian territories and territorial waters and exclusive economic zone of its subsidiaries are considered public ownership except for construction materials such as limestone and sand." Palestinian Legislative Council, Law No. (1) for Natural Resources (1999), quoted in Decolonizing Art and Architecture, *The Stone Industry in Palestine–Final Report,* Beit Sahour, January 2015, 40.

24. Basim Makhool and Mahmoud Abu-Alrob, *Quarrying, Crushing and Stone Industries in Palestine: Current Situation and Prospects,* Jerusalem and Ramallah: Palestine Economic Policy Research Institute, April 1999, palestineeconomy.ps, 6.

25. Palestinian Central Bureau of Statistics, *Press Release on the Results of the Labour Force Survey in Palestine, 2016,* April 2017, pcbs.gov.ps.

26. Canaan documents an earlier form of environmental devastation caused by the overuse of vegetation to feed the lime kilns of the artisanal stone craft: "The practice of uprooting thistles for kilns, as well as for household fuel, has denuded the mountains, and hills of the only vegetation which serves to hold in place the surface layer of the earth, since Palestine has not now any forests; thus in recent centuries, the heavy winter storms have washed down the earth and so exposed the bare rocks." *The Palestinian Arab House,* 21.

27. In 2015, Decolonizing Art and Architecture submitted a detailed report to the Ministry of Planning, outlining several recommendations for environmental regulation of the industry. Included was a proposal to rehabilitate the "dead space" of inactive quarries for community uses: "There is an evident lack of open-air communal spaces to compensate for the growing urban areas found in the West Bank. Public spaces are not only important as recreational areas but as places where society can interact and reflect on their past as well as construct a vision for their future. The unused quarries that are spread over the West Bank are therefore potential spaces that could be turned over to the community as a place to build an alternative sustainable future." *The Stone Industry in Palestine*, 87.

28. Artemis Kubala, *The Political Economy of Stone Quarrying in the West Bank (Palestine)*, M.A. thesis, University of Ghent, 2015, 26–27, available at lib.ugent.be.

29. Union of Stone and Marble, *Stone & Marble in Palestine*, 15.

30. Mohammad Najim, "New National Cement Plant; Will It Cut Costs of This Vital Product?" *WAFA*, February 2, 2017, english.wafa.ps.

31. Jon Shelbourne, "Gaza Residents Stand Firm in Opposition to New Cement Factory," *Intercem*, November 22, 2016.

32. See Eyal Weizman's discussion of the environmental crisis in the Negev (*Naqab*) in Eyal Weizman and Fazal Sheikh, *The Conflict Shoreline: Colonization as Climate Change in the Negev Desert*, Berlin and Brooklyn: Steidl Verlag and Cabinet Books, 2015, and Emily McKee's analysis of Bedouin community politics in *Dwelling in Conflict: Negev Landscapes and the Boundaries of Belonging*, Stanford, CA: Stanford University Press, 2016.

33. Kubala, *The Political Economy of Stone Quarrying*, note 126.

34. David Israel, "Bedouin Tribe, Gush Etzion Council, Cooperate Against PA Environmental Disaster [video]," *Jewish Press*, November 21, 2016, jewishpress.com.

35. UNESCO, World Heritage Site, tentative list, whc.unesco.org/en/tentativelists/5708.

36. See the report by Emek Shaveh (self-described as "an Israeli NGO working to prevent the politicization of archaeology in the context of the Israeli–Palestinian conflict, and to protect ancient sites as public assets that belong to members of all communities, faiths and peoples"), *The Role of Ancient Sites in the Political Struggle in the Bethlehem Area (Gush Etzion) and Their Economic and Educational Potential*, March 16, 2015, alt-arch.org.

5. Human Gold

1. A range of critical views can be found in Michael Sorkin, ed., *Against the Wall*, New York: Verso, 2005.

2. According to a survey prepared for the PGFTU by the Arab World for Research and Development for the Palestine General Federation of Trade Unions, *Palestinian Workers: A Comprehensive Report on Working Conditions, Priorities and Recommendations*, Ramallah: Arab World for Research and Development, 2013, 18, 27, awrad.org.

3. Quoted in Tovah Lazaroff, "Conflict Takes Back Seat to Commerce in Palestinian Village," *Jerusalem Post*, February 23, 2014.

4. Matthew Vickery, *Employing the Enemy: The Story of Palestinian Labourers on Israeli Settlements*, London: Zed Books, 2017, 49.

5. Chaim Levinson "Israel Preparing Major Expansions in Four West Bank Settlements: Kedumim, Vered Yericho, Neveh Tzuf, Emanuel Slated to Grow," *Haaretz*, February 9, 2015.

6. Moshe Semyonov and Noah Lewin-Epstein, *Hewers of Wood and Drawers of Water*, 11–15.

7. By 1996, the numbers had dropped to less than 63,000 but increased again to 135,000 in 2000, only to fall again to 40,000 over the next year. Leila Farsakh, "Palestinian Labor Flows to the Israeli Economy: A Finished Story?" *Journal of Palestine Studies* 32: 1, Autumn 2002, 16.

8. Semyonov and Lewin-Epstein, *Hewers of Wood and Drawers of Water*, 13.

9. Leila Farsakh, *Palestinian Employment in Israel: 1967–1997*, Ramallah: MAS, 1998, 21.

10. Leila Farsakh, *Palestinian Labour Migration to Israel: Labour, Land, and Occupation*, New York: Routledge, 2005, 94.

11. Sara Roy, *The Gaza Strip: The Political Economy of De-development*, Washington, DC: Institute for Palestine Studies, 1995; "De-development Revisited: Palestinian Economy and Society Since Oslo," *Journal of Palestine Studies* 28: 3, Spring 1999, 64–82.

12. Salim Tamari, "Building Other People's Homes: The Palestinian Peasant's Household and Work in Israel," *Journal of Palestine Studies* 11: 1, Autumn 1981, 31–67.

13. Joost Hilterman, *Behind the Intifada: Labor and Women's Movements in the Occupied Territories*, Princeton, NJ: Princeton University Press, 1991.

14. According to one estimate, "between 1996 and 2002, the number of Israeli workers [almost all Palestinian] in construction dropped by

35,000 while the number of migrants rose by 11,000." Workers Advice Center—Final Report of International Labor Delegation, "The Labor Market in Israel, 2004: The Construction Industry as a Test Case," June 20, 2004, labournet.net, 6.

15. Evan Goldstein, "Does Israel Have an Immigrant Problem?" *Foreign Policy*, January 22, 2010, foreignpolicy.com.

16. Israel Drori, *Foreign Workers in Israel: Global Perspectives*, Albany: SUNY Press, 2009, 10.

17. Following a 2006 High Court appeal, a one-time decision was made to grant legal status to 900 children (as permanent residents) and 2,300 of their family members (as temporary residents). Since then, it has been standard practice to deport children and pregnant mothers. "Children of Migrant Workers Israel," *Hotline for Migrants and Refugees*, hotline.org.il.

18. Rebeca Raijman and Adriana Kemp, "Labor Migration, Managing the Ethno-national Conflict, and Client Politics in Israel," in Sarah Willen, ed., *Transnational Migration to Israel in a Global Comparative Context*, Lanham, MD: Lexington, 2007, 31–50. The Israeli Minister of the Interior's comment about the "existential threat" is quoted in Jonathan Ofir, "Israel Passes 'Anti-Infiltration Law' to Speed Up the Deportation of African Refugees," *Mondoweiss*, December 14, 2017, mondoweiss.net.

19. In the mid-1990s, the Israeli government and the Association of Builders and Constructors initiated a training program for newly released soldiers, but few were kept on in construction after the subsidies to employers ran out. Drori, *Foreign Workers in Israel*, 118.

20. Netanel Katz, "Government Introduces Incentive Program for Construction Workers," *Arutz Sheva* 7, June 8, 2014, israelnationalnews .com.

21. Sawt El Amel (The Laborer's Voice), a Nazareth-based organization, is especially active in advocating for the rights of working poor and unemployed among the Israeli Palestinian minority population.

22. Moti Bassok, "Wage Gap Between Israeli Jews and Arab Counterparts Widens," *Haaretz*, November 23, 2016.

23. Farsakh, *Palestinian Labour Migration to Israel*, 24.

24. Ibid., 93.

25. Machsom Watch, an Israeli women's peace group, monitors conditions at checkpoints and issues regular reports: machsomwatch.org /en/daily-reports/checkpoints.

26. Arab World for Research and Development, *Palestinian Workers*, 51–2.

27. See Amjad Alqasis and Nidal al-Azza, eds., *Forced Population Transfer: The Case of Palestine—Installment of a Permit Regime*, Working Paper 18, Bethlehem: Badil Resource Center for Palestinian Residency and Refugee Rights, December 2015. The Histadrut's collaboration with South Africa in building and maintaining the infrastructure of apartheid is documented in Jane Haapiseva Hunter, *Israeli Foreign Policy: South Africa and Central America*, Boston: South End Press, 1987, 64–68, 75–89, and passim.

28. Report of the Director-General, International Labour Office, *The Situation of Workers of the Occupied Arab Territories*, Geneva: 2013, 25.

29. "Palestinians Told to Boycott Online Israeli Work Permits," *Gulf News*, April 10, 2017.

30. See B'Tselem, *Builders of Zion: Human Rights Violations of Palestinians from the Occupied Territories Working in Israel and the Settlements*, September 1999, 71, 68–73, btselem.org.

31. Firas Jaber, "How Palestinians Pushed for Social Security—and Won," *Middle East Eye*, November 1, 2016; Ahmad Melhem, "Will New Social Security Law Protect Palestinian Workers?" *Marsad*, May 10, 2016, marsad.ps.

32. About 25.5 percent of employees in the Occupied Territories were affiliated with professional unions or trade unions in the second quarter of 2015 (14 percent in the West Bank and 54.8 percent in Gaza Strip). Democracy and Workers Rights Center, *Overview of the Trade Union Movement in Palestine*, September 2015, dwrc.org.

33. Quoted in "The West Bank: A Dustbin for Israeli Industrial Waste?" *Demographic, Environmental, and Security Issues Project*, May 2001, desip.igc.org.

34. "In 2012, Israel reported to the World Bank that exports from settlement industrial zones to the European Union totaled $300 million in value annually … The World Bank put this figure much higher— suggesting a figure of $5.4 *billion* a year—because Israeli companies often transfer raw materials and manufactured components across the border into internationally recognized Israel before export." Jonah Walters, "The Settlement Industry," *Jacobin*, June 11, 2016.

35. Haggai Matar, "Court Denies Equal Rights to Palestinian Workers in Israeli Industrial Zone," *+972*, July 23, 2015, 972mag.com.

36. The labor conditions were more comparable to those inside Jordan's Qualifying Industrial Zones, hosting many Israeli–Jordanian joint ventures, where forced labor and trafficking were rife among the migrant workers. *The Good, The Bad, and the Ugly—Report on the*

National Labor Committee and United Steelworkers of America Delegation to Jordan, Institute for Global Labor and Human Rights, June 13, 2006.

37. The question of whether border-crossers could be organized lay at the center of factional struggle in the 1970s among trade union groups controlled by Fatah, the Palestine Communist Party, Democratic Front for the Liberation of Palestine, and the Popular Front for the Liberation of Palestine. Joost Hilterman argues that the efforts to unionize were critical in raising workers' nationalist consciousness. *Behind the Intifada,* 64–68.

38. Palestinian Central Bureau of Statistics, *Labour Force Survey in Palestine,* January–March 2017, pcbs.gov.ps.

39. Joshua Mitnick, "Israel Built a Wall. But Palestinian Laborers Continue to Sneak Through Daily," *LA Times,* July 14, 2017.

40. Israel's Central Bureau of Statistics records 115,600 in 1992. After 1994, no official data was collected, though the World Bank reported a peak of 146,000 just before the start of the al-Aqsa intifada. The World Bank, *Long Term Policy Options for the Palestinian Economy* (2002), 35.

41. Tali Heruti Sover, "Israel Mulls Increasing Number of Work Permits for Palestinians," *Haaretz,* December 19, 2016; "Israel Said to Okay Work Permits for 30,000 More Palestinians," *Times of Israel,* February 8, 2016.

42. In the preface to *Crossing the Green Line Between the West Bank and Israel* (Philadelphia: University of Pennsylvania Press, 2002), Avram Bornstein reflects on the moral challenges faced by an ethnographer in studying the experience of border crossing.

43. The age requirements are frequently altered, but these 2011 figures are cited in Kav LaOved, *Employment of Palestinians in Israel and the Settlements,* Tel Aviv, August 2012, 12.

44. B'Tselem documented many instances of abuse in *Human Rights Violations,* 19–32.

45. In December 2014, as many as 5,000 workers refused to cross the al-Tayba checkpoint as a protest against the degrading conditions. Nine days later, one of them lost his life in the crush. "Palestinian Man Crushed to Death Inside Overcrowded Israeli Checkpoint," *Ma'an News,* December 31, 2014, maannews.com.

46. Rashid Khalidi, *Palestinian Identity: The Construction of Modern National Consciousness,* New York: Columbia University Press, 1997, 1.

47. Drori, *Foreign Workers in Israel,* 202, citing a 2007 report by Kav LaOved and Workers Hotline.

48. "Chinese Workers Trapped in Land of Broken Promises," *RT News*, April 30, 2011.

49. Labour Start, "Israel/China: Stop Governments' Deal to Import Bonded Workers," December 4, 2015, labourstartcampaigns.net.

50. Barak Ravid and Yotam Berge, "Israel Accepts Chinese Demand Not to Employ Chinese Laborers in Settlements," *Haaretz*, April 23, 2017.

51. Andrew Ross, ed. (for Gulf Labor), *The Gulf: High Culture/Hard Labor*, New York: OR Books, 2015.

52. Noah Kosharek, "Chinese Construction Workers Go Out on a Limb to Get Paid," *Haaretz*, September 22, 2009; Lee Yaron, "Two Foreign Workers in Israel Barricade Themselves on a Crane, Demanding Pay," *Haaretz*, November 2, 2016.

53. Lee Yaron, "Israel Has One of Highest Rates of Construction Accidents in West," *Haaretz*, September 6, 2016.

54. Yael Darel, "Not Safe for Chinese: Israel's Poor Record on Construction Sites Irks Beijing," *Haaretz*, May 30, 2018.

55. On the causes of these disability rates, see Jasbir K. Puar, *The Right to Maim: Debility, Capacity, Disability*, Durham, NC: Duke University Press, 2017.

56. Bethan Staton, "Palestinian Workers in the Settlements Unite," *Al-Jazeera*, April 9, 2015.

57. Yoav Tamir, "Employers Fear 'Zarfati Precedent,' Raise Palestinian Workers' Wages," *WAC-MAAN*, May 17, 2018, at eng.wac-maan.org.il.

58. Shir Hever, *The Political Economy of Israel's Occupation*, London: Pluto Press, 2010, 34. Also, according to one 2005 estimate, 45 percent of aid to the Occupied Territories flowed back to the Israeli market. See Ghada Karmi, "With No Palestinian State in Sight, Aid Becomes an Adjunct to Occupation," *The Guardian*, December 31, 2005, 37.

59. Rashid Khalidi, "The Balfour Declaration from the Perspective of Its Victims," lecture at Hagop Kevorkian Center for Near Eastern Studies, New York University, September 25, 2017.

60. Richard Falk, *Palestine's Horizon: Towards a Just Peace*, London: Pluto Press, 2017. For a canonical explanation of the BDS campaign, see Omar Barghouti, *Boycott, Divestment, Sanctions: The Global Struggle for Palestinian Rights*, Chicago: Haymarket Books, 2011, and Audrea Lim, ed., *The Case for Sanctions Against Israel*, New York: Verso, 2012.

61. B'Tselem, "By Hook and by Crook: Israeli Settlement Policy in the West Bank," July 2010, btselem.org.

62. Cited in Adam Entous, "The Enemy of My Enemy," *New Yorker*, June 18, 2018, 30.

63. Stanley Fischer and Thomas Schelling produced one such estimate ($250 million) of the difference in payments made and benefits received between 1968 and 1993. See "Summary and Conclusions," in Stanley Fischer, Leonard Hausman, Anna D. Karasik, and Thomas C. Schelling, eds., *Securing Peace in the Middle East*, Cambridge, MA: The MIT Press, 1994, 21.

64. In *The Price of Occupation*, first issued in 2004 (and updated several times since), Shlomo Swirski has described and audited all the ways in which the Occupation has exacted an immense economic burden on Israel (and the Occupied Territories). He concluded, in the 2008 version of the report, that "we can clearly state that Israel's policy in the Palestinian territories, a policy that focuses on preventing the Palestinians from developing their own economy was short-sighted and, in a sense, comparable to 'biting off the nose to spite the face.' Rather than recognizing the potential of the simultaneous development of both sides of the Green Line, with the aim of creating a stronger and sounder regional economy in the long run, based on meaningful mutual interchange, consecutive Israeli administrations strove to strengthen only one of the two sides. The Israeli economy might reasonably have benefited if the standard of living in the Palestinian territories had risen higher than it did through the meager salaries Palestinian workers received in Israel, and if Israel had allowed Palestinian entrepreneurs—farmers, manufacturers, and service providers—to invest in their own businesses. Put simply, if there were more cash on the Palestinian side, both the Palestinians and the Israelis would be reaping the benefits. The close ties between the two economies, developed during the years of occupation, have created a situation in which if one is damaged, the other will inevitably be affected as well." *The Burden of Occupation: The Cost of the Occupation to Israeli Society, Polity and Economy*, Tel Aviv: Adva Center, 2008, 142.

65. See Yoav Peled and Nadim Rouhana, "Transitional Justice and the Right of Return of the Palestinian Refugees," *Theoretical Inquiries in Law*, 5: 2, 2004, 317–32; Anne Massagee, "Beyond Compensation: Reparations, Transitional Justice and the Palestinian Refugee Question," in Rex Brynen and Roula El-Rifai, eds., *Compensation to Palestinian Refugees and the Search for Palestinian–Israeli Peace*, London: Pluto Press, 2013; Roger Duthie, ed., *Transitional Justice and Displacement*, New York: Social Science Research Council, 2012.

66. Omar Barghouti, "A Secular Democratic State in Historic Palestine," in Antony Loewenstein and Ahmed Moor, eds., *After Zionism: One State for Israel and Palestine*, London: Saqi Books, 2012, 194–209.

Index

Also by Andrew Ross

Creditocracy and the Case for Debt Refusal

The Exorcist and the Machines

Bird on Fire: Lessons from the World's Least Sustainable City

*Nice Work If You Can Get It: Life and Labor in
Precarious Times*

*Fast Boat to China: Corporate Flight and the
Consequences of Free Trade—Lessons from Shanghai*

Low Pay, High Profile: The Global Push for Fair Labor

No-Collar: The Humane Workplace and its Hidden Costs

*The Celebration Chronicles: Life, Liberty, and The Pursuit of
Property Values*

Real Love: In Pursuit of Cultural Justice

The Chicago Gangster Theory of Life: Nature's Debt to Society

*Strange Weather: Culture, Science and Technology in the Age
of Limits*

No Respect: Intellectuals and Popular Culture

The Failure of Modernism: Symptoms of American Poetry